M000208240

THE ATTEMPT
TO UPROOT
SUNNI-ARAB
INFLUENCE

THE ATTEMPT TO UPROOT SUNNI-ARAB INFLUENCE

A Geo-Strategic Analysis
of the Western, Israeli and
Iranian Quest for
Domination

NABIL KHALIFÉ
TRANSLATED AND INTRODUCED BY
JOSEPH A. KÉCHICHIAN

sussex
ACADEMIC
PRESS
Brighton • Chicago • Toronto

Copyright © Joseph A. Kéchichian, 2017.

The right of Joseph A. Kéchichian to be identified as Author of this work has been asserted in accordance with the Copyright, Designs and Patents Act 1988.

2 4 6 8 10 9 7 5 3 1

First published 2017, in Great Britain by
SUSSEX ACADEMIC PRESS
PO Box 139
Eastbourne BN24 9BP

and in the United States of America by
SUSSEX ACADEMIC PRESS
Independent Publishers Group
814 N. Franklin Street, Chicago, IL 60610

and in Canada by
SUSSEX ACADEMIC PRESS (CANADA)

All rights reserved. Except for the quotation of short passages for the purposes of criticism and review, no part of this publication may be reproduced, stored in a retrieval system or transmitted in any form or by any means, electronic, mechanical, photocopying, recording or otherwise, without the prior permission of the publisher.

British Library Cataloguing in Publication Data
A CIP catalogue record for this book is available from the British Library.

Library of Congress Cataloging-in-Publication Data
Names: Khalifé, Nabil, author Kéchichian, Joseph A., translator, writer of introduction.
Title: The attempt to uproot Sunni-Arab influence : a geo-strategic analysis of the Western, Israeli and Iranian quest for domination / by Nabil Khalifé ; translated and introduced by Joseph A. Kéchichian.
Description: Brighton : Sussex Academic Press, 2017 I Includes bibliographical references and index.
Identifiers: LCCN 2016052473I ISBN 9781845198534 (hbk : alk. paper) I ISBN 9781845198541 (pbk : alk. paper)
Subjects: LCSH: Middle East—Politics and government—21st century. I Geopolitics—Middle East. I Islam and politics—Middle East. I Sunnites—Relations—Shi'ah. I Shi'ah—Relations—Sunnites. I Arab Spring, 2010–
Classification: LCC DS63.123 .K43 2017 I DDC 327.1/1409174927—dc23
LC record available at https://lccn.loc.gov/2016052473

MIX
Paper from
responsible sources
FSC® C013056

Typeset & designed by Sussex Academic Press, Brighton & Eastbourne.
Printed by TJ International, Padstow, Cornwall.

Contents

Targeting Sunnis
NABIL KHALIFÉ

Preface

In the aftermath of the late 2010 "Arab Uprisings" that unleashed the quest for freedom, governments scrambled to survive, preserve existing sources of authority, fulfill international obligations, maintain law and order, and limit sectarian divisions, though much of these efforts came to naught. Regrettably, weak governments fell into carefully laid out traps, which aimed to divide and rule. Much of those exertions succeeded, including protracted wars that further unglued fragile societies, destroyed Arab wealth, and shriveled whatever cohesiveness existed, while members of the majority Sunni communities saw their power bases marginalized in several countries, including Egypt and Syria. It was a given, and on cue, that extremist movements like the so-called Islamic State of Iraq and Syria (ISIS), would rise, which promised to further polarize the Arab and Muslim Worlds.

How to prevent ISIS, now popularly known through its Arabic acronym Da'ish [al-*Dawlah al-Islamiyyah fil-'Iraq wal-Sham*, sometimes written as Daesh] from gaining power in both Iraq and Syria, or to make a bid for Lebanon, or to even make inroads in such places as Yemen, Libya and elsewhere, is a serious question that can no longer be neglected. It is vital to ask what needs to be done to prevent the Arab disenfranchised from joining extremist groups within their dominant appeal that a charismatic Caliph is the ultimate guide for salvation. It is, therefore, critical to ask whether these radicalized Sunni fighters are embarked on a divine mission and whether they are the only ones making such fallacious arguments? How about Shi'ah extremists who feel no compunction to stand with bloody dictators ready to destroy everything in sight to fulfill Stalinist objectives and, simultaneously, serve God? Can Baghdad and Beirut stand up to pro-Iranian militias for example? Can the minority regime in Damascus impose its will over the majority, which no longer wishes to be ruled by the Ba'ath Party, and do so with impunity? Will sectarian tensions increase in Yemen and elsewhere throughout the Muslim World at a time when confrontations polarize awakened Arab societies caught in the whirlwind of modernization?

Such questions are neither easy to formulate nor answer, especially when few seem aware of dramatic geopolitical transformations that will permanently change the entire Muslim World in the twenty-first century. Media focus is on ISIS, al-Qa'idah and similar terrorist organizations, ostensibly because of a few bloody incidents; voluminous studies offer to decipher what motivates dejected Muslims anxious to restore past glories. Regrettably, most of what is available is little more than descriptive, journalistic observations, which provide instantaneous assessments at a time when thoughtful analysis is required. In fact, the vast majority of what has been written to date, in books, academic journals, magazines, newspapers and on a slew of social media outlets, skirt fundamental questions. Likewise, television programs everywhere delve on sensationalism, concentrating on gory footage even when bloody scenes were blurred so as not to offend alleged sensibilities. Our appetite to watch the 2003 War for Iraq live on television, when carpet combings or "smart weapons" devastated entire communities, gave way to aerial footage that illustrated routinized bombings without any connection to those caught under such fire. Drone attacks that mistakenly wiped out innocent civilians, which used to be referred to as collateral damage, have evolved into "precise" or "targeted" killings. It was easy to distance oneself from death and mayhem and only associate oneself with, or show sympathy towards, individuals in our neighborhoods that succumbed to violent acts.

What occurred over a very short period of time, and which is still largely unclear because so few of the socio-political repercussions were accurately digested, was a plethora of television shows, carefully organized and orchestrated productions that displayed and continue to broadcast executions and other abominable acts of violence. Western scholars and journalists were not and are not immune to these displays and absorb what millions of people see too. Understandably, few venture into the area, and even fewer nurture ties with those who upset the proverbial apple cart. A few European parents of youngsters recruited by ISIS trekked to Turkey, Syria and Iraq during the past few years, and wrote first-hand reports about their difficult experiences, though most of these essays concentrated on the fates that befell their children. Outside of intelligence services that, presumably, enjoy electronic access to what extremists contemplate and plan, few independent analysts offered anything resembling a comprehensive assessment of why ISIS and groups like it mushroom or why the joyful Arab Spring revolutions allegedly seem to falter.

Beyond short-term preoccupations with ISIS and other terrorist groups, however, the phenomena ushered in by the post-2010 revolutions was cavalierly dismissed by the same scholars and journalists, who saw failures, relapses, morbidity, breakdowns, bankruptcies, fiascos, letdowns, catastrophes, disasters, miscarriages, and assorted other calamities. Arabs, these erudite men and women concluded, were not ready for revolution. The fact that the chief accomplishment of the uprisings—a shedding of the fear factor at a time when anxieties returned with a vengeance to Western societies—was dismissed as an inconsequential event, spoke volumes. Removing the shackles of fear in outright dictatorships, where any opposition was punishable by unspeakable torture, was overlooked, dismissed as a local concern, or simply ignored, even if the transformation was epochal. Demonstrating against a regime like the Ba'ath dictatorship in Syria, for example, required genuine courage even if most Syrians knew that global powers stood by the regime. That too was dismissed as the logic evolved towards a preference for Bashar al-Assad over Da'ish and, in Iraq, to back corrupt leaders anxious to kowtow to Iran, over preserving what is left of Iraqi liberties presumably introduced after its 2003 liberation. Somehow, the priority was no longer freedom or liberty, but regime stability that protected Israel and, secondarily, sustained efforts to fight Sunni extremists. Even renewed Sunni–Shi'ah clashes, which were carefully nurtured by global powers, and which will preoccupy mankind for decades and centuries to come, were deemed far less important than what Da'ish intended to do.

Targeting Sunnis [*Istihdaf Ahl al-Sunnah*] by Nabil Khalifé, an established Lebanese Christian thinker with numerous publications to his credit, is an extraordinary book that offers erudite responses to many of the questions raised above. Khalifé advances the thesis that the post-2011 Sunni–Shi'ah struggle was carefully planned by leading Western powers, including Russia, to preserve Israel and impose the latter's acceptance in the Middle East as a natural element, even if it was not. He offers sharp distinctions between Sunnism, which he asserts evolved its political roots before it justified dogmatic aspects, and Shi'ism, which he affirms developed its religiosity before it aligned political agendas. Based on an extensive discussion of the 1979 Iranian Revolution that toppled the Shah, Khalifé advances the notion that the revolution was not "Islamic" but an "Iranian-Shi'ah" rebellion that ended the Pahlavi military monarchy. That alone deserves utmost attention for few scholars, including native Iranians who migrated to Western academies, broached the subject with such lucidity.

In many ways, Khalifé's book mimics Samuel Huntington's *Clash of Civilizations*, though it is far more honest, as it concentrates on how the world's three monotheistic religions perceive each other and "Political Sunnism." The Lebanese divides the Christian world into three branches: Protestantism (America), Catholic (Europe) and Orthodox (Russia), associated with a junior partner, Judaism and its Israeli Zionist corollary. The target of these communities, he avows, is the "Middle World" [a famous Henry Kissinger appellation, according to the author], which houses significant and indispensable oil resources that cannot possibly be entrusted to its natural owners because the latter harbor permanent and doctrinaire ideas that have little room for compromise. In other words, what makes "Political Sunnism" dangerous, according to Khalifé, is its rigidity. That is why these same powers have concocted various policies to check this undeniable force, and while one does not have to believe in conspiracy theories, which Khalifé does not, one is able to provide geo-strategic analyses that debunk facile journalistic interpretations that confuse far more than they elucidate.

The translation of Khalifé's book into English will now allow a wider audience to benefit from the insights of an indigenous Arab thinker, someone who is widely read and respected throughout the region and who, as a practicing Maronite (Catholic), cannot be accused of preferring Sunni extremism. What is relevant today, and what Khalifé brilliantly and objectively explains, is the way major powers act to rule the Arab World, not just control its fate. There seems to be agreement over key questions, ranging from a monopoly to determine whether the Palestinian Question can or ought to be resolved, whether the very notion of a strong nation [*Ummah*] can or ought to be rejected, and whether sectarian confrontations can or ought to be encouraged to give advantages to outsiders. Naturally, global powers prefer the Westphalian nation-state system that, presumably, protects minorities who require shields from extremists. Yet, what will ultimately protect minorities—Shi'ahs, Christians, Jews and others—are the ideas, policies and initiatives adopted by emancipated Arabs from all faiths and denominations. Khalifé provides various references to original Arab and Muslim thinkers like Mohammed Arkoun, Abul Hassan Bani Sadr, Tariq Ramadan, Shaykh Ahmad Al Tayyib, Michel Chiha and many others, to illustrate that significant options are available and that everything is not gloom and doom. Unless Arabs and Muslims adapt, he argues, they will remain on a collision course with themselves and fall prey to traps set by outsiders, victims of permanent struggles that will deny stability, wealth, and freedoms.

Transliterating is an arduous task that requires both accuracy and meticulousness, not only to transcribe what an author intended to convey in a foreign language with its own semantics and different sentence construction techniques, but also to avoid misinterpretations, because the same word may have multiple meanings. This is the case of Arabic, an incredibly rich tongue where vocabulary is a trove of knowledge and nuances, and in which a single word can be translated a dozen or more different ways.

This transliteration is my second effort after the *Sulwan al-Muta' fi 'Udwan al-Atba'* [Consolation for the Ruler During the Hostility of Subjects] by Muhammad Ibn Zafar al-Siqilli, which was published in 2003 as *The Just Prince: A Manual of Leadership*. That experience was complicated in its own right, as I worked on a twelfth-century manuscript, though several Italian and Egyptian writers updated the Arabic renderings that facilitated my tasks. In this instance, I dealt with a hot topic, but wanted to render Nabil Khalifé's text carefully without altering its profound analysis. Though some of his observations are scathing, I found his analysis superlative, one that conveyed a society's angst, which Westerners ignore at their peril.

Fortunately, and while I consulted frequently with Khalifé to avoid errors, the author was kind enough to entertain my frequent requests to add footnotes to supplement his work. Although readers who are familiar with international affairs may know who Friedrich Ratzel is, for example, additional details were added to the book to highlight the German father of geopolitics for those who may not be acquainted with the subject. In addition to such adaptations, Khalifé makes various assumptions in his essays, including the notion that his reader will be conversant with specific regional matters that concern Iran, Sa'udi Arabia and several other Arab countries, including his native Lebanon. That is the prerogative of the essayist though an effort was made to clarify obscure points and provide supplemental information where deemed necessary. It is also critical to note that Nabil Khalifé started his book in 2012, completed two chapters in 2013, and concluded his work in 2014. Moreover, and because he did not follow a chronological approach—as two chapters written in 2014 are placed ahead of two others written in 2013 and 2012, respectively—the reader may find some of the theoretical discussions repetitive. Once again, it is crucial to underline that the purpose of the essay is not to offer a descriptive analysis of the Arab Spring, or what various analysts opined about and continue to provide detailed assessments of ongoing events. Rather, Khalifé is drawing a geostrategic evaluation, based on his theoretical understandings. In that sense, and though the reader may find some of the theoretical reiterations distracting, his purpose is to alert Arab readers, and now English-language bibliophiles, to the fundamentals.

A few technical clarifications must be added to this Preface to under-score the author's writing techniques. As a French-educated scholar Nabil Khalifé relies chiefly on Arabic and French sources, which were duly annotated to maintain the book's integrity, although I have added various English-language sources to update his text with materials that may be more accessible to the English-language reader. Several of the author's sources are from *Le Monde,* a peerless French media institution with top-notch researchers who also dabble in journalism. I verified and updated Nabil's sources as best as I could though I could not verify all of them. Whenever possible, I located original English sources instead of keeping the French or Arabic translations, including references to books authored by Henry Kissinger and Philip Hitti, for example. Transliteration theory is not easy, especially when both Arabic and French notions are intermixed, which may include universal features but can also differ from Anglo-Saxon fare. That is why I kept several orig-inal terms inside the text intact but added what I assumed were necessary clarifications for the English reader—again, with the author's approval. His six appendices, numbered 1 to 6 in this volume, are supplemented by several others as well.

Arab political writers pepper their studies with bullet points that make books look like Power Point presentations. In turn, these summary presentations assume that the reader is already entirely familiar with the author's arguments and that there is no need to provide detailed expla-nations. Khalifé is no exception to this rule though I eliminated dozens of such bullet points and adapted the text to academic standards.

Although the Arab World witnessed dramatic transformations between 2011 and 2016, readers will find Nabil Khalifé's essay to be right on the mark. The Introduction before the essay is a modest attempt to update some of the author's affirmations, even if every effort was made to keep the integrity of the theoretical arguments developed by the erudite geo-strategist intact, given his wide experience that stretches over five decades and that draws on both French and Arabic materials. Even if the reader may not agree with Nabil Khalifé's geopolitical analysis, or with my own updated analyses of developments that occurred after 2011, his views are worthy of the utmost attention because they reflect the perceptions and opinions of over a billion human beings who crave for freedom but who are caught between the rocks of authoritarianisms and the hard place of fanaticisms.

About the Author

Nabil Kamal Khalifé is the director of the Byblos Center for Research and Studies [Markaz Byblus lil-Dirasat wal-Abhath] in the city of Byblos [Jbayl], Lebanon. The Center, which specializes in the Arab and Muslim worlds, focuses on geopolitical and geo-strategic concerns, including religious affairs and the roles of minorities throughout the Middle East.

Khalifé holds a Diplôme d'études approfondies (DEA) in Arab and Islamic Civilization from the Sorbonne University in Paris (1979) and a doctorate in Literature from the Lebanese University (1997). Between 1995 and 2002, he served as an advisor to the President of the Holy Spirit University of Kaslik (USEK), a private Catholic higher education institution founded by the Lebanese Maronite Order in 1938.

A linguist who mastered Arabic over the course of a quarter century, Khalifé devoted years to perfect his proficiency of Arabic poetry, and contributed to 25 scientific studies of language and its structure, including the study of morphology, syntax, phonetics, and semantics. He published several poems to wide acclaim, including "Thalith al-Khalidayn" [The Third Immortal], which was a 1970 ode to the late President of Egypt, Jamal 'Abdul Nasir. Presidents Anuar al-Sadat and his Sudanese counterpart, Ja'afar al-Numayri, congratulated the author on the poem. The al-Azhar Shaykh Muhammad al-Faham declared that this was "the only verse on Nasir he framed and hanged in his home."

Over the course of several years, the author worked in several media outlets, both as a political analyst for the Paris-based *Al Mustaqbal* [Future] magazine (1978–1980), and in Lebanon until 1988. In 1980, he became a broadcaster on *Radio Monte Carlo*, which beamed its voice throughout the Arab World, and published scores of essays in *al-Nahar*, *al-'Amal*, *Lisan al-Hal*, *al-Mustaqbal*, *al-Usbu' al-'Arabi* (all Lebanese dailies), as well as *al-Siyasah* and *al-Watan* (both in Kuwait), and *al-Wahdah* (Morocco). During his years in Paris, Khalifé assumed a key post in the political section of the Arab Center for International Studies (1979–1980), and participated in dozens of conferences and television programs on religious affairs, political and strategic questions, as well as numerous cultural programs. He frequently appears on Arab television stations and is widely quoted among intellectual circles for his expertise and the breadth of his knowledge.

The author of twenty books on geopolitics and geo-strategy, his most renowned publications include: *Lubnan al-Jadid* [The New Lebanon], 1977; *Lubnan wal-Khayar al-Rabih: al-Hiyad wal-Tah'id* [Lebanon and the Fourth Choice: Neutrality and Unity], 1984; *Lubnan al-Hadari baynah al-Tahadudiyyah wal-Wahdah* [Contemporary Lebanon between Identity and Unity], 1984; *Majlis al-Ta'awun wa 'Urubat al-Qarn 21* [The Gulf Cooperation Council and Arabism in the 21st Century], 1989; *Lubnan fi-Istratijiyyat Kissinger* [Lebanon in Kissinger's Strategy], 1991; *Al-Istratijiyyat al-Suriyyah wal-Israilliyyah wal-Urupiyyah Hiyal Lubnan* [The Syrian, Israeli and European Strategies Concerning Lebanon], 1994; *Madkhal fil-Khususiyyah al-Lubnaniyyah* [An Introduction to Lebanese Particularities], 1997; *Qira't Jadidah lil-Shar'iyyah al-Duwaliyyah fi Mawdu' al-Niza' al-'Arabi-al-Israili* [A New Reading of International Legality over the Arab-Israeli Question], 2003; *Ta'dil Hudud Lubnan al-Duwaliyyah 'Indah al-Muthalath: Min al-Wazani . . . la Wadi al-'Asal* [Adjustments to Lebanon's International Borders over the Tripoint: From the Wazani River to the al-'Asal Valley], 2003; *Lubnan 'Ashiyat al-Tahawulat al-Kubra* [Lebanon on the Eve of Major Transformations], 2005; *Jiupolitik Lubnan: al-Istratijiyyat al-Lubnaniyyah* [The Geopolitics of Lebanon: Its Strategy], 2007; *Ahamiyyat al-Khayarat al-Siyasiyyah fi Taqrir al-Masir al-Watani* [The Importance of Political Maps that Determine National Destiny], 2009; *Masihiyyuh al-Sharq al-Aswat: Dirasat Jiupolitikiyyah* [The Christians of the Middle East: A Geopolitical Study], 2011; *Michel Chiha: Awal Anbiya' Lubnan wa Akhir Anbiya' Filastin* [Michel Chiha: Lebanon's First Prophet and Palestine's Last], 2013; *Hududunah al-Bahriyyah Fawqah al-Nafd wal-Gaz: Lubnan 'Indah al-Nuqta 61* [Our Sea Borders on Top of Oil and Gaz Fields: Lebanon Along Point 61], 2013; *Khamsun Sanah fi-Khidmat al-Khalimah: Shakhsiyat Qadamtuhah wa Munasabat Sharaqtu Fihah* [Fifty Years in the Service of the Word: Personalities I Presented and Occasions I Participated In], 2014; *Istihdaf Ahl al-Sunnah: Man Yataza'am al-'Alam al-'Arabi-al-Islami—Al Sa'udiyyah am Iran? Al-Mukhattat al-Istratijih lil-Gharb wa Isra'il wa Iran lil-Saytarah 'ala al-Sharq al-Awsat wa Iqtila' al-Nufuz al-Sunni al-'Arabi Minhuh!* [Targeting Sunnis: Who Will Lead the Arab-Islamic World, Sa'udi Arabia or Iran?—A Western–Israeli–Iranian Strategic Plan to Dominate the Middle East and to Uproot all Sunni-Arab Influences from It], 2014.

About the Translator

Dr. Joseph A. Kéchichian is a Senior Fellow at the King Faisal Center for Research and Islamic Studies (KFCRIS), in Riyadh, Sa'udi Arabia; the CEO of Kéchichian & Associates, LLC, a consulting partnership that provides analysis on the Arabian/Persian Gulf region, specializing in the domestic and regional concerns of Bahrain, Iran, Iraq, Kuwait, Oman, Qatar, Sa'udi Arabia, the United Arab Emirates and the Yemen; and a Senior Writer with the Dubai-based *Gulf News*, which is the top-ranked English-language news daily in the United Arab Emirates, available online at http://www.gulfnews.com. Between 2006 and 2011, he served as the Honorary Consul of the Sultanate of Oman in Los Angeles, California.

Dr. Kéchichian received a doctorate in Foreign Affairs from the University of Virginia in 1985, where he also taught (1986–1988), and assumed the assistant deanship in international studies (1988–1989). In the summer of 1989, he was a Hoover Fellow at Stanford University (under the U.S. State Department Title VIII Program) and, between 1990 and 1996, an Associate Political Scientist at the Santa Monica-based RAND Corporation as well as a lecturer at the University of California in Los Angeles (UCLA). Between 1998 and 2001, Kéchichian was a fellow at UCLA's Gustav E. von Grunebaum Center for Near Eastern Studies, where he held a Smith Richardson Foundation grant (1998–1999) to compose *Succession in Saudi Arabia* (New York: Palgrave, 2001), which was translated into Arabic as *Al-Khilafat fil-'Arabiyyat al-Su'udiyyat* in 2002, and reprinted in a second edition in 2003 (Beirut and London: Dar Al Saqi)]. In 2003–2004, he held a Davenport fellowship at Pepperdine University in Malibu, California, to produce *Power and Succession in Arab Monarchies* (also on a Smith Richardson Foundation grant), (Boulder, Colorado: Lynne Rienner Publishers, 2008), which was translated into Arabic as *Al-Sultah wa-Ta'aqub al-Hukm fil-Mamalikah al-'Arabiyyah*, 2 volumes (Beirut and London: Riad El-Rayyes Books, 2012).

Kéchichian published *Political Participation and Stability in the Sultanate of Oman* (Dubai: Gulf Research Center, 2005), *Oman and the World: The Emergence of an Independent Foreign Policy* (Santa

Monica: RAND, 1995), and edited *A Century in Thirty Years: Shaykh Zayed and the United Arab Emirates* (Washington, D.C.: The Middle East Policy Council, 2000), as well as *Iran, Iraq, and the Arab Gulf States* (New York: Palgrave, 2001). In 2003, he co-authored (with R. Hrair Dekmejian) *The Just Prince: A Manual of Leadership* (London: Saqi Books), which includes a full translation from the Arabic of the *Sulwan al-Muta'* by Muhammad Ibn Zafar al-Siqilli, which appeared in Turkish as *Adil Hükümdar*, (translated by Bariş Doğru), (Istanbul: Kırmızı Kedi Yayınevi, 2009). Among his more recent contributions are *Faysal: Saudi Arabia's King for All Seasons* (Gainesville, Florida: University Press of Florida, 2008), translated into Arabic as *Faysal: Al-Malik wal-Dawlah* (Beirut: Dar al-'Arabiyyah lil-Mawsu'at, 2012), *Legal and Political Reforms in Sa'udi Arabia* (London: Routledge, 2012), translated into Arabic as *Al-Islahat al-Qanuniyyah wal-Siyasiyyah fil-Mamlakah al-'Arabiyyah al-Sa'udiyyah* (Beirut: Riad El-Rayyes Books, 2013), and *'Iffat Al Thunayan: An Arabian Queen* (Brighton, Chicago, Toronto: Sussex Academic Press, 2015). The Seoul-based ASAN Institute for Policy Studies published his updated report on *Succession Challenges in the Arab Gulf Monarchies*, in English (December 2015) and Korean (January 2016).

The author of a dozen book chapters, close to fifty peer-reviewed academic essays, over 200 encyclopedia entries, and 350 book reviews, his latest studies are *From Alliance to Union: Challenges Facing Gulf Cooperation Council States in the Twenty-First Century* (Brighton, Chicago, Toronto: Sussex Academic Press, 2016), and *The Arab Nationalist Advisor: Yusuf Yassin of Sa'udi Arabia*, forthcoming with Sussex Academic Press.

Acknowledgments and Credits for Cover Illustrations

Four years into the uprisings that shook the Arab World and that continues to evolve in front of our eyes, Ayed Noweisser, a retired airline pilot, introduced me to Nabil Khalifé's book *Istihdaf Ahl al-Sunnah* [Targeting Sunnis]. He told me that he discovered it by chance in a Beirut bookstore and purchased the few copies on display to distribute to his friends. We agreed to discuss it after I read the 196-page-long book, which I started doing the next day. Forty-eight hours later, and after a first reading, I decided to embark on its translation into English as quickly as possible and I thanked Ayed for sharing the book with me. We quickly tracked down Nabil Khalifé and drove to Byblos [Jbayl] to meet with him. Our frank conversation acted as added persuasion to introduce this Maronite [Catholic] thinker's ideas about what befell Arab Sunni Muslims and what kind of assaults were mounted to weaken them on a more or less permanent basis. Both Ayed and I focused on our target audience on the drive back to Beirut and settled on senior Western decision-makers, scholars, writers, journalists and clerics, as well as lay men and women anxious to know the truth. At a time when Iran promoted sectarian policies and as Sunni–Shi'ah clashes gained momentum, coupled with cavalier anti-Arab and anti-Sunni declarations uttered in numerous Western audiences, the urgency of the book to be in the hands of senior leaders was imperative. We both wanted *Targeting Sunnis* to be widely read.

Faysal Kamal Adham proved to be the generous philanthropist who ensured that Nabil Khalifé would be compensated for his efforts and that the translated volume would be distributed to various groups. I thank Shaykh Faysal for his generosity, and extend my appreciation on behalf of Nabil Khalifé, in writing.

When I mentioned the project to HRH Prince Turki al-Faisal bin 'Abdul 'Aziz, the Chairman of the King Faisal Center for Research and Islamic Studies [KFCRIS] in Riyadh, he quickly approved it and encouraged me to embark on the translation. Prince Turki requested that I add an introduction both to update the book and, equally important, to share with readers my own perceptions of the impact. As I devoted dozens of columns to the "Arab Uprisings" in my weekly *Gulf News* contribution, I assembled several thematically and updated them as necessary, adding original materials as required.

Finally, many thanks to Anthony Grahame at Sussex Academic Press for the care that he and his staff devoted to the production of this volume.

Sources and credits for the cover illustrations. All photos are in the Public Domain and are primarily sourced via "commons.wikimedia. org" unless specifically alerted below.

Saddam Hussein was the fifth President of Iraq, serving in this capacity from July 1979 until April 2003. *Source*: https://commons.wiki-media.org/wiki/File: Iraq, Saddam Hussein (222).jpg. *Credit*: 172 at English Wikipedia [Public domain or Public domain], via Wikimedia Commons.

Major General Qasem Soleimani is an Iranian senior military officer in the Army of the Guardians of the Islamic Revolution and since 1998 commander of its Quds Force. *Source*: https://commons.wikimedia.org/wiki/File:Qasem Soleimani in Sepah Sarallah.jpg. *Credit*: By Hamed Malekpour [CC BY 4.0 (http://creativecommons.org/licenses/by/4.0)], via Wikimedia Commons.

Ayatollah Khamane'i is the second and current Supreme Leader of Iran and a Muslim cleric. *Source*: https://commons.wikimedia.org/ wiki/File: Hossein Fardi and Supreme Leader Ayatollah Khamenei (cropped). jpg. *Credit*: By Ataei86 [CC BY-SA 4.0 (http://creative commons. org/ licenses/by-sa/4.0)], via Wikimedia Commons.

Grand Ayatollah Ruhallah Khumayni was an Iranian Shia Muslim religious leader, revolutionary and politician. *Source*: https://commons. wikimedia.org/wiki/File: %E2%80%8C   .jpg. *Credit*: Unknown author [Public domain], via Wikimedia Commons.

Benyamin Netanyahu is an Israeli politician and is currently prime minister. *Source*: https://commons.wikimedia.org/wiki/ File:Portrait of Benjamin Netanyahu.jpg. *Credit*: Official White House Photo by Lawrence Jackson derivative work: TheCuriousGnome (Benjamin_

Netanyahu_with_Obamas.jpg) [Public domain], via Wikimedia Commons.

Arnold Joseph Toynbee was a British historian, philosopher of history, research professor of International History at the London School of Economics, and a leading specialist on international affairs. *Credit*: Arnold Joseph Toynbee in 1969. Godfrey Argent; © National Portrait Gallery, London.

Henry Kissinger, former U.S. Secretary of State and national security advisor for Presidents Richard Nixon and Gerald Ford. *Source*: https://commons.wikimedia.org/wiki/File:Henry_Kissinger_at_the_LBJ _Library_(2016).jpg. *Credit*: LBJ Library photo DIG13877MM_0050 by Marsha Miller [Public domain], via Flickr. https://www.flickr. com/ photos/lbjlibrarynow/26667223635/in/album-72157667635816275/.

Salman bin 'Abdul 'Aziz Al Sa'ud is the King of Sa'udi Arabia whose official title is Custodian of the Two Holy Mosques. *Source*: https://commons.wikimedia.org/wiki/File:Prince_Salman_bin_Abd_al-Aziz_Al_Saud_at_the_Pentagon_April_2012.jpg. *Credit*: By DoD photo by Erin A. Kirk-Cuomo (Flickr: 120411-D-BW835-028) [Public domain], via Flickr. https://www.flickr.com/photos/ 68842444@ N03/ 7067812455.

Tony Blair is the former Prime Minister of the United Kingdom of Great Britain and Northern Ireland, and was a Quartet Representative on the Middle East. *Credit*: Marc Müller / MSC [CC BY 3.0 de (http:// creative commons.org/licenses/by/3.0/de/deed.en)], via Wikimedia Commons. This file is licensed under the Creative Commons Attribution 3.0 Germany license.

Rafiq Hariri, the former Prime Minister of Lebanon, was killed along with 21 others in an explosion in Beirut on 14 February, 2005. *Credit*: Rafiq Hariri Foundation, Beirut.

Barack Hussein Obama, 44th President of the United States and the first African American to hold the office. *Source*: https://commons.wiki-media.org/wiki/File:President_Barack_Obama.jpg. *Credit*: By Official White House Photo by Pete Souza (P120612PS-0463 (direct link)) [Public domain], via Wikimedia Commons.

A Note on Transliteration

A modified version of the Library of Congress transliteration system is adopted throughout this book, even if rendering Arabic words and names into English is a nearly impossible task, something that Arabic readers know well. As in the past, I relied upon the style used by the *International Journal of Middle East Studies* and, for practical purposes, eliminated all diacritical marks for long vowels and velarized consonants, save for the hamza (') and the ayn ('). Thus, a name that is commonly rendered in English, for example Mohammed, becomes Muhammad, and Mecca becomes Makkah. Quotations that refer to "Mecca" or "Sheik" were not tampered with.

In modern Arabic, even when using standard pronunciation, the feminine -ah is often ignored, with the h usually silent and not recorded. Consequently, we see it as -a, like in fatwa, Shia, Sharia or even Ulama. Strangely, however, the h is kept in other circumstances, including Riyadh or Jiddah or even Shaikh when it is not written as Sheikh. Throughout this book, an effort is made to be both consistent and accurate, which is why the h is recorded in all instances, including when it refers in the Arabic alphabet to the diacritical marks on the *ta' marbutah* [the final Arabic letter], the *alif* (Abhah, Hasah), the *alif maqsurah* (Shurah, fatwah), or even the *hamza* ('Ulamah, Fuqahah). Thus, all transliterated words that qualify include the silent h, as in fatwah, 'Ulamah, Shari'ah, Shaykh, and Shurah. Several Arabic names entered our lexicon though the spelling is journalistic and often inconsistent. Da'ish [al-*Dawlah al-Islamiyyah fil-'Iraq wal-Sham*], is sometimes written as Daesh, and is interchangeably used with ISIS [Islamic State of Iraq and Syria] or ISIL [Islamic State of Iraq and the Levant], while we have Houthis for Huthis in Yemen and, of course, al-Qaeda for al-Qa'idah.

The preferences adopted in this volume may look odd but, at least, the approach is consistent and meets academic transliteration standards. Readers interested in how best to transliterate can refer to the protocols established by the Library of Congress and the *International Journal of Middle East Studies*, the authorities on the matter. Again, Arabic speakers will know the correct references and while special care was devoted to standardize the spellings of as many transliterated words as possible, there are—inevitably—a few inconsistencies that, I trust, readers will understand and forgive any linguistic transgressions.

Finally, it is equally important to note that because the author [Nabil Khalifé] relies on French sources in numerous instances, there are a few cases when the transliteration went from the Arabic into English for text that was first written in French. While an effort was made to locate the original French sources, this was not always possible, though in those instances when I was successful and deemed their inclusion necessary, I copied the original French in a footnote.

Translator's Introduction to *Targeting Sunnis*

JOSEPH A. KÉCHICHIAN

Nearly six years into the "Arab Uprisings" that continue to shake societies exposed to ingrained political fragility, hundreds of exposés, erudite articles and books wonder why things are going so badly wrong. One of the more erudite appeared in the highly respected London *Guardian*, penned by Adam Roberts, a Senior Research Fellow at the Centre for International Studies at Oxford University.[1] Roberts co-edited a new volume with Michael J. Willis, Rory McCarthy & Timothy Garton Ash, titled *Civil Resistance in the Arab Spring: Triumphs and Disasters*, which includes eleven chapters and covers most of the developments that toppled several dictators without necessarily empowering ordinary people to assume their fair share of authority.[2] Is this an accurate reading of what is going on?

To his credit, and even if the real uprisings started in Lebanon in 2005, Roberts highlights the major victory that is Tunisia. When Muhammad Bu'azizi [Bouazzi] immolated himself in late 2010, he ushered in a new paradigm that empowered the meek and brought down a pro-Western dictator. President Zayn al-'Abidin bin 'Ali [Zine al-Abidine Ben Ali] fled the country, but what took place afterwards was epochal too. Roberts recognized that Tunis achieved significant political changes because Tunisians devised a new constitutional order and credited the al-Nahdah Party for its foresight. It was not easy, of course, but we are now told that whatever success came Tunisia's way occurred as a result of the "cultural affinity to Europe" and, equally important, because of the "Tunisian army's traditional apolitical ethos." These may indeed be accurate readings and while other countries were not as lucky, allegedly because they lacked the democratizing bug, cultural affinities and apolitical militaries were not the only reasons why short-term disasters struck Egypt, Yemen, Libya and especially Syria. Rather, it seems that the chief reason why so many peaceful demonstrations turned violent was due to leaderships that refused to tolerate uprisings and insisted on outcomes acceptable only to the ruling body.

Real dictators, like Husni Mubarak (Egypt), 'Ali 'Abdallah Salih (Yemen), Mu'ammar al-Qaddafi (Libya), and Bashar al-Assad (Syria), among others, could not possibly imagine that they could be superfluous. On the contrary, they believed, and Assad continues to hold onto the notion, that they were indispensable lest disaster envelop their respective societies. Even more problematic is the false notion that these regimes were in the process of building democratizing institutions and that they were doing so only in the context of upholding law and order in support of the regime. Dictatorial impositions were made easier by powerful regional and international actors that muddied the waters in several of these countries by extending outright financial and/or military assistance, or after "interested parties" opted to observe rather than to comment and recommend various steps for a variety of geo-political and strategic reasons.

There is no doubt that "getting rid of a dictatorial and corrupt ruler is not enough" for success, as Roberts concluded in his *Guardian* essay, and that careful planning about what comes after is a key ingredient for revolutionaries who intend to change the systems of government in various Arab societies. At times, change will be relatively peaceful like in Tunisia; and as we have seen it may be confrontational, bloody, and outright calamitous as in Syria. In fact, there is no choice but to live through the growth of anomalies of extremist Islamist movements which take advantage of nascent opportunities to fill existing voids where regimes collapse. But that's the price to pay for revolutionary transformation. Likewise, and while revolutions are messy affairs, the lame excuse that an outgoing tyrant retains some portion of any particular society's support does not negate the calls for change. Power vacuums are usually filled, naturally or otherwise, and even if civil resistance is untested and haphazard, it usually settles down over a period of time. That's what occurred in Europe, and it may be useful to recall that it took hundreds of years of sectarian battles, bloodshed and ugly wars for France, Britain, Germany and many other countries to develop democratizing societies. The civil wars in the United States and Russia were equally bloody though both powers glossed over some of their respective citizens' notoriety for mayhem. To now expect Arabs to develop democratic structures overnight after everything that unfolded during the past thousand years of autocracy is naïve and, more important, unbecoming.

Alexis de Tocqueville, the brilliant Frenchman who studied and probably understood American democracy better than most, once suggested that revolutions are usually gory affairs and that "a state is at its most vulnerable when it attempts to reform."[3] Both conditions are now visible in the Arab world that will live through a period of revolutionary change. Under the circumstances, it may be better if we stop presenting post-mortems that entertain, but fail to explain. Better to wait for a while before we pass judgment and let us remember what the former Chinese Prime Minister Zhou En Lai apparently told President Richard Nixon in 1972. During his key visit to Beijing, and aware that the Chinese studied at the Sorbonne in France, the American asked his host about the impact of the French Revolution. Even if there was a mistranslation—Zhou believed that the question was about the event that took place in 1789 whereas Nixon may have meant the events of May 1968—the Chinese leader's comment that it was "too early to say" spoke volumes.[4] Arabs, like the Chinese, have innate abilities to take the long view of history. We need to update our mentalities whenever we evaluate epochal public discourses, and perceive ongoing developments from a less sanguine perspective.

The purpose of this Introduction to Nabil Khalifé's book is to provide an assessment as to whether the visible sectarian divisions that aim to emasculate Sunni Islam—in the political sense—are spontaneous or part of a carefully laid out plan long before the latest Arab uprisings surfaced. It aims to discuss, as the author affirms, whether the Iranian plan to seek a domination of the Arab World and, if possible, the entire Muslim World, is an acceptable quest to leading powers. It also proposes to gain insights into Israeli thinking regarding the consequences of the uprisings on regional stability and how the State of Israel can benefit from the ongoing chaos. Indeed, and as discussed by Nabil Khalifé, it is critical to understand whether the international community is now determined to weaken, perhaps even destroy, political Sunnism because of a belief that only such an outcome will save minority populations including Arab Shi'ahs, Christians, Druzes, 'Alawis, Yezidis, Kurds and Jews. As the former Director of the U.S. Central Intelligence Agency R. James Woolsey declared in 2013—at the annual Herzliya Conference in Israel no less—there is even a blanket desire to bankrupt all Muslims if the West is to win World War III (a conflict that apparently started some time ago).[5] With this logic, even if it is highly doubtful, it is vital to weigh the repercussions that such policies will inevitably create. Will World War III truly serve Western interests by embarking on an open-ended confrontation with over a billion Sunnis? Will Sunni–Shi'ah clashes initiate bloody collisions and unforeseen spillover effects? Who stands to truly gain from unending hostilities? In the end, are strategists and senior decision-makers in leading global powers willing to engage in perpetual wars with determined Sunnis, who display an uncanny capacity to resist, and whose primary goal is liberty?

To better answer these questions, this Introduction is divided into three parts, starting with a very preliminary assessment of the uprisings that rocked the Arab World from Tunis to Sana'a. An effort is made in this section to highlight what led to various democratization failures, or at least what appear to be catastrophes, as well as the rise of extremism. The second part provides an analysis of leading thinkers, from Henry Kissinger to Barack Obama, who planned, devised, adopted strategies, and introduced policies to divide and rule. Were there specific preferences to weaken Sunnis that can be identified, and what were/are the selected mechanisms on how best to achieve those goals? The third and final part deals with the rise of sectarianism that will surely lead to added chaos in classic clashes of civilizations, which will generate fresh catastrophes, lest dramatic changes are introduced before long. The Introduction closes with observations on how not to embark on permanent enmities.

FROM TUNIS TO SANA'A

Five years after a young university graduate, Muhammad Bu'azizi, immolated himself in the central Tunisian town of Sidi Buzid because of a routine infraction that prevented him from making a living as a fruit seller, a second street vendor set himself on fire in Sfax after authorities seized his merchandise—3,000 packs of contraband cigarettes according to a local official. The incident occurred a few days after the Norwegian Nobel Peace Committee awarded the 2015 prize to the Tunisian Quartet, composed of Abdessattar Ben Moussa, Houcine Abbassi, Fadhel Mahfoudh and Widad Bouchamaoui, representing the Human Rights League, the General Labor Union, the Order of Lawyers, and the Confederation of Industry, Trade and Handicrafts. These four brave individuals and their respective institutions stood as pillars of Tunisian civil society, excelled in their respective fields, and were models of democratization in what was an authoritarian regime that failed to uphold the law, defend the nation, and improve the lives of citizens. At a time when gloom and doom permeates private and public discourses over the fate of the uprisings that are permanently changing Arab societies, the conscientious award, a rarity in recent times, will further seal the inevitable democratization process. It is thus fair to ask whether pioneering Tunisians will bear the reform torch further and seal the epochal transformations under way?[6]

To be sure, Bu'azizi ignited the 2011 Arab Uprisings that quickly spread to several Arab capitals and brought down leading autocratic regimes that, truth be told, are not missed no matter the nostalgia for dictators among the intellectually challenged, or the so-called realists who seldom shy away from accepting brutality as a means of governance. Happily, the Tunisian National Dialogue Quartet presents an alternative model to such realism, and is worthy of emulation. Indeed, Oslo recognized the Quartet's "decisive contribution to the building of a pluralistic democracy . . . in the wake of the Jasmine Revolution in 2011." Still, and beyond the need to address poverty and corruption, what Arabs often complain about, and what ails their body politics, are the inabilities of various branches of society to work together to serve their respective nations. Few can deny that abject poverty brings to the fore survival instincts, which lead one to practice any and all means to ensure a living, provide for one's family and, when all else fails, resort to violence. In fact, corruption is rampant in many Arab societies because ordinary citizens see their elites practice it with a vengeance, despite the existence of laws that are supposed to suppress and forbid such stances. Consequently, an entire generation may be said to have adopted the status quo habit that, along with effective police behavior, were some of the reasons why uprisings took so long to manifest themselves. Until 2011 that is, when elite ways and means reached catastrophic levels, with the subsequent revolutionary results unfolding in front of our eyes.

To be sure, Tunisian patriots drew correct lessons from everything that unfolded throughout the region, even if few concentrated on the assiduous work that the Nobel Peace Committee members noted. What members of the Quartet have done was to work for the benefit of the nation and whatever progress was made during the past five years intended to transform Tunisia into a functioning country. Of course, Tunis was not out of the woods as several political assassinations and bombings in 2013 shook it to the core, followed in 2015 by killings at the Bardo Museum as well as ugly mowing down of sunbathers at a Sousse beach resort, but what was undeniable was the resilience to oppose viciousness. Indeed, after every incident, anti-violence manifestations mobilized large masses. The very creation of the Quartet—and the role it played to avert confrontations—was a perfect example of how ordinary people rejected political violence as a vehicle for reforms. Such efforts were the mechanisms that paved the way to the relatively free and fair 2014 elections that opened a new chapter for all Tunisians.

Towards that end, the Tunisian Quartet worked in earnest to establish a constitutional system of government that guaranteed fundamental rights for the entire population, irrespective of gender, political conviction or religious belief. Theirs was the ideal model that avoided a civil war, though leaders will now need to stay focused on improving economic conditions, something that President Muhammad Mursi neglected in Egypt, and that other leaders overlooked. For no matter how unpalatable such requirements may be, only concerted economic action can eliminate the stagnation that increases joblessness—which stands at nearly 30 percent in Tunisia—and that channels the energies of young people towards profitable trades. Otherwise, we should not be surprised when another young man immolates himself, precisely to escape the scarcities that keep one in six Tunisians below the poverty line. For the Quartet's Nobel award to be symbolically shared by all Tunisians, therefore, the reform torch must continue to burn. Peacefully and in the best traditions of a proud nation that seeks evolutionary change rather than revolution and war.

Economic Development and Political Legitimacy

Naturally, one must be optimistic and hope that this will occur notwithstanding disparaging comments about Arabs in general and revolutionary forces in particular. Still, it is difficult to dismiss lamentations that a dictator like bin 'Ali allegedly kept dangerous Islamists away from power, fought al-Qa'idah, and helped prosecute the perpetual war on terrorism. Lest we forget, he "was fêted by the West," which illustrates Western cynicism about democracy in the Arab World.

According to the "theory of modernization," first developed in the 1950s by the American sociologist Seymour Martin Lipset, democracy is the direct result of economic growth. Lipset's observations generated one of the largest body of research on any topic in comparative politics. Not surprisingly, many social scientists contested it, but the theory has withstood various trials and over time, gained momentum. In summary form, the theory posited that democracy emerged when accurate economic development blossomed, a phenomenon that could be tested through per capita gross national income (GNI) and other indicators.[7] Lipset articulated how every kind of government eventually transitioned to democracy if a certain level of development occurred. With a single exception in contemporary history, Argentina in 1975, this proved to be highly accurate, true even for authoritarian regimes. Although Buenos Aires posted a per capita GNI of $6,055 in 1975, the year the benevolent dictator Isabel Perón signed several decrees that empowered security forces to "annihilate opponents," no other country in recent memory experienced a revolution if its GNI was above the $6,000 level. Over this carefully measured threshold, dictatorships mimicked democratic regimes, as they became far more stable because a majority of their inhabitants attained unprecedented levels of affluence. Paradoxically, dictatorships often survived in countries where per capita income seldom crossed the $1,000 figure, which proved that utter poverty was an incredible useful tool to dominate nations.

Equally important, and over the years, Lipset and others demonstrated that economies that posted incomes between $1,001 and $4,000 were those that were truly in danger, because increasingly educated populations rejected tangential promises that were never fulfilled. Many resented the cronyism and blatant corruption among privileged elites, especially when illegally acquired wealth was openly flaunted, the writ of tasteless minions.[8] Except for the six Gulf Cooperation Council (GCC) States—composed of Bahrain, Kuwait, Oman, Qatar, Sa'udi Arabia and the United Arab Emirates—and Libya, whose per capita GNI topped the $10,000 per year mark, few Arab countries managed to cross the $6,000 threshold. More recent research on the "theory of modernization" confirmed that countries whose GNI oscillated between $2,001 and $4,000, both democratic or dictatorial regimes, fell within 20 years. Nicolae Ceauşescu ruled over Romania from 1974 to 1989 (15 years) while General Augusto Pinochet governed Chile, via a military junta, from 1973 to 1990, for a total of 17 years. Zayn al-'Abidin bin 'Ali orchestrated his 1987 palace coup against Habib Burghibah, to rule for 23 years. Romania and Chile, like Tunisia, posted data within the bracket.

Based on this proven theory, it is thus clear that dictatorships are far less stable when they reach the per capita income of $4,000, which means that the current regimes in Algeria, Jordan, Morocco, Syria and Egypt are in the danger zone. While Iraq is mired in a long-term chaotic political situation, the Sudanese (even after its division into two separate countries) and Yemeni governments may manage to hold on for a while longer, although other concerns could create serious destabilizing threats. Only Lebanon is safe from such upheavals, which is a major reason for its longevity as a growing democratic republic since 1 September 1920 under French mandate, and 22 November 1943 as an independent country, even if its citizens' appetite for violence should not be underestimated.

Target Tunisia

Between 2011 and 2016, Tunisians struggled with reform programs, and managed to adopt a new constitution.[9] Tunisian parliamentarians debated difficult topics, including the approved article that guaranteed "freedom of opinion, thought, expression and information," along with one that authorized the government to propose legislation that would ban torture and safeguard rights. That these discussions were carried out in a country that barely emerged from five decades of dictatorship was downright amazing. In the end, Tunisians showed that Arabs can reform democratically, when the head of the Nida' Tunis Party, Biji Qayd al-Sibsi [Sebsi], won the country's first free presidential elections since independence in 1956. Many were persuaded that this political cycle would be a transitional term and, regardless of the controversies associated with the campaign, Tunisians affirmed the notion that Sunni Arabs were capable, willing, and ready to exercise one of the basic features of democratization. Elections were held with limited violence and most observers confirmed that irregularities were very limited because civilized Tunisians, yes civilized Arab voters, exercised their constitutional rights in a peaceful climate even if media outlets anticipated gloom and doom. A reality despite serious challenges: the jihadist threat that lay dormant finally met its patriotic foes.[10]

Tunisia is not out of the woods yet as the traumas created by years of dictatorship could easily resurface unless effective programs are introduced to meet popular needs. The Islamist question, a Damocles Sword that hangs over Tunisia as it also threatens most Arab societies, is still there. Still, voters were categorical as they rejected heavy ideological commitments and the potential of an "Islamic State" that threatened to polarize the entire nation. Instead, Tunisians voted for security, stability and political accountability and created a "Truth and Dignity Commission" help cement democracy in an impeccably civilized way.[11]

Egypt Confronts New Demons

Unlike Zayn al-'Abidin bin 'Ali, who was rapidly ousted by the Tunisian military, President Husni Mubarak enjoyed the backing of the Egyptian generals at the time of the revolution, which meant that he lingered on for several weeks before he was forced out on 11 February 2011. Mubarak conceded because Egyptians, like Arabs everywhere, were and are truly angry and tired of "unending rule." Still, while Arabs lived through dramatic changes in Algeria, Egypt, Lebanon, Libya, Palestine, Syria, and Yemen, it is important to ask what else was necessary to establish genuine democratic regimes in this part of the world?

To be sure, there were and are significant differences among countries, and although Husni Mubarak was dissimilar from bin 'Ali, Saddam Husayn of Iraq, or even Bashar al-Assad of Syria, this much is certain: elected Arab "Presidents" promoted cronyism, tolerated corruption and practiced the worst forms of torture, including the rendition variety that shamed them in the eyes of their own populations.[12] Moreover, if most Arab regimes are authoritarian, this is partly the result of unnecessary reverence. Throngs of people routinely fill Arab streets, chanting "Bil Ruh Bil Dam, Nafdiq yah . . . [fill in the name of your favorite potentate]", as if their "Soul and Blood" were so cheap to squander on mere mortals. Truth be told, Arabs generated the kind of slogans—"With Our Souls and Our Blood we Sacrifices Ourselves"— that would make Genkhis Khan's followers red with envy. Ironically, the same crowds that chanted with abandon for dictators, vented their fury against them. Therefore, to say that the experiences were cathartic would be an understatement, although such shifts usually called for serious psychological reappraisals. One hopes that Arabs will eventually leave "Bil Ruh Bil Dam, etc. . . . " to Najwah Karam or Majidah al-Rumi, two Lebanese singers whose divine voices can soothe hardened souls far better than any promise to meet basic living needs.

Beyond cheap theatrics, and as events in Egypt amply demonstrated, Arabs were no longer willing to adulate elected officials if for no other reason that they no longer wished to be disappointed. Even if one agreed with a statesman's policies, the post-2011 uprisings demonstrated that Arabs wished to respect themselves and those officials who added value. Regrettably, Arabs tended to lift their leaders to great heights, and to trample over their decaying political bodies when they inevitably fall out of grace. That showed, above all else, limited political maturity and in Egypt at least the people showed that the times were changing. In the event, Arabs learned from others and ascertained, for example, how the French treated Nicholas Sarkozy, the Italians perceived Silvio Berlusconi, or in the ways that Americans regarded Barack Obama. While some ridiculed their elected officials, the French, Italians and Americans stood by them, at least for the periods when these men held office, because they respected their institutions (thus themselves). Many merely accepted ordinary officials so that they could tell the difference when extraordinary ones showed up (Charles De Gaulle, Faysal bin 'Abdul 'Aziz Al Sa'ud, John F. Kennedy, Konrad Adenauer, etc.).

Egyptians felt betrayed by Mubarak and his successors who tested the patience of the docile and malleable.[13] After Mubarak and the February 2011 Supreme Council takeover, which dissolved Egypt's parliament and suspended the constitution in response to demands by demonstrators, elections were held in June 2012 that ushered in the Muslim Brotherhood and its candidate Muhammad Mursi. He became the first Islamist to be elected head of an Arab state, and Egypt embarked on unending constituent assemblies that drafted a post-Mubarak constitution. Mursi, who took a symbolic oath of office in Tahrir Square and affirmed that the people are the source of power, wasted an entire year on social and religious concerns instead of concentrating on what the Egyptian population wanted—economic prosperity. Millions protested against him as he drove tourists away. On 3 July 2013, the President of Egypt was overthrown, martial law was imposed, and though a civilian senior jurist, Adly Mansur, was appointed interim president, it was clear that a military coup was inevitable. On 26 March 2014, the head of the Egyptian Armed Forces, General 'Abdul Fattah al-Sisi, resigned from the military, announced he would stand as a candidate in the presidential elections, and with a 47% turnout, posted a resounding victory. Sisi was sworn into office on 8 June 2014.[14]

Law and order returned to Egypt but it will be a while before freedom returns, and time will clarify whether the military will submit to the rule of law or whether they will uphold and enforce dictatorial authority. What will not change, however, are the basic desires by millions of ordinary people who crave prosperity and stability as they oppose extremism.

Libya Caught between a Rock and a Hard Place

The Wars in Libya—a rebellion as well as an international anti-Mu'ammar al-Qaddhafi offensive—added loud salvos to tectonic changes that shook the Arab World in 2011, and while it is impossible to know whether Arabs will ever produce a leader as entertaining as the late Qaddhafi, Libyans were no longer subjugated. Simply stated, the "King of Kings," as he modestly crowned himself in 2008 during an Organization of African Unity gathering, was only surpassed by equally enigmatic titles. For nearly 42 years, which made Qaddhafi the longest-serving Arab leader, the "Brother Leader" insulted one and all, seldom discriminating against those who disagreed or held a different view. It is fair to ask what will occur to Libya after this successful business model?

How the "Guide of the Revolution" mistreated his own population, denounced freedom fighters who stood up to his tyrannical rule as "rats," and introduced so many bizarre laws over the years that few Libyans escaped unscathed, cannot be forgotten.[15] Qaddhafi's 1975 political opus, *The Green Book*, included strange explanations, bordering on the comical, though in a tragic way. "Women, like men," wrote this self-appointed philosopher, "are human beings," which came as a shock to Libyans.[16] His claim that "mandatory education is a coercive education that suppresses freedom," explained the country's poor record.

Qaddhafi's excesses were tolerated because of Libya's wealth. In fact, a slew of Western leaders flocked to Libya to kiss him (Tony Blair, Jacques Chirac, Nicolas Sarkozy, among others) or profusely shake his hands (Condoleeza Rice and several impressionable U.S. Senators anxious to sign contracts on behalf of their multi-national corporation clients), thereby displaying genuine ugliness. Mercifully, this is no longer possible as Qaddhafi's "all my people love me" declaration was proven wrong. His ousting subjected Libya to utter destruction and at least 50,000 killed or maimed, as well as years if not decades of future instability. His violent assertion that Libyans who did not love him did not deserve to live literally guaranteed his own brutal execution that, ironically, contained a lesson for other Arab autocrats. In the post-Bu'azizi world, dictators were warned that, even if they were entertaining, identifying citizens as "rats" or "microbes" guaranteed their demise.[17]

Of course, the War for Libya reflected a weakening of the new Libyan regime, though the ongoing civil war in Syria, along with the crises in Iraq, Lebanon, Bahrain, Yemen, Egypt, and Tunisia, contributed to the malaise. Regrettably, the world witnessed rival Islamist groups in Libya gain importance and strength, some supported by the General National Council while others were backed by the military, though it is too early to know how events will unfold. Belligerents seem anxious to position themselves on the checkerboard as they enter into temporary coalitions of armed groups, though time will tell whether they will gain the upper hand, or whether the United Nations brokered December 2015 ceasefire—which was reiterated on 31 March 2016 when the leaders of a new UN-supported "unity government" arrived in Tripoli—will prevail. A government of national unity may emerge though Libya is deeply immersed in a dangerous situation. Notwithstanding the ongoing chaos, few should lament the fact that a brutal dictator is gone for good, while significant efforts are under way to deny putative successors fresh gains. Indeed, so-called jihadists may succeed in terrorizing ordinary Libyans, though chances are excellent that most would be defeated especially when locals see what ideologically challenged militants offer them. To be sure, al-Qa'idah factions probably overlapped with clans, militias, and criminal networks, but the majority of these latter-day wannabes were of the fleeting, opportunistic variety that enriched the wily and gave significance to the irrelevant. Moreover, it was a mistake to assume that dictators like Qaddhafi and his fallen counterparts kept in check various ethnic and tribal factions, or acted as a lid by keeping volatile elements repressed, or that Islamic militants were engaged in "holy war." Such assessments were nothing more than insults to those who sought liberty, and while gangsters took advantage of the chaos that followed epochal politico-military changes, most were exposed for being nothing more than passing cults. Five years is far too short a time to write off democratizing efforts and it behooves analysts to assess the learning process with utmost care.

The Yemeni Killing Fields

Unlike Bashar al-Assad, who prematurely claimed that Syria would be bypassed by the ongoing Arab uprisings, 'Ali 'Abdallah Salih knew his end was near and negotiated an orderly departure. Like other paragons of absolute authority whose very survival depended on how well they seduce gullible masses, Salih entertained "proposals" to ease him out of power. One of the most effective was made by the Gulf Cooperation Council Secretary General 'Abdul Latif Al Zayani, who met with Salih in Sana'a to deliver a package deal. Reportedly, the arrangement consisted of what came to be known as the "30-60 Plan," which offered the dejected President and his family immunity from prosecution if he left the country.[18]

A gambler who frequently bet on regional losers, Salih's political genius at home was evident after he manipulated various constituents to triumph within the General People's Congress. For all his prowess, however, it was unclear which major military victories prompted him to seek, and receive from parliament in 1997, a promotion to the rank of field marshal. In the event, the first directly elected president in the country's history, Salih apparently won over 96 percent of the vote in 1999. This was standard operating procedure for dictators even if few could match Saddam Husayn's 100% mark in 2002. Unlike Saddam Husayn, however, Salih was interested in leaving office if a sweet deal could be cut. The former Yemeni leader promised to step down in 2013 without passing the torch to his son Ahmad, who was then serving as the Commander of the Republican Guard, and even offered to amend the constitution to give more powers to parliament. "We will continue to resist," he declared, "undaunted and committed to constitutional legitimacy, while rejecting plots and coups," adding that "those who want the chair of power have to get it through ballot boxes."[19] Still, his shameful negotiations to orchestrate a departure, while seeking immunity for countless family members along the way, perfectly illustrates an "Ali Baba and his 40 Thieves" mentality.[20] Beyond acolytes who benefited from his largesse, Yemenis perceived Salih for what he was and is, an expert manipulator who craves power.

No wonder his rule came to an end, as decent Yemenis no longer wished to be ruled by an official who made the army of thieves in 'Ali Baba's legendary story look good.

Yet, and a few months after they first made a run for Sana'a, Yemen's Huthi rebels, who were and are supported by Salih and his acolytes, gave the country's political factions a three-day ultimatum to reach a political agreement on power sharing before, or so they claimed, their challenged leaders would take over. It was a realistic threat that allowed Huthis to grab power even if it meant that they were ready, on Iran's explicit orders, to destroy the country in the process. As Nabil Khalifé discusses in his study, how Huthis came to power and how they exploited conditions on the ground deserves careful attention as the development is nothing if not a perfectly orchestrated coup.

Huthis, who name themselves after Husayn Badriddin al-Huthi, a renegade commander who was reportedly killed by the Yemeni army in a September 2004 battle but who boastfully also refer to themselves as "Supporters of God" (Ansar Allah), are an insurgent group. They happen to be Zayidis, followers of the second largest branch of Shi'ah Islam, named after Zayd bin 'Ali, and may constitute approximately 40% of the Yemeni population, although no proper statistics confirm this figure. Today, the nominal leader of the militia is Husayn's father, Badriddin, though it is unclear whether he is merely a spiritual leader or also a warrior. In the world of religious competition Zayidi laws are not that much more different from Sunni rulings, although Shi'ahs in general and Zayidis in particular believe in the Imamate as a cornerstone of religion. This is a vexing point to say the least, because the effort mimics Iran and, more important, because it negates much of the contemporary history of Yemen after the fall of the Imamate, or the Mutawakkilite Kingdom of Yemen, in 1962. The three monarchs of the Imamate—Yahyah Hamid al-Din, Ahmad bin Yahyah, and Muhammad al-Badr—were Zayidis, but also diehard Arab nationalists. This is the critical feature to bear in mind at a time when Huthis continue to benefit from the military assistance that Iran extends, since Sana'a was a founding member of the League of Arab States in 1945 and, as such, could not, or at least ought not, to be hijacked by intruders.

In the event, Huthis first organized themselves as a militia in 1992—long before the U.S. invasion of Iraq in 2003 that set in motion the current uprisings throughout the Arab World. They repeatedly asserted that their actions fought Salafi extremism—the term they use evolved as Iran updated the narrative to Salafi-Takfiri-Wahhabi—even if this was disingenuous because President 'Ali 'Abdallah Salih, who emerged as a Huthi ally, was the head-of-state allegedly responsible for the widespread and systematic discrimination against them. What characterized Huthis was their anti-Sunni and anti-American slogans, which displeased the then pro-American Salih. In fact, the first confrontations between Huthis and government officials occurred in 2004 when hundreds of Huthis were arrested, followed—on Salih's explicit orders no less—by the systematic hunting of Husayn al-Huthi who resisted, and was presumably killed on 10 September 2004. More recently, and in the aftermath of the uprising that ended Salih's dictatorship, Huthis found it convenient to participate in the 2011 National Dialogue Conference but rejected the provisions of the Gulf Cooperation Council peace plan, probably on orders emanating from Tehran.[21]

Fierce fighters gnawed at Sa'adah, Al-Jawf and Hajjah governorates in late 2011, Huthis attacked the capital in September 2014 and consolidated their holding when they gained access to the Red Sea, which meant that Iran could resupply them with fresh weapons. Today, parts of Sana'a, including government buildings, are under the control of the militia even if their actions have led to confrontations with an increasingly wary population that rejects extremism. Of course, and in addition to the legitimately elected President of Yemen 'Abid Rabbu Mansur al-Hadi—who was in limbo because parliament could not meet to deliberate his fate—as well as the ongoing American drone attacks on al-Qa'idah in the Arabian Peninsula, Huthis were still unable to persuade Southerners to accept their vision for the country. What irritated Huthis was the 2014 constitutional panel recommendation to divide the country into six regions, four in the north and two in the south, thereby creating a federalist model of governance that they believe weakens their position. Al-Hadi, a Zayidi too, disagreed and, in turn accused insurgents of intending to overthrow the government not in order to institute Shi'ah religious laws as they claimed, but to destabilize the government, stir anti-American sentiments, and otherwise do Iran's bidding in the area. Not surprisingly, Huthis countered with allegations that al-Hadi was backed by the allegedly anti-Shi'ah Sa'udi government, and now gave political factions time to agree on a way out of the crisis or submit to its own undetermined solutions.

The worst occurred in 2015 as Iranian miscalculations in the Arab World, especially after Tehran sought to project power everywhere, led to a war in Yemen. After President al-Hadi fled his residence in Sana'a, where he was under virtual house arrest, and took refuge in the southern city of Aden, events unfolded rather quickly. Hadi rescinded his 22 January 2015 resignation, resumed his presidential duties, and called Huthi actions taken after September 2014 illegitimate. Buoyed by hundreds of thousands of Yemenis who protested in Sana'a, Ta'iz and elsewhere against the Huthis, Hadi's move nullified what rival factions agreed to—to create UN brokered transition councils—that, for all practical purposes, established equality among warring factions that did not deserve such parity. Although what happened next was murky, the fate of the embattled nation is at the time of writing (November 2016) very much in the air, with a distinct possibility of renewed civil war. Few should doubt that Tehran will back the Huthis given that Iran is determined to hold on to its gains. Strangely, Washington seems baffled by the Huthis, unaware of or unwilling to label Iranian-backed militias as terrorists, since the American narrative is to more or less exclusively reserve that label to al-Qaʻidah and Daʻish [ISIS]. It was an eerie tale that belied reality on the ground. Indeed, the Obama Administration seldom tackled the crisis from the perspective of what was actually occurring in reality and concluded that Iran was the key to its preferred solutions whereas Tehran was the problem. Much like the mistaken Nixon Administration, whose 1971 "Twin Pillars" policy intended to create a balance of power between Iran and Saʻudi Arabia, Obama opted to copy that stale model to resurrect a regional security architecture in which Tehran and Riyadh would compete. Nabil Khalifé raises various questions on this point, including whether such preferences are not aimed to neutralize both countries and, through them, two alleged proxies, al-Qaʻidah for Sunni Saʻudi Arabia and Hizballah for Shiʻah Iran. As meticulously explained in his study, Khalifé deciphers the evidence for this American preference, even if the choice set the stage for more or less permanent confrontations (see also Appendix 7).

In Yemen, and unlike what brainy U.S. decision-makers concluded, everyone discovered that the Arab World was more than al-Qaʻidah and Hizballah. Nevertheless, this was a secondary concern since President Obama initiated secret negotiations with Tehran starting in July 2012, which sealed the fates of both Iraq and Syria. Obama chose to overlook the use of chemical weapons by the Damascus regime in August 2012, saying that he would change his calculations significantly if this proved to be accurate. It was accurate. But no change of policy came from the White House. The thousand or so human beings who perished in that attack, and similar ones at other times, were mere statistics even if the evidence was incontrovertible. For Obama, there were more important geopolitical negotiations underway, and the priority was elsewhere. In fact, neither Iraq nor Syria nor Lebanon nor, for that matter, the conservative Arab Gulf monarchies, were considered important to the American administration. What motivated the American president was his Iran policy to reinforce a "geopolitical equilibrium" that was anything but.

In the words of one of America's intellectual paragons, former Alaska Governor and one time Vice Presidential candidate, Sarah Palin, "Let Allah sort it out," which was what everyone thought in private but were too diplomatic to reveal.[22] Such an avowal would have been humorous were it not woefully illiterate. Obama administration minions echoed similarly obtuse views of the "pity they can't both lose" variety that, sadly, ignored the fate of millions of human beings. What Obama missed in the Middle East, which proved to be a significant error in retrospect, was the notion that Iran would be satisfied with a minor regional role. On the contrary, and as it is now amply evident in Yemen, Iranian leaders intend to win everywhere. Indeed, it is safe to conclude that Iran now controls four Arab capitals—Baghdad, Beirut, Damascus and Sana'a—and for some commentators even holds Washington captive. As discussed below, both the U.S. and Iran seem to be led by leaders immersed in vanity, unaware that their actions will generate counter-actions.

To Sacrifice Iraq and Serve Iran

Cicero, a statesman who ruled Rome and who was murdered on the orders of the tyrant Anthony [of Anthony and Cleopatra fame] in 44 BC, once opined that a leader ought to issue commands that were just, advantageous to the nation, and in keeping with the law. He added that the laws of a state were the ultimate sources of legitimacy and that even the just ruler ought to obey them because, in the end, the law was the "silent" leader. Cicero's recommendations were harsh, and as recorded by history he paid the ultimate price—his head was cut off—when he defended the republic at a time when tyranny gained the upper hand. Although he supported a moderate and balanced form of government, he concluded that the most preferable type of rule was monarchy because royal qualities were essential for justice, especially since man generally speaking failed to create full equality among citizens.

Twenty centuries later, the vast majority of the seven billion inhabitants on Earth are still far from such an ideal, as tyranny has led to the rise of oligarchies in many lands, mob rule governs directly or indirectly, and anarchy pokes its ugly face from time to time. In the absence of effective and just laws, nation-states toyed with forms of oppression, including the sophisticated types that pretended to rule under the law when the latter were selectively applied to benefit tiny minorities. That was the chief reason why chaotic movements turned into revolutions with no end in sight. The latest such development in the Arab World was the gradual unraveling of Iraq that entered a new phase of its ongoing wars since 1918. Notwithstanding his parliamentary victories several years ago, Prime Minister Nuri al-Maliki pursued policies that ensured mayhem for over a decade after Saddam Husayn was forcibly removed from power. Few should now be surprised that Iraq as we knew it is no longer a viable state or that al-Maliki's initiatives guaranteed its disintegration. Indeed, most Iraqis prepared for that outcome, as Baghdad lost its bearings. In the words of the prime minister of Iraq's autonomous Kurdish region, Natchervan Barzan, it was "almost impossible" for Iraq to return to the situation that existed before the city of Mosul was captured by the Islamic State in Iraq and Syria, Da'ish, even if al-Maliki's successor, Haydar al-'Abadi, vowed to liberate it—an operation that started in mid-October 2016 and continued as this book went to press. Barzan condemned the Sunni jihadist group's blitzkrieg over Mosul with less than a thousand fighters in 2015 but said nothing as to how two Iraqi Army brigades, presumably well trained and equipped, could come apart so fast? Moreover, he said even less about his own Kurdish fighters, the peshmergas [literally "those who confront death"], who stormed Tikrit as additional Iraqi army troops fled that city.[23]

Beyond Da'ish or what regional powers attempted to accomplish in Iraq, it was increasingly clear that the country would not remain unified, which meant that the post-World War I design by Gertrude Bell, an extraordinary woman who forcefully morphed four governorates together, was slated to end.[24] This reality emerged in the aftermath of the U.S. invasion and occupation of Iraq when Senator, later Vice-President, Joe Biden championed an effective federal system that was "explicitly allowed by the Iraqi constitution (at the insistence of the Kurds)," which devolved power away from Baghdad. Biden denied he had made the proposition in 2006 but he was ahead of his time because he understood that Prime Minister al-Maliki and other Iraqi officials could no longer rule with justice.[25] Al-Maliki failed to impose law and order as Iraqis were subjected to routine atrocities that targeted civilians from all communities. Under both Maliki and 'Abadi terms, Baghdad became gradually disunited, as various factions prevented each other from finding the necessary ways to live together in relative peace and harmony. Both blamed so-called Sunni extremist militants while Shi'ah leaders disenfranchised many, sided with Damascus against the vast majority of the Syrian people, acted as a conduit for Iran throughout the region, and insulted most Arab Gulf rulers on a more or less continual basis. High-ranking Shi'ah officials did not engender confidence but increased raw sectarianism across the country despite the devastating consequences of the War for Iraq, which generated more terrorism than previously acknowledged (see also Appendix 8).

Of course, Cicero believed that there were universal laws that governed human relations, which were topped by fundamental freedoms that imposed certain rules on leaders. He stressed that those who embraced a balance of power ruled with justice, although he also noted that true leaders were those who displayed exceptional character and integrity. He counseled the latter to keep their friends close and their enemies even closer, hoped that they would rely on intelligence to reach sound decisions based on facts, and recommended that they learn the art of compromise to advance the interests of the nation. He also added two specific prescriptions that apply to Iraqis and others: namely that good leaders ought to realize that corruption destroys societies, just as much as unjust wars.[26]

The Emasculation of Syria

In his classic *Muqaddimah: An Introduction to History*, Ibn Khaldun, the father of Muslim sociology, wrote that prestige in one lineage lasts four generations before it dissipates. Five years into the Syrian Revolution, it is doubtful whether the al-Assad lineage will last that long, though the "Ba'ath Crown" pretended to rule with 'asabiyyah (solidarity, group feeling, as well as group consciousness). What few doubted was the ironclad resolve of the president who understood, perhaps better than most, what he and the 'Alawi community stood to lose. It was his destiny to complete the Sulayman, Hafiz and Bashar al-Assad trilogy, though history is poised to record the last two leaders' ferocious appetites for violence. Will future generations of Syrians comprehend their insatiable hunger for power?[27]

As discussed by Nabil Khalifé, and though Bashar al-Assad told *The Wall Street Journal* that Syria was stable because of its ideological strength, confrontations continue with no end in sight.[28] Arguably, the president's enthusiasm for bloodshed and his oft-repeated willingness to fight until death, stands out, although few anticipate that the regime will successfully crush the opposition and emerge victorious. Despite a steady stream of defections from the ranks, one of the primary reasons for the prolongation of the war is the unwavering backing of the army leadership to the Ba'ath government. Of course, while the military and various security forces suffered and continue to sustain significant losses, their willingness to defend the regime sealed their fate even if the time to settle differences was probably in the distant future. Nevertheless, despite undeniable losses of large swathes of territory in northern and eastern Syria, President al-Assad has persuaded himself that he would emerge victorious from the civil war. Somehow the conservative United Nations estimates of 250,000 fatalities—which in reality are probably twice as high—along with the wholesale destruction of a relatively modernizing society, were tangential matters. Amazingly, the Syrian head-of-state devoted precious little attention to his nation's total destruction in several carefully orchestrated presentations, which led commentators to conclude that al-Assad was unable to contemplate reality.

What was equally delusional was his conviction that he and his military could actually win, oblivious to grave errors that incorrectly measured the Syrian thirst for freedom. Although debatable, the president's undoing probably started after he refused to condemn members of the security forces who savagely tortured Hamzah al-Khatib in early 2011. It was worth recalling that the thirteen-year old was arrested—along with several of his peers—after he scribbled anti-regime graffiti on a school wall in Dar'ah. His body was returned to his family nearly a month later, bearing signs of horrific torture, which redefined barbarism. Such misconceptions notwithstanding, another reason for the prolongation of the war was the unprecedented level of indecision within the resistance. Despite one of the early Syrian Opposition Council leaders' visit to liberated Aleppo in 2012, Shaykh Mu'az al-Khatib and his successors were caught in interminable negotiations over the establishment of a government in exile, which extended the time when anti-regime ranks would be united. Such dissonance played into the regime's hands, even if Syrians rejected autocratic rule and no longer wished to have leaders who measured their prowess by the number of decades they governed.

Five years into the revolution and with soaring casualties as well as a huge refugee crisis that threatens to linger on for years if not decades to come, contradictory political initiatives loom over the horizon, as fresh weapons flood warehouses and further lengthen the war, especially now that Russia became a warring faction (see Appendix 9). In 2017, Syria faces an existential crisis, even if Bashar al-Assad advances various political cards that portray him as the indispensable player in future negotiations led by Washington and Moscow. Indeed, Syria hopes that Russia will continue to stand by the dejected president, though President Vladimir Putin carries a double-edged sword in his hands. It remained to be determined whether Russia feels any compunction to bleed the Syrian regime dry. Nevertheless, where Assad blundered was to believe that the revolution was a foreign conspiracy, though fewer and fewer Syrians shared the "anti-imperialist" ideological tune he cavalierly hummed. Nearly five decades of such rhetoric has brought Syria to its current state, which is to say, nowhere worthy of a great nation that protects its citizens and creates wealth.

In his opus, Ibn Khaldun pointed out that injustice, despotism, and tyranny were clear signs of the downfall of a ruler, though he foresaw the possibility to make corrections. "Throughout history," he wrote, "many nations have suffered a physical defeat, but that has never marked the end of a nation." Yet, when a nation became "the victim of a psychological defeat," he warned, then that marked its end. There was no chance for such an emotional reversal in Syria, because Syrians were not weak and the mere fact that a significant portion was willing to sacrifice itself, confirmed it.

Who is Winning the Arab Spring?

As the discussion above highlights, the Arab Spring has proved to be far more complicated than many assumed, and is truly at its very beginnings. There are several specific consequences, topped by the creation of the so-called Islamic State, which will need sorting out although it is too early to determine final outcomes. The term "Arab Spring" was inadvertently coined by Marc Lynch writing about the first uprisings in January 2011 in *Foreign Policy*, even if few believed at the time that a seasonal development could unravel entrenched regimes, usher in democratizing governments, and resolve all types of ills—domestic or foreign. Rather, what actually started in late 2010/early 2011 were a series of revolutions in the best traditions of the word, which effectively meant that dramatic transformations under way throughout the region were bound to take decades to mature. As such, it might also be far too early to talk about "winners and losers" as the erudite John Simpson proposed in one of his BBC "comments."[29]

For Simpson, Libya was ruined by the fall of the Qaddhafi dictatorship; Egypt was "back in a condition of stasis"; the Syrian system persisted against revolutionaries because Western countries, "though they won't say so, have decided they would rather have" Assad than the so-called Islamic State; Iraq weathered the Da'ish storm; Jordan remained under threat but endured; Lebanon held together; Algeria and Tunisia settled down; and Turkey, "watching from the sidelines, has often been worried, but has survived unscarred" notwithstanding a failed coup attempt in mid-2016.

One is not sure whether Libyans, Egyptians, Syrians, Iraqis, Jordanians, Lebanese, Algerians, Tunisians and even Turks were losers but what was certain was the fact that they could not possibly be winners, according to Simpson, since the transformations under way did not result in cleaner changes like in the former Eastern European environment. Still, a strong argument can be made that Arabs in general, and those confronting dictatorial regimes in particular, have demonstrated impeccable resilience. Half-a-million Syrians have paid the ultimate price for freedom, killed during the past five years under atrocious conditions. The same can be said about others who died for liberty; Arabs have become pawns in the hands of amoral powers.

Simpson hinted that the outside world led by the United States and the United Kingdom tergiversated. Notwithstanding the art of diplomatic initiative, President Obama's warning to his Syrian counterpart that the use of chemical weapons against insurgents would not be tolerated and then conveniently overlooking events when Damascus did precisely that, stands as a perfect illustration of American weakness and loss. Similarly, when Prime Minister David Cameron conceded a key parliamentary vote not to bomb Syria in August 2013—by a mere 13 votes—it was because Labor Party leader Ed Miliband had the better line: "Evidence should precede decision, not decision precede evidence."[30] Of course, and in the aftermath of the more recent spectacular "Da'ishi" proofs, ranging from televised beheadings to minting currency, few raised critical questions regarding such gains. Was Da'ish a winner or a loser? Was the sale of Da'ish-controlled oil a winning or a losing proposition?

Despite the brutality that permeated the Arab World, an honest assessment of what was gradually unraveling was sheer determination to slowly change the way Arabs were and are governed. Ironically, this became evident in the Arab Gulf monarchies more than in the secularizing republics, but that was one of the paradoxes of contemporary affairs. That conservative rulers would be far more attuned to the needs of their populations rather than entrenched parliamentary or presidential regimes that neglected constitutional responsibilities was, truth be told, an amazing development. A small win by any stretch of the imagination. Nevertheless, there is no denying that ISIS, which was allegedly created in 2003 and pledged its loyalty to the so-called al-Qa'idah terrorist organization, resurfaced in 2013 when Ayman al-Zawahiri disbanded its Syrian faction. While the self-appointed successor to 'Usamah bin Ladin spoke with authority in an audio recording on the *Al-Jazeera* television network, several ISIS leaders rejected this decision, as fighters gained ground. Was ISIS part of the poorly defined and largely meaningless "global jihad" movement? How effective was it? Were accusations that Sa'udi Arabia financed it accurate? Was it a coherent group led by a central hierarchy that promoted a clear ideology or was this a fly-by-night operation created by the Ba'ath regime to further confuse conditions in Syria?

Few doubted that some of ISIS' estimated original 2,500 rebels believed in the Caliphate—the ideal Muslim government that would eventually rule the entire world—that, with a little luck and a lot of work, would end the nation's decline and restore it on the path to glory. Indeed, many of its adherents contemplated a return to the "Islamic Golden Age," one that was cleansed from foreign influences, to live under just rule. It was towards that end that the Iraqi ISIS leader, Abu Bakr al-Baghdadi, committed his forces to fight alongside Jabhat al-Nusrah, an indigenous Syrian group led by Muhammad al-Jawlani that conveniently changed its name to Jabhat Fatih al-Sham in July 2016.

How to fight the so-called Islamic State was at the very heart of the matter; it is not the invincible multi-pronged hydra that no one can destroy. In reality, Da'ish is little more than a collection of Internet-savvy misfits that rely on technology and rudimentary weapons to earn attention. Confronted by formidable opposition from Western and Arab countries, the few thousand Da'ish fighters will not be long allowed to assassinate, behead, starve, rape, destroy, exile, and otherwise stand as vulgar barbarians who pretend that their acts are divine will. Although these modern Hashashin are their own worse enemies, why are sophisticated analysts mesmerized by their prowess and, even worse, why are they gullible enough to think that thirty or fifty thousand hooligans can destroy relatively powerful nation-states?[31] Naturally, any long-term military commitments are worrisome because of casualties, and must only become last resort options though few appreciate the devastating consequences that such deployments have on large numbers of civilians.

FROM KISSINGER TO OBAMA

As Nabil Khalifé discusses in his important study, the "Arab Uprisings" occurred within the framework of major power strategies, best articulated by Henry A. Kissinger, who served two American presidents as National Security Council advisor and Secretary of State, and who identified Realpolitik as diplomacy based on power and practical concerns. Kissinger rejected ideological notions, dismissed moral considerations, and derided ethical premises in the conduct of foreign policy. In one of his latest rants, published in *The Washington Post* under the title "Meshing Realism and Idealism in the Middle East," he offered a carefully laid out variation.[32] What stood out in this essay were the nonagenarian's oft-repeated arguments that Washington ought to remain focused on its core interests in the region, even if he colored his classic comments with a remarkable assertion that the U.S. ought to embrace "intermediate stages." To his credit, Kissinger opined that revolutions are primarily judged "by what they build, not what they destroy," which was a fair assertion. In fact, events that followed the four classic revolutions (British, French, American and Russian) changed humanity as we know it, although a fifth must now be added to this list. Mao's revolution, which completely redesigned China even if that experiment was a work in progress, transformed the Middle Kingdom into the rising power it is. Lest we overlook particularly violent chapters, revolutions almost always destroyed at first, before embarking on various corrections that allowed for emancipation and progress. Kissinger and many others who focus on the Arab World routinely reject this premise, pointing out how little has changed since 2010, although five years is hardly enough time to provide an accurate assessment of the level of destruction under way, or of the potential for reconstruction.

Of course, Kissinger rejected the premise that the Syrian Revolution was a struggle for democracy and while he welcomed the removal of President Bashar al-Assad from power, the former Secretary of State was utterly mistaken when he claimed that the real concern in Syria was the nascent "struggle for dominance between Assad's 'Alawites, backed by many of the other Syrian minorities, and the Sunni majority." This was and is a largely incorrect reading of what is under way even if religious overtones cannot be ignored. In fact, Damascus has unleashed its fury against all Syrians, shelling Latakiyyah from the sea, bombarding Aleppo from the air, and otherwise running its tanks through most cities without asking whether its victims were Sunnis, Shi'ahs, Druzes, or Christians. Yet, by underlining the religious equation in the Syrian Revolution, Kissinger wanted to prepare public opinion to the "day-after" when, presumably, 'Alawites could engage in a long-term "struggle for physical survival." While it is impossible to predict whether Syria will break into component ethnic and sectarian entities, with grave repercussions in a sustained civil war as well as serious consequences to neighboring countries, chances are excellent that this wishful thinking will not occur even if, as Khalifé argues, that seems to be the Western objective. Indeed, today's belligerents are more likely to quickly embark on democratizing values, precisely to maintain the unity of the country but without its dictatorial anchor. Like Cairo under the interim Tantawi/Mursi duopoly that was overthrown by Sisi, Damascus will also go through a transition period, and though no-one can accurately predict what its ultimate outcome may be, relative success stands as much of a chance as gloom and doom scenarios especially if opposition forces that call for the birth of a free Syria reached administrative power. The latters' eventual writ was to emphasize the value of the "nation" instead of concentrating on those who destroyed it, especially the Ba'ath

Party, even if the political tasks required to rebuild the broken country are as daunting as any eventual physical reconstruction efforts.

Sykes–Picot: Take One and Two

Syrians of all ethnic and religious groups are loyal to their country, and history demonstrates that a century of Sykes–Picot-led, British-inspired, French-administered, and Ba'ath-dominated power centers did not prevent the rise of true revolutionary spirits.[33] Naturally, Kissinger disagreed, as his primary audience was the Boston—New York—Washington corridor elite, though it was interesting to note that he formulated the U.S. goal as any new regime in Damascus that will end the Syria–Iran alliance. It was Tehran that stood out on his radar screen, precisely as Israel has been clamoring for years, and it is important to highlight that Kissinger had nothing to say about the influence of Israeli politics on everything that Washington contemplates in the area. Be that as it may, Kissinger knew that the Israeli–American record in the Middle East was poor, with wars galore, and double, triple, quadruple, and even quintuple standards applied by the veto-yielding superpower against 375 million Arabs. What befell the Palestinian nation, for example, and continues to harm generations that will never give up cannot but be self-evident though the foresightful know the difference between right and wrong. The confirmation that Washington undermined democratically elected governments—Islamist or otherwise—since the 1950s, stretching from Algeria to Iran, cannot be denied. Thus, although it may be accurate to state, as Kissinger does, that Islamists have a poor record of democracy in the Middle East, he simply chooses to overlook the causes for that failure.

Perhaps the day will come when Westerners in general and Americans in particular will not conclude that Arabs espouse hard-line Islamism because that is part of local "culture," as so many politicians boldly assert from time to time, oblivious to reality.[34] All Arabs, the Muslim majorities as well as the Christian minorities, desire the same things that people everywhere hope for: freedom. They neither want blatant consumerism nor the more extreme application of laws designed centuries ago. It is worth repeating, Arabs want to be free, and it remains to be determined whether Islamist governments or more enlightened rulers will ensure that people re-discover their dignities at a time of great hostility towards them. Of course, every conflict cannot be framed in ideological terms to serve intrinsic interests affirmed by Kissinger and others, even if that is precisely what the American did in Vietnam, Chile, Cambodia, and in so many other places. In the past, he projected

American power and exceptionality, sometimes implemented through raw force. He called for the development of strategic interests in the Arab World, but now wants to embrace "intermediate stages"—a clever stance since reconciliation between realism (interests) and idealism (values) prolongs Western hegemony. Still, his audience may be better served if it understood that the Arab Spring has permanently changed this part of the world, and while it might take several decades to reach a modus vivendi, there simply is no going back.

Kissinger, who is still America's leading realist, perceived power through the prism of the Cold War. At its height, the state of enmity between capitalism and communism defined the second part of the 20th century, when Western powers lamentably relied on Israel, Turkey and Iran to help them dominate Arabs. Remarkably, Israel marketed itself as a strategic bulwark against the Soviet Union while Iran offered its services as the policeman of the Gulf. Turkey, a member of the North Atlantic Treaty Organization (NATO) alliance, was deemed a model Muslim democracy even if it was under military rule. With the fall of the Soviet Union in 1990, Israel's putative value as a strategic American asset vanished, while the 1979 Islamic Revolution toppled an Iranian dictator only to replace it with another. In light of a plethora of military coups that rocked Ankara for decades, Turkey's democratizing institutions, which ushered in the Justice and Development Party [Adalet ve Kalkınma Partisi (AKP)] in 2002 under Recep Tayyip Erdoğan, were perceived as a reliable model. In light of recent developments, all three countries are now searching for regional significance as leading experts raise grave concerns on their political capabilities and, perhaps far more important, whether all three societies may be willing to oppose the inevitable rise of political Sunnism.

Naturally, and in addition to strategists of Kissinger's status who explored these concerns, a number of academics added their own analyses too. The most prominent to join the chorus is none other than Bernard Lewis, the Cleveland E. Dodge Professor Emeritus of Near Eastern Studies at Princeton University. Should we heed his warnings as Arab societies adjust to epochal uprisings against tyranny?

Academic Prowess

Few doubt the British-American professor's detailed and sophisticated capabilities. A genuine specialist of the history of Islam and the interaction between Islam and the West, Lewis authored over thirty books, including the popular *What Went Wrong?: The Clash Between Islam and Modernity in the Middle East*, which became a bestseller in the aftermath of the 9/11 attacks.[35] In his books and other writings, Lewis argued that the Muslim World was archaic, whose self-inflicted decline resulted from both cultural and religious shortcomings. Regrettably, President George W. Bush and Vice President Dick Cheney lent credence to such nonsense by listening to Lewis, although one wonders what they would make of the good professor's more recent regurgitations.[36] Speaking to *The Wall Street Journal* in early April 2011, Lewis posited that tyrannical regimes were "doomed," and that he was "delighted" by the popular movements that shook Arab governments from Tunisia to Syria. Nevertheless, he cautioned against the pace of rapid change and, especially, on any insistence to usher in Western-style elections. Although Lewis' views were surprisingly positive, he raised alarms about the growing "Islamization of Turkey," and expressed serious fears regarding a nuclear-armed Iran. Lewis hoped that the so-called "Green Movement" would successfully topple the Iranian regime although he did not think that Iran "can be contained if it does go nuclear." According to the erudite scholar, mutually assured destruction [MAD] would not work with nuclear-armed mullahs, allegedly because the latter were "religious fanatics with an apocalyptic mindset." "In Islam, as in Christianity and Judaism," he clarified, "there is an end-of-times scenario—and they think it's beginning or has already begun."[37] Consequently, if Iran managed to acquire nuclear warheads, this convoluted logic went, one can comfortably assume that irrational Iranian leaders might use such weapons for fear of an American or Israeli counter-strike. For Lewis, the MAD theory was "not a deterrent . . . [but] an inducement." Such a tragic view is not level-headed, for there are no reasons to believe that Iranian leaders would be that unwise.

Because Bernard Lewis wrote seminal works on Turkey, his comments on that country's recent developments raised eyebrows too. "In Turkey," declared Lewis, "the movement is getting more and more toward re-Islamization. The government has that as its intention—and it has been taking over, very skillfully, one part after another of Turkish society. The economy, the business community, the academic community, the media. And now they're taking over the judiciary, which in the past has been the stronghold of the republican regime," he declared. It is unclear whether the professor's concerns were colored by ongoing Turkish–Israeli socio-political divergences, though the 100-year-old pro-Turkish intellectual believed that Turkey could become the next Iran, overtaken by so-called radical forces that reject secularism and/or pro-Western preferences.

Towards the end of his interview, Lewis insisted that the Muslim World espoused a long tradition of diffuse and limited government, which formed the bases of modernizing societies. He acknowledged that Islamic tradition was replete with examples of anti-autocratic rule, especially since Muslims favored governments that were legal, based on justice. His sharp criticisms of what he labeled the "mistreatment of women" apparently were the chief causes for the decline of the Muslim World. "My own feeling," he chimed, "is that the greatest defect of Islam and the main reason they fell behind the West is the treatment of women." In what passed for an off-hand sociological commentary, the eminent historian posited: "Think of a child that grows up in a Muslim household where the mother has no rights, where she is downtrodden and subservient. That's preparation for a life of despotism and subservience. It prepares the way for an authoritarian society." When an eminent scholar on Arab culture and politics utters such fare, one wonders what else needs to be said beyond shaking one's head, especially in the Spring of 2017. Why is it so hard for leading historians like Bernard Lewis to accept that both the cold and hot war models were flawed and that, beyond political considerations, there were simple cultural norms to respect? Lewis and others were caught by surprise when ordinary Arabs rose up against ossified regimes. Few anticipated or wished to see dictators vacate their posts and even fewer contemplated similar fates for those still clinging to their seats, incredulous that their days were numbered, as evidence of Arab emancipation. Indistinguishably, today few commentators perceive Sunni Arab masses with anything but fear, which raises a key question: Why was it so difficult for Washington, London, Paris, Moscow and Beijing to side with those who strove for liberty?

Part of the diplomatic answer must fall under the idiom "Better the devil you know than the devil you don't," even if this is in poor taste. Over the longterm such attitudes are worrisome, because millions are now developing specific mind-sets. How Arabs will judge Western societies whose companies pursue wealthy contracts with Arab states without buttressing democratization and freedom? Egyptians, for example, were bewildered and will long remember after senior American officials fell into delay tactics in February and March 2011 when President Husni Mubarak was barely able to withstand popular pressures to resign his post. Millions still shake their heads in what must be politely termed as confusion emanating from Washington. Even more questioned the Obama Administration's policies during the past few years, asking themselves whether there is a deliberate policy to divide and rule, even to crush Sunni Arabs.

Of course, the United States was not the only paragon of confusion as France embarked on a similar preference. Many remember the 13 July

2008 Paris Summit called by President Nicolas Sarzoky to launch the Union for the Mediterranean that, a day later (14 July 2008), honored 43 Heads of State and Government gathered to observe France's annual military parade on the Champs-Elysées. Even if Stefan Simons labeled the gathering as "Nicolas Sarkozy's New Club Med" in *Der Spiegel*, it was hilarious to see the Syrian President Bashar al-Assad receive a red carpet treatment, barely a few years after the 23 October 1983 bombing of French barracks in Beirut that killed 58 servicemen, an attack that was most probably ordered by Damascus. Mercifully, the kings of Morocco and Jordan, as well as then favorite Libyan leader [Mu'ammar al-Qaddhafi], were not in attendance. But the Assad invitation, ostensibly made to open a new diplomatic chapter between France and Syria, highlighted French diplomatic amateurism.[38]

Truth be told, few Western politicians foresaw the brewing uprisings in the Arab World, as scholars, including several French academics, were seldom optimistic regarding far-reaching change for these societies. That is why Western silence on developments in Syria is now so deafening. Even Russia and China, alleged epitomes of mundane populations, distinguished themselves with diplomatic mendacity and, at least in Moscow's case after 2015, to military activities that substantively increased the number of the dead. When heavily equipped Syrian Arab Army troops entered cities like Hamah or Hums [Homs], where thousands of residents defiantly opposed their government's crackdown, little more than peeps were heard from the morally challenged. Random killings were conveniently overlooked for political expedience. Interestingly, little or no commentaries were offered after a video from Hamah, which was posted on YouTube in 2012, and which showed a crowd fleeing from uniformed gunmen firing from a short distance. When a lone protestor picked-up a rock and hurled it at the emptiness, one could clearly see how the demonstrator's life was instantly snuffed out. Far worse videos were posted online but that one summarized the level of violence that will now linger. Of course, the greater calamity was the global gag against the increasingly violent aerial bombardments of Syria's largest city, Aleppo, which illustrated the bankruptcy of every argument one could make to find a peaceful solution to the ongoing civil war. Aleppo now resembles Grozny, Stalingrad or even Dresden and one wonders whether this is a victory against terrorism. Is this what presidents Barack Obama, Vladimir Putin, Xi Jinping, François Hollande, and Prime Minister David Cameron, who was succeeded in mid-2016 by Theresa May, truly believe?

How many must fall in Syria and Yemen before one can hear an unambiguous statement that human life, every human life, is precious and must be preserved at all costs? When will we understand that real-politik cannot, and must not, triumph over ethical values? Why should ordinary people everywhere accept the conduct of power politics to serve material factors rather than moral standards? While it may be too soon to reach final conclusions as to who lost and who won in the ongoing Arab Uprisings, an honest even if largely preliminary assessment cannot but identify the major world powers as the greatest losers. Israel, along with surviving Arab dictators, ought to also be added to this list, for few Arabs will henceforth accept to be ignored or mistreated by wily deal-makers, especially as Prime Minister Benjamin Netanyahu displayed a unique aversion to the peace process. Bloody crackdowns will, naturally, kill many more since armored personnel carriers, tanks, helicopter gunships and other instruments of war will continue to inflict serious damage on unarmed civilians. In the Syrian case, one wonders why some of these tools were not used to liberate the occupied Golan since 1967, or whether a model battalion will one day join the Champs-Elysées parade if real-politik requires it. It thus behooves decision-makers to look into their crystal balls and see how fast the world is changing, for awakened Sunni Arab populations will never again be subjugated to the whims of autocratic rulers who have no compunction but to mow them down. Indeed, because ordinary Arab citizens have very long memories, and will remember friends and foes alike, one should applaud their courage to stand up against tyranny. Few should be surprised that an increasingly educated mass of young Arabs, especially Sunnis, will insist on proper governance and on leaders who will represent them in the true sense of the word.

Sykes–Picot: Take Three

There is, at least for now, a tendency to accept Western leadership of the world, though this is becoming an increasingly difficult proposition to support—a question that requires an honest assessment.

Whether Rudyard Kipling, the 1907 Nobel Prize winner for Literature and renowned English poet who celebrated British imperialism, ever set foot in London's Westminster Hall, is impossible to determine. Barack Obama, the 2009 Nobel Peace Prize laureate and 44th President of the United States, was invited to address a joint session of the British Parliament gathered for the occasion on 25 May 2011.[39] Obama was only the fourth foreign dignitary since World War II bestowed with this honor, preceded by Charles de Gaulle, Nelson Mandela and Pope Benedict XVI, which underscored what followed. In an emotional and highly charged oratory, Obama served notice to the entire world that the growing influence of nascent powers like China and India, among others, did not mean a diminished global role for the West. On the contrary, "the time for our leadership is now," intoned the first African-American President, which begged the question so eloquently raised by Ian Morris, a Stanford University professor: "For how long?"

Obama's impressive presentation covered a litany of topics though the most relevant section was his assessment of significant challenges emerging from the BRICS [the economic grouping composed of Brazil, Russia, India, China, and South Africa] that was, at least once, a promising quintet. Aware of genuine socio-economic trials that today confront more mature countries, he ironically asked whether the stiff competition from, as well as rise of, leading developing economies meant that Western leadership was safely nestled in the past. "It was the United States and the United Kingdom and our democratic allies," underscored Obama, "that shaped a world in which new nations could emerge and individuals could thrive. And even as more nations take on the responsibilities of global leadership, our alliance will remain indispensable to the goal of a century that is more peaceful, more prosperous and more just." Herein lay a fundamental issue that tied economic prosperity with freedom.

There was certainly food for thought in the claim that Western societies invented the Magna Carta, introduced parliamentary democracy, and ensured the rights of man, although Obama glossed over the actual behavior of Western colonialism, which achieved successful global economic prosperity, at least partly, with cheap resources "harvested" from the developing world. Somehow that legacy was conveniently overlooked even if Westminster Hall witnessed several of the best chapters of imperialist monopolies. Of course, Obama was right to focus on democracy as a specific Western asset, a universally acknowledged contribution to mankind. It was equally important to hear that the values embedded in democratization were destined for all even if actual implementation might follow different courses in various societies. "Let there be no doubt," asserted Obama, that "the United States and the United Kingdom stand squarely on the side of those who long to be free," which necessitated that both Washington and London step away from interest-based preferences. For democracy to thrive everywhere, one ought to "proceed with humility," but also with consistency—a rare commodity in the practice of what passes for diplomacy.

If Western leadership was "essential to the cause of human dignity," as affirmed by the American President, then it was critical to lead without falling into the East—West trap that was colored in political terms during the Cold War, and masqueraded in economic overtones since. Even if geography shaped the rise of world powers, the current conundrum was honestly addressed by Ian Morris, the Jean and Rebecca Willard Professor in Classics and History at Stanford University in Palo Alto, California. Published in 2010, Morris' opus anticipated "a single posthuman world civilization."[40] Morris closes his book with an examination of Rudyard Kipling's "The Ballad of East and West" poem, which remains one of most widely recited verses, even if most focus on its first line. Yet, when one reads the poem's opening stanza, one might conclude that Kipling exhibited self-satisfaction, although he probably foresaw a great deal more.

"Oh, East is East, and West is West, and never the twain shall meet
Till Earth and Sky stand presently at God's great Judgment Seat;
But there is neither East nor West, Border, nor Breed, nor Birth,
When two strong men stand face to face,
tho' they come from the ends of the earth!"[41]

For Morris "there will be neither East nor West, border nor breed, nor birth when we transcend biology. The twain shall finally meet if we can just put off Nightfall [nuclear annihilation] long enough."[42] Unlike 19th and 20th century geography-based power sources, we now live in a rapidly shrinking world, and one can no longer bank on Anglo-Saxon hegemony—elegant oratories notwithstanding.

As Nabil Khalifé affirms, in the Arab World, the fear factor is now in oblivion, buried alongside Saddam Husayn and other dictators who no longer scare awakened populations. While the second part of the twentieth century ushered in avowedly secularized Arab rulers who pretended to fight against Western imperialism to establish "Unity, Liberty, Socialism" (*wahdah, hurriyyah, ishtirakiyyah*), none of these lofty goals saw light but were supplanted by what one astute observer labeled "The Republic of Fear."[43] In Iraq and elsewhere, dictators fought hard to retain power though stale ideologies, which added little or no value to Arab societies for much of the past century, sealed their demise. As discussed in the first part of the Introduction, "From Tunis to Sana'a," several Arab societies experienced the pangs of revolutions that may, just may, give rise to genuine freedom and the spread of concrete liberties. The question that needs to be raised at this juncture is whether the major Western powers will back such quests? It may be useful at this stage to assess several examples of contemporary Arab leaderships and the types of solutions they advanced to promote national interests.

Arabs have been living lies for at least the past 100 years with young people tired of concealing mistakes committed by their ancestors. Remarkably, and perhaps because of the 1979 Iranian Revolution paradigm, few Arabs looked to puritanical Salafis or any combination of Islamists, as answers to their economic and social predicament. Nevertheless, there is no denying that many Arab men and women were inspired by the 2009 "Twitter Revolution" in Iran, where the notorious paramilitary *basij* forces beat protesters with impunity. Peaceful demonstrations that objected to election gerrymandering by the President of the Islamic Republic resulted in open confrontations that resulted in the deaths of between 36 and 72 people, including Neda Soltani, a 25 year-old martyr who lost her life to a well-trained sharpshooter. Though Iranian authorities blocked Twitter, Facebook, and other websites, they could not stop every cell phone transmission and text message. Ostracized Arab governments have, and are, using similar methods with identical results. Oblivious to stale promises, many Arabs—and this needs to be reemphasized time and again—are no longer afraid, as most reject failed post-World War II ideologies. From Cairo to Dira'ah, and from Misurata to Sana'a, Arabs no longer fancy *wahdah* and *ishti-rakiyyah*. They simply long for *hurriyyah* from dictators generous with orders to kill but who, in the end, cannot endure, since all they offer is death.

The Conundrum that is Israel

The Question that we ought to ask, however, is whether liberty can be part of the Sunni Arab World or whether it is, or ought to be, reserved for minority populations spread inside the Muslim World. The conundrum presented by Israel is probably one of the more pertinent cases worthy of attention as carefully annotated by Nabil Khalifé.

Over the decades, Israeli leaders played on highly emotional notes to garner Western sympathy, and some engage in impeccable theatrics at a time when the country is a major military power with inherent military capability, including nuclear. To their credit, numerous Israeli intellectuals reject absurd contentions, aware of the damage their country's leaders could inflict. In fact, and despite stringent censorship rules on media working inside Israel, many creative minds highlight existing farces. Perhaps the best known case is that of the Israeli nuclear arsenal, now estimated to top 400 warheads, which is routinely denied. A former Israeli nuclear technician, Mordechai Vanunu, provided explicit details and photographs to a British daily in 1968, which revealed the weapons program "including equipment for extracting radioactive material for arms production and laboratory models of thermonuclear devices."[44]

Notwithstanding denials, cartoonists all over the world repeatedly showed rare talent whenever Israeli leaders complained about Muslims in general and Arabs in particular, a phenomenon that reached comical levels as Israel honed on the Iranian nuclear program and warned that it might take military action to protect its interests. In 2012, many cartoonists depicted Israeli Prime Minister Benjamin Netanyahu's "Wylie Coyote" presentation in colorful montages, one illustrating his head in the shape of a bomb, and an imaginary red line above which the fuse ignited (see Appendix 11). Stated mildly, the prime minister's 2012 appearance at the UN General Assembly meeting was a debacle, especially as U.S. President Barack Obama telegraphed his opposition to any "red line" demands. Lacking finesse, Israel cranked up its displeasure of the Obama White House, as it courted the Republican Party presidential candidate Mitt Romney.[45]

It was within such a context that the nascent news of a secret 82-page report entitled *Preparing for a Post-Israel Middle East* received additional attention, even if leaks on its putative existence circulated for several months before it was made public. Of course, the document was not available, presumably because the only format for such a document would be a classified National Intelligence Assessment (NIA), though Kool-Aid experts opined that they knew what it said and how grave its contents were. Whether the alleged report described how much of the U.S. military and intelligence infrastructure distanced itself from Israel could thus not be verified. Be that as it may, the report purported to reveal that the undefined American national interest on this matter was fundamentally at odds with that of Zionist Israel, as Franklin Lamb, a Beirut-based journalist, opined at the *Foreign Policy Journal* online site. He affirmed that Israeli "actions prevent[ed] normal U.S. relations with Arab and Muslim countries and, to a growing degree, the wider international community."[46] Obama supposedly concluded that struggles like the moribund Arab–Israeli conflict ended up "costing [Washington] significantly in terms of both blood and treasure," which contained an element of truth, although the wily politician was also on record for explicitly supporting Israel over all Arabs. Reportedly, the secret paper further claimed that Obama wished to develop "normal U.S. relations with Arab and Muslim countries," which he apparently started doing with the June 2009 Cairo speech that "praised Islam and the Muslim Brotherhood in an unprecedented and an ahistorical manner."[47] Pro-Israeli writers noted that President Husni Mubarak did not to attend the Cairo oration in 2009, and pointed out how Obama threw Mubarak "under the bus and supported the Muslim Brotherhood's takeover of Egypt" in 2011.[48] Many Arabs were pleased that President Muhammad Mursi and other Egyptians did not kowtow to Obama, although few know what kind of relationship developed between Washington and Cairo and other Arab capitals at the time. More recently, the Obama Administration allegedly revised federal counter-terrorism training materials that eliminated references to Jihad and Islam, which were excellent steps if true. Regrettably, that was not the case, but the idea was to link a "Muslim" Obama with presumed anti-Israeli initiatives. Anyone with the slightest notion of how U.S. intelligence agencies functioned, including the Federal Bureau of Investigation (FBI), would know that few politicians have the power to limit what such agencies can teach their agents. That was not the point of such accusations, however. Rather, the effort was to depict Obama undercutting Israel in the peace process by ignoring Netanyahu, though in a presidential election year Obama would commit political suicide if he were to telegraph that the U.S. withdrew its assurances from Israel. Even worse, Obama purportedly opposed Israeli plans to attack Iran, refusing to become complicit in any unilateral steps, although he reiterated time and again that he would do everything in his power to prevent Iran from acquiring such a weapon.

Secret or otherwise, *Preparing for a Post-Israel Middle East* was probably a classic sham operation, revealing nothing new. If Israel was supported by well-placed allies in the U.S.—to the tune of over $150 billion in direct aid since 1948—it was because its leaders knew how to play the democratic game rather well. Over the years, they nurtured the American people through their representatives, invested in those politicians that stood with them who, for sheer political survival, backed Israel. The practice, pejoratively known as lobbying, was as American as apple-pie. Arabs in general and Palestinians in particular relied on the U.S. view of justice and fair play instead. They failed to heed David Ben-Gurion's views who summed it up best in 1948 when he said: "Let us not delude ourselves, we (Israelis) are the aggressors, they (Palestinians) fight to defend their Land." Strangely, every American official, including Obama, neglected to see the inlaid problem in this provocative pronouncement, which was the real threat to U.S. national interests in the Muslim World.[49]

Iran—From Policeman of the Gulf to Nuclear Power?

Much like their Pavlovian defense of Israel, the five permanent members of the UN Security Council—China, France, Russia, the United

Kingdom and the United States (P5)—along with Germany, embarked on a similar quest with Iran, after they signed the Geneva interim agreement, officially titled the Joint Plan of Action (JPOA), on 24 November 2013. Under the terms of the JPOA, the P5+1 concurred that Iran would implement a short-term freeze of portions of its nuclear program in exchange for a limited decrease in economic sanctions—including access to frozen accounts in Western financial institutions—while negotiations continued towards a long-term accord.[50] It was an amazing concession as it explicitly acknowledged that whatever accords could be reached, this would not prevent Tehran from eventually joining the nuclear club, notwithstanding temporary setbacks.

Given rekindled sectarianism that further divided the Gulf region, several Western observers advanced the notion that Iran, a country with hegemonic ambitions throughout the Arab World, including over Sa'udi Arabia, Yemen, Egypt, Jordan, and especially Iraq, Syria and Lebanon, was well poised to impose specific conditions to reach a final agreement with the P5: nuclear power vs. policeman of the Gulf. Was this even possible? Notwithstanding intense discussions in Geneva, Vienna, and Muscat, diplomats granted themselves several additional months to overcome existing deadlocks that ended in a serious accord. Although few believed that a felicitous outcome could be hatched fast, it was eminently clear that the bazaar mentality prevailed, which effectively meant that negotiations would resolve lingering differences. Before JPOA became the Joint Comprehensive Plan of Action (JCPAO) in 2015, it was critical to make two critical points: first what was included in the accord and, second, why Iran accepted its terms.

JPOA emasculated Tehran, which accepted strict interim conditions following extensive secret bilateral negotiations with Washington, even if it did not kill the nuclear program permanently. Reality finally sank in largely because of the post-2008 cyber-attacks that disrupted Iran's uranium processing capability even as the accord threatened to permanently alter regional security arrangements. Although few commentators made the link, National Security Agency whistle-blower Edward Snowden confirmed to *Der Spiegel* in July 2013 that the U.S. and Israel collaborated on the matter and, more importantly, succeeded in crippling Iran's nuclear ambitions.[51] Indeed, the U.S./Israeli Stuxnet cyberweapon—a computer worm that literally shook Iranian centrifuges to pieces—was so successful that Tehran re-evaluated its plans to replace several thousand costly machines at a time when its economy was in dire conditions. As it turned out, Iran only agreed to stop enriching uranium above 5 per cent, and dilute its stock of uranium enriched to 20 per cent. The latter was a significant concession although it was not clear how large that stock was. Still, doing so addressed a major proliferation concern, a key French condition at the time. Consequently, no new increases of low-enriched uranium were expected over the course of several months, an issue that required further negotiations. Moreover, as Tehran pledged not to install new centrifuges to replace the estimated 8,000 inoperable machines, this vow was a confirmation that several Stuxnet hits were effective.

Without enrichment capacity and with intrusive nuclear inspections by the International Atomic Energy Agency (IAEA), including daily visits to some facilities, Iran's nuclear ambitions were severely curtailed. Even more telling was Foreign Minister Muhammad Javad Zarif's concession that his country would not fuel or try to commission the heavy-water reactor at Arak, or even build a reprocessing plant that could produce plutonium from the spent fuel, again for the duration of the interim accord. In exchange for these important allowances, the deal promised to remove several economic sanctions and release between $4 and 7 billion in Iranian oil revenues from frozen accounts. In other words, Iran received some of its own funds, along with a suspension of various restrictions that had prevented it from trading in gold, petrochemicals, car and aircraft parts and a few other items. Under the circumstances, the hailed victory was particularly hollow, since the restrictions were far more intrusive than many assumed. In fact, the ubiquitous presence of IAEA inspectors ensured that Iran completely abided by its commitments, something that Israel's assassination-of-nuclear-scientists-plan failed to accomplish to date.[52] Challenged Israeli leaders huffed and puffed but the acting was worthy of an Oscar given what transpired and what Prime Minister Netanyahu knew. He and U.S. President Obama exchanged several telephone calls and, more importantly, their respective advisers coordinated what was on the table and what transpired under it. Indeed, Israeli officials were aware of, and approved, the secret talks between American and Iranian diplomats in Oman and other locations as the capable deputy secretary of state, William Burns, and Jake Sullivan, a foreign policy adviser to Vice-President Joe Biden, met with their Iranian counterparts on several occasions. The *Washington Post* reported that at least five meetings were held starting in March 2013, which meant that the first overtures occurred when Mahmud Ahmadinajad was president of Iran.[53]

This caveat put to rest the canard that the U.S. saw the election of the reformist Hassan Ruhani as a window of opportunity. Instead, embarking on serious discussions of Iran's nuclear program three months before Ruhani was elected, confirmed that the U.S. felt no compunction about extending lines of communication as it pursued its interests. Washington cooperated with Iran under the Shah, continued doing so under Ayatollahs Ruhallah Khumayni and 'Ali Khamane'i, and was likely to do likewise under any other leader.[54] To believe otherwise is to underestimate American political flexibility. Of course, the rapprochement between Washington and Tehran upset the proverbial security applecart in the Gulf region, with leading Arab Gulf States misreading what actually transpired in Geneva. Most saw the accord as a further Western, especially American, compromise after the flip-flop over Syria. It was not.

What was comical was President Bashar al-Assad's quick hailing of the "historic accord," unaware that the inevitable strangulation of Iran was nearly identical to the treatment that stripped Syria of its strategic chemical weapons. In the aftermath of the infamous 21 August 2013 Ghouta chemical attack on the outskirts of Damascus, which killed hundreds and that showered the big powers with shame when they failed to assign blame on the real culprits—the regime—Moscow arranged for, and Western countries agreed to, an Organization for the Prohibition of Chemical Weapons (OPCW) deal to remove prohibited weapons from Syria. This prevented Western cruise missile strikes on Syria's chemical weapons and heightened concerns among U.S. allies because the Gulf States, led by Sa'udi Arabia, were not persuaded that the Syrian government would fully comply.[55] It is worth underscoring that the openly expressed goal—to accelerate al-Assad's downfall—was doable and stood a better chance after these two recent agreements, provided certain decisions were made. But that was not to be because such an outcome necessitated the transfer of effective arsenals to those fighting the Syrian regime, something that Arab States and Turkey were reticent to introduce, no matter various pressures on all regional governments. Unlike Russia, Iran and Hizballah, all of which backed the al-Assad regime with arms, men, and expertise, Arab Gulf states provided financial support and some weapons, which were useful but not sufficient. In the post-2013 period, the choices were either to embark on the political bandwagon, that is, support the long-delayed Geneva 2 negotiations scheduled for late January 2014, or accelerate the transfer of the kind of weapons that would make a difference on the battlefield.

On 14 July 2015, U.S. Secretary of State John Kerry, along with the other P5+1 countries' foreign ministers, signed the Joint Comprehensive Plan of Action (JCPOA) with Muhammad Javad Zarif. In exchange for major sanctions relief, the agreement introduced a decade-long moratorium on Iran's ongoing military nuclear programs. To its credit, Iran implemented the initial phase of the accord and shipped 25,000 pounds of low-enriched uranium to Russia, leaving it without enough material for a bomb. This is a vital step because it is irreversible while Iran is nearing completion of other requirements, including dismantling the requisite number of centrifuges, reconfiguring the Arak heavy water reactor, and allowing for more intrusive inspections. Still, not everything has gone smoothly, as Tehran conducted provocative ballistic missile tests, which was not technically a violation of the JCPOA but violated, nonetheless, UN Security Council resolutions. The Obama Administration has stated that it will continue to enforce sanctions that are not part of the agreement, but caused confusion by sending mixed signals when it notified Congress about new sanctions aimed at Iran's missile program, only to then pull back.[56]

While undeniable progress was achieved on the implementation front, regional reactions over the nuclear accords were negative. Leading Middle Eastern countries were affected by what the P5+1 discussions entailed, even if they were not represented in Vienna. Sa'udi Arabia and the United Arab Emirates, in particular, felt the pressure of potential Iranian hegemonic aspirations and it fell on Frank-Walter Steinmeier, the German Foreign Minister, to clarify: "We bear responsibility not just for us six but for many states in the world . . . that have legitimate security concerns about the development of the Iranian nuclear program."[57] While it was unclear whether Steinmeier hinted that a long-standing request made by his Sa'udi counterpart, Prince Sa'ud al-Faysal, would eventually be honored to have a GCC representative join the discussions, this was indeed on the table. Naturally, Iran opposed such an addition and rejected the very notion that a looming crisis pitted it against neighboring states. Nevertheless, there is no denying that Iran's future geo-strategic role in the Middle East and Southeast Asia is critical to them, and Iran's leaders would not hesitate to bargain in earnest to transform the country, once again, into "the policeman of the Gulf."

Iran negotiated its nuclear program masterfully for nearly twelve years and did not walk away when the going was tough. It stuck to its guns to accomplish several objectives simultaneously, including to secure the removal of devastating economic sanctions and the right to eventually proceed with its nuclear program. By these means it may well impose its will on the region. Save for a few statements issued by Ayatollah Khamane'i, Tehran never provided any guarantees that its long-term goal was not to try and build a nuclear weapon. Moreover, it is also worth remembering that the November 2013 extension was only reached after Israel appeared to be ready to launch a military assault on Iran, something that cannot be ruled out in the future. That was why Iran dragged the talks and why the June 2015 deadline was only met in extremis.

The Suspicious Iran Deal: An Obama Victory

What the deal achieved was to highlight the looming conflicts between Arab and Western interests in the region, as Arab Sunni perceptions of American neglect crystallized. Between the "Persian Pivot" and "America hates Sunnis," two propositions advanced by Daniel Twining (*Foreign Policy*) and Hussain Abdul-Hussain (*NOW*), many are persuaded that leading Western powers, led by the United States, have now ushered in a fresh balance of power in the Gulf region.[58] How realistic are these options for Washington and its allies at a time of significant upheavals throughout the area and beyond?

First, a word about Twining's intriguing "Persian Pivot" that was a play on words after President Barack Obama's 2012 still-born "Pivot to Asia" regional strategy, which purported to shift U.S. foreign policy from a Middle Eastern/European focus to an East/South Asian one. According to Twining, Obama borrowed a page from Richard Nixon, whose 1972 visit to the People's Republic of China normalized relations between the two countries and ended 25 years of separation. To his credit, even if he lacked Nixon's dexterity and strategic depth, Obama may well have perceived the nuclear deal with Iran in a similar vain, reaching the conclusion that Tehran in 2015 was as weak as Beijing in the 1970s. Under Mao Zedong, a vulnerable China sought an alliance against the relatively stronger Soviet Union, whose leaders seldom abandoned aggressive foreign policy initiatives to destabilize the world. Nixon and his Machiavellian policy wonk, Henry Kissinger, played the geo-political strings with rare expertise. Obama and his advisors, who are not in the same league as the former national security advisor/secretary of state, could well believe—or at least may have persuaded themselves—that Washington pursued an equivalent strategy. After all, this perception concluded, Iran was relatively weak too, bending under effective sanctions that crippled its economy. In fact, Iran's revolutionary zeal created an undeniable overstretch that was not sustainable, as Obama concluded that the mullahs were bound to mimic Mao and seek an alternative alliance against regional and global foes.

The trouble with this logic, and as Nabil Khalifé explains, is that Iran is far less pragmatic than either China or Russia were, as it pursues its revolutionary agenda that, for lack of a better description, intends to destabilize the region and the Muslim World for two specific goals: to militarily dominate the Gulf region's oil resources and to lead Muslims in the *wilayat-al faqih*. Although the latter definition is tied to Shi'ah theology, it is nevertheless the foundation on which the Islamic Revolution is built, namely to exercise power over the nation through guardianship. Regrettably for Iran, the vast majority of Muslims are Sunnis who find tangential merit in the theory and, in the case of Sa'udis, the custodian nationals of the two holy mosques in Makkah and Madinah, discern none. To be sure, the "Persian Pivot" could usher in a U.S.–Iran rapprochement that will erase the sequels of the 1979–1981 U.S. hostage crisis, but it was unlikely to create a gulf balance of power, not because Sa'udi Arabia loathed neighborly ties with Iran but simply because it rejected Tehran's above cited objectives. It is fair to conclude, therefore, that the chimerical pivot towards Iran was bound to produce an imbalance of power in the Middle East because Iranian mullahs have done more harm than others to violently destabilize the Arab world.

Abdul-Hussain's narrative, if true, highlights a far more dangerous proposition that merits careful evaluation as well. In the words of the Washington Bureau Chief of the Kuwaiti newspaper *Al-Rai'*, not only does Obama believe that American national interests are best "served by defusing the Iranian nuclear program," but that his "zeal for democracy waned" after the "pro-Shiite [Bashar al-] Assad started killing his Sunni opponents en masse" [in Syria].[59] Abdul-Hussain hammers Obama for looking the other way and for arguing that the only way out of the bloodbath is through a political settlement. Moreover, the Kuwaiti writer affirms that "when Syria's Sunnis formed militias in self-defense, Obama starved them of funds and arms and accused them of either extremism or amateurism." He cites several examples from Iraq under Saddam Husayn as well, to further illustrate why Washington rekindled ties with Tehran, and may well plan to return to the period of time when the U.S. considered Iran to be one of its two pillars in the region—perhaps even its best friend and ally.

Given Iran's four-decades old record in the Arab World, which redefined "interference" in the internal affairs of Iraq, Syria, Lebanon, Egypt, Jordan, Bahrain, Kuwait, Qatar, Sa'udi Arabia, the UAE and Yemen, one can understand the primary reason why Obama and some of his supporters opted to pivot towards Tehran. While it is facile to state that America as a nation was predisposed to hate Sunnis after 9/11, the propinquity to favor Iran was manna from heaven or, to use another idiom, Washington found in Tehran the goose that laid a golden egg— a power that added to regional tensions that, in turn, allowed outsiders to dominate—even if revenge and greed were not the ways to conduct a country's foreign policy much less protect its national security goals.

This last observation was buttressed by an extraordinary John Kerry declaration in September 2016 on the sidelines of the annual UN General Assembly, when the affable and overworked official blurted out: "Hizballah is not plotting against the U.S.," which overlooked that

Washington continues to list Hizballah as a terrorist organization.[60] The truly bizarre declaration sullied the memories of at least 241 U.S. Marines, and 58 French paratroopers (as well as six Lebanese civilian bystanders), who were killed in the 23 October 1983 Beirut bombings. Earlier, Hizballah was responsible for the kidnappings and, in several instances, the executions of U.S. hostages, whose sacrifices were reduced to naught by a careless political spin that was egregious as well as unbecoming.

FROM SECTARIANISM TO CHAOS

In the final and third part of this Introduction, an effort is made to highlight how the push for renewed sectarian preferences led to a chaotic environment that targets Sunnis in general and Sa'udi Arabia in particular. This part is, in turn divided into two sections, the first assessing various sectarian developments, and the second providing specific evaluations of perpetual wars against Arabs and Muslims. The third part closes with an examination of the proposition that Iran will not triumph and that the "Arab Uprisings" will redefine the fate of over a billion human beings.

Devout Tunisians Embark on Separating Church from State

There is no better example of the evolution of sectarian clashes than Tunisia, the premier laboratory for the Arab Spring that is unfolding in front of the entire world. What is underway in the North African country is worthy of detailed attention for Tunisians are rewriting history.

It was John Stuart Mill—the author of *On Liberty*—who opined that the masses are nothing more than "collective mediocrity," since they have taken "their opinions from dignitaries in Church or State," a viewpoint part and parcel of human history for millennia. But a renaissance emerged and ushered in—at least in Europe—the kind of separation that allowed for religious devotion to be practiced away from political diktats. It is thus fair to ask whether we are now on the verge of a similar experiment in the Arab World.

The surprise came when the leader of the Tunisian Al-Nahdah Party pledged to separate politics from religion. At a time when just about every commentator concluded that the 2011 Arab Uprisings were utter failures, what Rashid Ghannouchi said was epochal. His assertion is simple: there is no room left for political Islam within the Tunisian constitution. Though time will tell whether this is the real deal, a separation between religious activities from political ones bodes very well for both his country and just about every other Arab country. "Tunisia is now a democracy," Ghannouchi affirmed, as he underscored constitutional limits on both "extreme secularism and extreme religiosity."[61] In a moment of candor, the Islamist leader declared that what he wanted was for "religious activity to be completely independent from political activity . . . so that religion would not be held hostage to politics." Even if Ghannouchi's latest declarations raised doubts in certain minds—that a full separation of church and state could not be envisaged in the Arab context—the latest Al-Nahdah declaration prompted debate around political Islam which will slowly but surely address, perhaps even repair, outdated and extremist concepts that shaped several generations, transformed disillusioned believers into extremists, and empowered competitors to label them enemies that ought to be destroyed. Tunisia's burgeoning democracy, the result of a gradual separation of powers, tolerated every vanguard idea but practiced genuine participation, which was the essence of democracy away from Mill's "collective mediocrity." Tunisia is showing that Arabs and Muslims can practice democratization, as long as leaders adapt to the will of increasingly educated and alert citizens. How one adjusts to political circumstances and encourages ideological moderation will surely confirm whether the necessary transformations will become reality.

It's Political Salafism, Not Sectarianism, Stupid!

As discussed by Nabil Khalifé, and in the words of the erudite Moroccan cleric Shaykh Muhammad 'Abdul Wahab Rafiki, the message of the so-called Islamic State is effective because young people are predisposed to identify with religion first, rather than with their nations. Rafiki, who spoke in 2015 at a Carnegie Middle East Center event in Beirut, is well known for arguing that the time was long overdue to give young Arabs new dreams. His message is powerful: without dreams to taste freedom and enjoy life to the fullest, which allows one to become a productive member of society, individuals are mere fodder for those who do not value life. No wonder extremists from all faiths manipulate innocent souls, deny followers essential freedoms, and subjugate masses to authoritarianism. Theirs, Rafiki clarified before he condemned the approach, is based on a simple proposition: "One must 'die to advance causes that one seldom comprehends in the name of the Creator."[62] In fact, the political–religious schisms dividing Arabs, regrettably presented as a Sunni–Shi'ah tussle of wills are not religious per se, though most carry religious overtones, but strategic in the classic sense of the term, and it behooves us not to fall into traps that allow sectarianism to triumph. For Khalifé, a strategy, by definition, is a plan to achieve goals through specific means. According to this definition, Iran allegedly enjoys a considerable advantage over Saʻudi Arabia, because Tehran can rely on a much more homogeneous bloc than Riyadh. Teheran's allies in Iraq, Syria, Bahrain, Lebanon and now Yemen, can ostensibly rely on it because Iran, through the Pasdaran, Basij, and the Quds Force can prevent the collapse of the Syrian regime, the re-conquest of Iraqi provinces now under Daʻish's influence (although this might be short-lived because of the Iraqi-led assault on ISIS to liberate Mosul and destroy the extremist organization), the backing of Hizballah in Lebanon, and the resupply of Huthi rebels in the Yemen as the latter reject national reconciliation. Somehow, Baghdad, Damascus, Beirut and Sana'a can overlook Iranian control of Arab Shiʻahs, ʻAlawites and Zayidis. Indeed, in the Iranian lexicon, existing tensions within Shiism are tangential, which is an inaccurate reading of conditions on the ground.

Naturally, one could make the argument that offensives launched by extremist Sunni groups like Jabhat al-Nusrah, Ahrar al-Sham and Daʻish, among others, do not bode well for conservative Arab governments either. It is with that goal in mind that critics of Saʻudi Arabia point to inconsistencies in the impressive Sunni coalition that launched *Operation Firmness Storm* in Yemen, arguing that Riyadh will not succeed because, this skewed logic affirms, the Sunni world is divided.

The Kingdom, anti-Saʻudi analysts avow, is no match against Iran since regional upheavals forced the Al Saʻud to change their foreign policy direction after they realized they were about to be overwhelmed by indigenous opposition forces. Somehow, the intervention in Bahrain and the rehabilitation of military rule in Egypt persuaded Riyadh to alter its perceptions, abandon traditionally passive military preferences, and adopt assertive steps. Why such changes, if true, were seen as a sign of weakness is never explained. Moreover, and equally puzzling, critics point to the 23 January 2015 death of King ʻAbdallah bin ʻAbdul ʻAziz as a watershed. They maintain that King Salman bin ʻAbdul ʻAziz had little choice but to adopt a new doctrine, called the Salman Doctrine, which relied on the military option without opposing extremist movements like the Muslim Brotherhood or Daʻish. Of course, this was an incorrect reading too, since Riyadh opposed all extremist movements without exception. Anti-Saʻudi analysts further focused on the reconciliation between Saʻudi Arabia with Qatar and the rapprochement with Turkey as examples of such policy shifts, even if the argument can be made that, on the contrary, it was Riyadh that successfully persuaded

Doha and Ankara to distance themselves from militias and join it in the Yemen campaign to restore a legitimate government. Even the refusal of Pakistan to participate in the coalition is interpreted as a serious setback for Sa'udi Arabia, after the Pakistani parliament voted for neutrality. While it is correct to surmise that Islamabad preferred not to inflame tensions with neighboring Iran, it did so only to prevent a sectarian conflict at home given the presence of a significant pro-Iranian Shi'ah minority.

Time will tell whether Turkey, which cannot afford to antagonize Iran on account of the latter's massive assistance to Damascus, will move to tackle the Syrian crisis that, truth be told, is its primary concern. Likewise, we will see whether Egypt will change its policies vis-à-vis the Muslim Brotherhood, although Cairo cannot possibly end its fight against extremists either. Whether President 'Abdul Fattah al-Sisi agreed to concentrate on domestic matters and, perhaps, on neighboring Libya, instead of sending troops to fight in Yemen, were mere speculation even if entirely logical. For at the end of the day, it was rational to assume that the coalition would tackle the rise of extremists on various fronts, without jeopardizing the core national security interests of participants. Remarkably, there are those who today argue that a new Sunni strategy is in the works towards a more conservative Islamism that aims to seduce Arab populations, carefully camouflaged to advance the ambitions of the "Wahhabi" Kingdom. This is strong on imagination but weak on substance for Sa'udi Arabia—whose legitimacy is based on its religious identity—and its conservative Arab partners are not embarked on either a crusade or on any other proselytizing project. Still, sectarian terminology of the "Wahhabi–Takfiri–Israeli–American" variety, which is loosely tossed around by extremists, will fully entertain the naïve, while Riyadh will persist to advance its real strategy, which is to counter extremism no matter its origin.

Is the Islamic State the First Caliphate of the 21st Century?

Much has been written about Sa'udi Arabia and ISIS though little of what is in print resembles reality. In an undated image posted by the Raqqah Media Center on 30 June 2014, verified by Associated Press that confirmed its veracity, fighters from the al-Qa'idah-linked ISIS paraded in the Syrian city. Militants from the al-Qa'idah splinter group displayed in this military parade what passed for the trappings of a state, displaying U.S.-made Humvees, heavy machine guns, and missiles captured from the Iraqi army for the first time since taking over large parts of the Iraq–Syria border. ISIS gained significant momentum between 2014 and 2015 and, emboldened by its successes, heralded Abu Bakr al-Baghdadi to announce the establishment of a caliphate. Naturally, al-Baghdadi designated himself as the new ruler of the Islamic *Ummah* (community), a modest initiative by the Rolex watch-wearing Caliph. The exercise was the first time such a display was recorded in the 21st century and was bound to lead to serious confrontations as a Lebanese television network boasted that ISIS appointed an "emir" over Lebanon even if the LBC channel could not provide any evidence to confirm this assertion. It would not be long before similar emirs emerged in Syria, Jordan, Palestine and elsewhere, which reminded one of ancient satrapies in the Persian Empire—which continued the tradition of appointing governors under the Sassanid and Hellenic empires—who ruled as surrogates in the name of larger powers.

Abu Bakr al-Baghdadi announced that his caliphate would restore order, which was akin to a declaration of war not only against the post-Westphalia nation-state system that resulted in the independence of 23 Arab states, but also against challenged extremist movements like al-Qa'idah. The ISIS attempt was little more than a consolidation effort, especially after one Abu Muhammad al-'Adnani, an alleged "spokesman" for the group, urged those living in areas under the group's control to swear allegiance to al-Baghdadi. The "restoration of the caliphate" was apparently made by a Shurah Council, al-'Adnani affirmed, without any identification of its members or their qualifications to reach such a momentous decision. Indeed, past failures attributed to al-Qa'idah may well have encouraged "ISISites" [both self-appointed leaders as well as blind followers] to make a bid for the extremist agenda, although it was too early to determine whether ISIS was the final repository of such goals. The caliphate remained the ultimate objective in historical terms but it was nearly impossible to conclude whether the world's Sunni populations were ready to jettison their *bay'ahs* (oaths of allegiance) from existing rulers, and to grant their allegiance to al-Baghdadi and men of his ilk. Of course, it was easy to assume that ISIS succeeded because the Iraqi armed forces melted in front of a few thousand rag-tag elements, though that short-term collapse was more the result of Prime Minister Nuri al-Maliki's poor leadership skills than al-Baghdadi's prowess. Be that as it may, the declaration of a caliphate cannot and should not be ignored because it threatens all 23 independent Arab states, even if the principal battlefield was concentrated in Iraq and Syria.

Caught in a premier sectarian inferno—Sunni versus Shi'ah extremists volunteering to butcher each other on command—Iraqis confronted two terrifying options. ISIS on one side and 'Asa'ib ahl al-Haqq, a powerful Shi'ah militia under the direct control of Iranian officers, on the other; remarkably, this situation did not elicit any concern from Prime Minister al-Maliki. It was as if 'Asa'ib was untouchable in Baghdad even if its actions encouraged ISIS to reciprocate and drag the country into yet another civil war. For al-Baghdadi and his crack ISISite team to succeed, however, it was not enough to defeat al-Maliki, the 'Asa'ib or even a variety of elements supported by the Iranians directly or even indirectly. Rather, al-Baghdadi faced the following challenges: First, would Muslims in general and Arabs in particular, accept the very idea of a caliph since doing so necessitated unanimity within the realm? Second, would harsh interpretations of Shari'ah Law, which re-evaluated established ideological and theological norms that were settled over centuries, be tolerated by the vast majority of Muslims who are moderate and practical believers? Third, how could Muslim theologians and political leaders abide by the killings of large numbers of opposition forces, whether they happened to be deviant Sunnis or Shi'ahs? Fourth, how would Arab monarchs, presidents, and prime ministers co-exist with caliph al-Baghdadi? Fifth, where was the urgency that these officials presumably felt since no one called for a summit to coordinate anti-ISIS efforts? Finally, and beyond al-Baghdadi's cult of personality theatrics, how long was ISIS likely to rule over areas under its control once financial and material backers reassessed their putative commitments?

How al-Baghdadi understood, and responded to, these challenges and, equally important, how Arab leaders perceived "ISISite" goals, were neither easy to unravel nor draft policy rejoinders. Most Arab rulers were perplexed that such phenomena would occur in their midst in the 21st century though, mercifully, very few Muslims and fewer Arabs supported extremist "caliphs." What most desired was freedom and the opportunities to create wealth. The rest was passing theatre.

Why the Ibrahim Caliphate is a Dud?

Notwithstanding such desires, it is critical to assess what value the putative Caliphate offered, particularly to Sunni Arabs. A few weeks after the self-declared Caliph Ibrahim—who, it is worth underlining, is not a renowned religious figure and has no publications to attest to his accomplishments—harangued followers in a Mosul Mosque, and in the aftermath of what appeared to be a carefully orchestrated expulsion of that city's established Christian population, Islamic State militiamen blew up a mosque and shrine dating back to the 14th century.[63] This was not their first accomplishment in Iraq or Syria though one wondered whether any of the perpetrators, or their "handlers," understood what they were doing. The latest achievement, the destruction of the Prophet Jirjis (George) mosque and shrine that was built over a cemetery that apparently belonged to the Quraysh tribe, came on top of earlier desecrations, including the bombing of the mosque of the Prophet Shith (Seth) and the mosque of the Prophet Yunis (Jonah), that may also be the burial place of Jonah, who, according to both the Bible and the Qur'an, was swallowed by a whale. "Religious militants" justified their sacrilegious behavior on the grounds that such mosques were no longer places of worship but facilities to practice apostasy.[64]

Earlier, IS fighters bombed several churches and expelled nearly 25,000 Christians from Mosul, most of whom found refuge in Iraqi Kurdistan. The President of the Kurdish Regional Government, Massud Barzani, welcomed the refugees and lamented IS actions, underscoring that the bombing of churches and mosques in Mosul was "against all the principles of the heavenly religions and humanity," as he asserted that such behavior targeted "the culture and demography of the area" without elaborating on who benefitted from such prowess. Indeed, it was no longer a mystery that the IS managed to gain control over a good chunk of Iraq with a mere 10 to 20,000 fighters, whose origins remained murky, training grounds carefully hidden from sight, financial wealth debunked after bankers acknowledged that their facilities were not robbed, and foreign supporters falling back into obscurity when several allegations hinted that Iranian and several Western powers may have facilitated the march onto Mosul. To say that the IS was even more enigmatic than its alleged predecessor, the so-called al-Qa'idah organization that most of us swallow hook, line, and sinker, is an understatement.[65]

In the event, what interested Western media outlets were the many rumors associated with the IS, including its alleged plans to perform female genital mutilation (FGM) on nearly four million women who lived in that part of Iraq (and presumably Syria), or the diabolical machinations that Sa'udi Arabia apparently orchestrated to expel Arab Christians from the Arab World. Various voices emerged in Western countries, and even in parts of the Arab World, that wanted to know where the moderate Muslims were, and why they weren't denouncing the IS and its plans? (see also Appendix 13).[66]

Of course, had any of them done their homework, they would have taken note that the Organization of Islamic Cooperation (OIC) condemned the forced displacement suffered by Christians in Mosul, and concluded that the deeds were a crime which could not be tolerated. In fact, the OIC Secretary-General, 'Iyad bin Amin Madani, revealed that the organization would provide necessary humanitarian aid to the displaced, look after their needs until such time when they could return to their homes, and insisted that what passed for IS ideologies were alien to Islamic principles that called for justice, fairness, and tolerance.[67] In Iraq itself, a popular Muslim newscaster, Daliah al-'Aqidi, launched a televised campaign to defend her fellow citizens under the rubric "We are all Christians." Al-'Aqidi, a Muslim, wore a cross around her neck in solidarity and declared that she rejected what was happening to the Christians of Mosul. In an interview with the Lebanese daily *Al-Nahar*, al-'Aqidi explained her gesture as a defense of "religious and sectarian diversity that made Iraq the cradle of civilization, science and culture." On her television show, she declared: "You Takfiri unbelievers detest apostates . . . but I am a simple human being ready to defend the rights of everyone in the nation." She concluded: "Our religion is a religion of tolerance whereas your political fascism makes moderate Muslims like myself ashamed of our faith and pushes many to silence out of fear, but I will not be ashamed, nor will I be silent about this injustice"[68] (see Appendix 14).

Ironically, the self-appointed Caliph said nothing about the carnage that befell the martyred city of Gaza at the height of the 2014 war against Isael, nor the fact that nearly 2,000 hapless individuals found refuge at the Greek Orthodox church in Zaytun in Gaza, another impoverished town living under occupation as well as a blockade, while his militiamen were rounding up people in Mosul. At St. Porphyrios (Gaza City), entire families slept on mattresses in the corridors and rooms of the church and adjoining buildings, and survived. On the last day of Ramadan, many gathered in the Church courtyard to perform their prayers, simply because most worshippers were afraid to visit the mosque next door.[69] For like the IS, the Israelis also bombed dozens of mosques, allegedly because Palestinian fighters were hiding there, even if families found refuge in them after their homes were destroyed. As Fred M. Donner demonstrated in his monumental *Muhammad and the Believers: At the Origins of Islam*, Christians welcomed Islam as an open-minded religion with universalistic aspirations, and concluded that believers were not the enemy and did not routinely tear down churches as propagandists claimed over the centuries. On the contrary, many shared their churches with fellow monotheists, when no mosques existed. In other words, Muslims prayed inside churches in Palestine and elsewhere, because these were considered places of worship for all believers. This was something that Caliph Ibrahim—who probably build his credentials inside Camp Buca prison near Baghdad, Iraq, with American assistance—was unaware of, and something that commentators chose to ignore, which affirmed the notion that mutual ignorance created perfect opportunities for manipulation.[70]

A Congruence of Christian and Muslim Extremisms

Perhaps one of the best examples of manipulation was what former Lt. General William "Jerry" Boykin, once a Deputy Under Secretary of Defense for Intelligence in the United States, practiced. Boykin told the Pro-Family Legislators Conference in Dallas, Texas that "Jesus will return with an AR-15" [assault rifle].[71] In his capacity as executive vice president for the Family Research Council, an ultra-conservative organization, the retired officer—who served in the Army's elite Delta Force and participated in several high-profile missions throughout his career—insisted that the "Son of God" would be armed, "coming back as a warrior, carrying a sword." Boykin further declared: "And I believe now, I've checked this out—I believe that sword he'll be carryin' when he comes back is an AR-15."[72] In 2003, Boykin boasted to church audiences that his work in Somalia, and since then, was God's labor. At the time, his remarks to a Somali warlord who told the General that he would be protected by Allah, drew the ire of many, as Boykin concluded: "I knew that my God was bigger than his. I knew that my God was a real God and his was an idol."

Although time passed and America elected a president whose father was a practicing Muslim, what was disturbing in this latest prophecy was the laughter and the applause that grew from his latest audience. After everything that happened in the aftermath of 9/11 and the unending wars that spread nothing but ruin, little seems to have changed among fundamentalist Christians, whose beliefs went beyond the building of an empire. Various reports that highlighted the dangers of fundamentalism that usurped religious norms failed to register, with no corrections made, and none contemplated. Similarly, equivalent threats spurted throughout the Muslim World with Jabhat al-Nusrah or ISIS coming online in the Levant, while dormant Muslim Brotherhood cells were activated elsewhere.

Of course, religion and politics always represented a volatile mixture, even if Christianity was founded on love and peace and Islam combined peace with the quest for justice. Still, what was remarkable about the latest Boykin revelation was its similarity to extremist outbursts, which mobilized indigenous scoundrels who shared a similar outlook. For example, so-called al-Qa'idah leaders presented their analyses of the putative ideological struggle with the West in general and the U.S. in particular as an "us-versus-them dichotomy," precisely the same language used by their Western counterparts. Such a perspective seldom allowed for anything but extremist violence because one could not adopt an opposite position to that of those arguing for violence. Throughout the Levant, especially in Syria, extremist forces used language that denigrated the Holy Qur'an, which resembled Boykin's reinterpretations of the New Testament. What was remarkable was the General's reliance on Luke 22:36, where Jesus tells his disciples: "Let the one who has no sword sell his cloak and buy one," to make his case. Nevertheless, neither Boykin nor fellow Christian fundamentalists bothered to read the rest of the text, which rejects violence. Indeed, when one of Jesus' followers used his sword on a hapless servant of the high priest in the temple, the disciple was sharply rebuked. Therefore, the real meaning of this scripture was precisely not to rely on violence, and though Boykin may believe that Christ would pack an assault rifle to defend himself, the Bible clearly states: "Thou shall not kill."

Muslim fundamentalists use the same exact logic when they "interpret" the Qur'an, and while several verses offer ambiguous interpretations, most believers reject the justification for violence. Sadly, extremists recruit miscreants, empowering them to commit atrocities, which does not augur well for tolerance and peace. What escapes most are clear warnings that gratuitous aggression begets cruelty to one's souls as well, which was best described by the German philosopher Friedrich Nietzsche. In his remarkable book *Beyond Good and Evil*, Nietzsche wrote that "he who fights with monsters should look to it that he himself does not become one," and warned that if a person gazes into an abyss for a long period of time, he should understand that the abyss will gawk back.[73] The trouble with fundamentalists is that they always pick and choose, no matter the religion, without realizing that men of Boykin's ilk, or 'Usamah bin Ladin, Ayman al-Zawahiri, or any number of recent jihadists, fail to add any value to mankind. Of course, one must accept that freedom of speech, especially in a country like the United States, means that the government ought not punish you for what you say, even if what you say is idiotic. For in the end, one should not resent extremist beliefs, as long as the Boykins of this world keep their views to themselves. When they incite to create wars, or bring about apocalyptic outcomes, however, it then becomes everyone's business to thwart them, whether they are in Dallas, Texas or Aleppo, Syria.

A Breath of Fresh Air in Inter-Religious Dialogue

How to deal with extremists has never been and will never be easy. It is, nevertheless, doable if Christian and Muslim leaders commit to rekindle ties to uphold common values, despite periodic errors that, mercifully, can and are easily corrected. When Pope Benedict XVI labeled the 1 January 2011 attacks on an Alexandria Coptic Church that killed 23 people as 'terrorism', and characterized the attacks as part of a 'strategy of violence' against Christians, Shaykh Ahmad Al Tayyib, the Imam of al-Azhar, suspended its ongoing dialogue with the Catholic Church. Five years later, a successor pontiff and the imam restarted the Sunni–Catholic conversation, aware that they shared far more than what separated the two largest religious communities on earth.

If al-Azhar reacted negatively to Pope Benedict XVI's criticisms—Al Tayyib blamed Benedict for 'interference' in Egyptian internal affairs—it could no longer ignore Pope Francis, who reiterated time and again that dialogue with Islam was a core issue for the Holy See. In fact, Vatican officials reported that the Pope asked to meet the Sunni imam, and instructed the Pontifical Council for Interreligious Dialogue, headed by Cardinal Jean-Louis Tauran, to reach out to al-Azhar. Towards that end, a secretary of the Pontifical Council, Father Miguel Ayuso Guixot—a bishop-designate and an expert on Islam who lived and taught in Egypt—visited Cairo in mid-February to communicate with deputy imam Shaykh 'Abbas Shuman, to make arrangements for the 16 May 2016 Vatican gathering.[74]

Francis prayed at several mosques in Turkey, Azerbaijan and several African countries, and planned to visit the Rome Mosque, which was built after the Second Vatican Council (1964). His mission was to reaffirm that dialogue must continue because "the plan of salvation also includes those who acknowledge the Creator, in the first place among whom are the Muslims." Vatican II affirmed that Muslims adored "the one, merciful God, mankind's judge on the last day" that, Francis reminded everyone, meant that Muslims and Christians shared profound values.[75] Such declarations were not mere words but build on the work of the late King Faysal bin 'Abdul 'Aziz, who visited Rome in 1973, and secured approval for the construction of the city's Islamic Cultural Center and Mosque. Faysal persuaded his religious advisors, Shaykh Muhammad al-Harakan, Shaykh Rashid bin Khunayn, Shaykh Muhammad bin Jubayr, as well as Shaykh 'Abdallah al-Musnad, to visit the Vatican in 1974 and participate in the Catholic Church's dialogue between Christians and Muslims. In turn, the late King received Cardinal Sergio Pignedoli in Riyadh, who conveyed "the regards of His Holiness [Pope Paul VI], moved by a profound belief in the unification of Islamic and Christian worlds in the worship of a single God, to His Majesty King Faisal as supreme head of the Islamic World."[76]

Sa'udi Arabia led the way but it fell to Pope Francis to re-emphasize commonality. Indeed, the world was stunned when Francis took twelve Syrian refugees, all of them Muslim, back with him to the Vatican after an emotional trip to the Greek island of Lesbos on 16 April 2016.[77] To be sure, the three families, including six children, represented a mere gesture but it was an incredibly powerful statement that was meant to nudge morally challenged officials that perceived life through the prisms of unadulterated interests. Francis provoked not for its own sake but to remind believers everywhere of what was the right thing to do. In a recent interview with the French Catholic newspaper *La Croix*, Francis confided that he "sometimes dreaded the tone" of statements heard throughout Europe where people spoke about the continent's "Christian" roots. "It is true that the idea of conquest is inherent in the soul of Islam," he declared but added that Christianity, too, had its "triumphalist" undertones. "It is also possible to interpret the objective in Matthew's Gospel, where Jesus sends his disciples to all nations, in terms of the same idea of conquest," he clarified.[78] These were not typical declarations and were addressed, first and foremost, to clerics, officials and believers, asking them to combine reason with compassion.

Francis and Al Tayyib carried the dialogue torch in a 25-minute meeting in the Pope's private library. As the men bid each other farewell, Al Tayyib leaned forward and embraced Francis, who was touched by the move and offered a broad smile. The Vatican said the meeting held a "great significance" for Catholic–Muslim dialogue and, according to Church sources, the two clerics deliberated on the best mechanisms for "authorities and the faithful of the world's great religions to show a common commitment to peace in the world." Both rejected violence and extremism, and the Pope requested that al-Azhar look into the plight of Christians "in the context of conflicts and tensions in the Mideast."[79]

As Nabil Khalifé concludes in his essays, the world is now challenged more or less on a regular basis with mundane Sunni–Shi'ah clashes, periodically supplemented by Salafi–Takfiri–Muslim Brotherhood extremists that are opposed to the contradictory alliance between an Iranian inspired *wilayat al-faqih* and the secularist Ba'ath ideology. And this just in Syria and Lebanon; similar groupings exist in other countries of course. Still, while extremists relied on religion or, more accurately, stressed their interpretation of Shari'ah Law as being the correct one, huge differences emerged between all of these groups and hundreds of millions of believers. Even in the supposedly secular Turkish Republic, allegedly the "model" of a moderate Islamist government under the Justice and Development Party (AKP), the Gezi Park attacks showed Prime Minister Recep Tayyib Erdoğan's political mantle. The concern that Ankara could slide so deep into authoritarianism was not foreseen before mid-2016 even if the AKP's supremacist and utopian goals shocked millions of Turks.

Though difficult to see through the fog of sensational coverage that aggrandizes lunatic fringes to spread their venom, there was plenty of good news, led by the wonderful constatation that extremist ideologies were no longer acceptable to a vast majority that sought peace and decency. Intolerance and xenophobia were out and it was amply evident that Arab and Muslim civilizations were safe from the temporary damage that fringe elements caused. Like most extremist groups, al-Qaʻidah could only conduct acts of violence, but then fail miserably since there was no unity or a nation-building vision. While dissension among opposition movements were not unusual, the very inabilities for self-appointed leaders from working with each other ensured that nothing substantive could ever come out of stale agendas. That was not what most folks wanted from their leaders and it should come as no surprise that the overwhelming majority of Arabs and Muslims have turned their backs on such groups. They overwhelmingly rejected sectarianism even if little of what they believed in, or wished to convey, ever reached Western eyes and ears.

In the final section of this third part, an attempt is made to evaluate the perpetual wars that now confront the Arab World, before testing the proposition that Iran may be engaged in an existential confrontation with political Sunnism.

How Jewish Prophecy Prepares for Perpetual Wars

Whether by design or through sheer coincidence, anti-Muslim venom has seeped into Western mentalities, especially in the United States. If past American presidential and congressional elections took on entertaining features, the 2016 cycle won rave reviews, with a reality television candidate whose motto—"You're Fired"—rings truly hollow. Of course, such television-propelled drivel is nothing new, as televangelist-entertainment filled the airwaves for decades, ranging from Jimmy Swaggart—whose 1980s telecasts were transmitted over 3,000 stations and cable systems—to Jerry Falwell—whose Lynchburg Christian Academy in Virginia became a university and who was responsible for creating what was once known as the "Moral Majority." Several of these iconic personalities confronted scandals—in 1991 Swaggart was arrested with a prostitute, while numerous parties sued Falwell for slander over the years—even though they claimed divine inspiration.

Most of these preachers disgraced themselves, as only they knew how, but the phenomenon endured. All were staunch allies of Israel and sometimes referred to themselves as "Christian Zionists." Falwell in particular displayed abject intolerance towards Muslims. In his epistle,

Listen, America!, he referred to the Jewish people as "spiritually blind and desperately in need of their Messiah and Savior."[80] What these men and women created was an industry of unprecedented hate that seeped through the body politic in the United States. Beyond traditionalists or even neoconservatives, the Republican Party espoused extremist ideals from the religious right, which came to be known as the "Christian Right," and which pretended to support conservative social policies like opposition to abortion, affirmative action, and same-sex marriage. How Donald Trump, who carefully hid his liberal preferences on socio-cultural matters, survived this vetting was a mystery that will long be debated after the 8 November 2016 elections that propelled him to the presidency of the United States. Notwithstanding this caveat, we now have an entire gloom and doom industry that prevails over naïve fundamentalists (the Christian and Jewish variety in these instances) who await the End of the World in earnest and whose proponents prepare to occupy high-ranking positions in the Trump Administration. Donald Trump's early appointments, including retired Lieutenant General Michael Flynn as his national security adviser, Stephen Bannon as a strategic counselor, Representative Mike Pompeo and Senator Jeff Sessions, have all expressed hateful rhetoric about Muslims and Islam. While the President-elect told CNN in March 2016 "I think Islam hates us," Flynn has called Islam "a cancer" and in a July 2016 tweet wrote that he "dare[s]" Muslim world leaders to "declare their Islamic ideology sick." In February 2016, Flynn tweeted a link to a YouTube video titled "Fear of Muslims is RATIONAL," which highlighted his state of mind. Bannon, who ran a conservative news outlet, promoted a nationalist line that portrayed Muslims as a dire threat to the U.S. while Frank Gaffney, under consideration for a high-ranking Department of Defense position, warned of "an Islamist Fifth Column operating inside our own country." Representative Mike Pompeo, a vocal critic of the Obama Administration's security policy was appointed director of the Central Intelligence Agency, and opined that "Muslim leaders across the U.S. who fail to condemn terror attacks motivated by radical Islamic beliefs are 'potentially complicit in these acts, and more importantly still, in those that may well follow'." For his part, U.S. Senator Jeff Sessions warned Americans in June 2016 to "slow down" on foreign born admissions into the United States, particularly those with Islamic backgrounds. The next attorney general's supporters believed that the Sessions appointment would now end what "Attorney General Loretta Lynch" allegedly did, which is to be "more concerned about protecting Muslims from criticism than they are about Muslim crimes and Islamic terrorism."[81]

In his heydays, Falwell spewed apocalyptic views, called Islam "satanic" and identified the Messenger as a "terrorist" though he added that he did not mean to offend "honest and peace-loving" Muslims.[82] The disingenuous apology was, however, a perfect illustration of what happened to the Christian Right industry, and it is one, according to *The Washington Post*, which estimated that Americans donated nearly $84 billion in charitable contributions to religious groups in 2013. In comparison, the sports market in North America was only worth $60 billion in 2014, and few realized that these churches owned $600 billion in property—considered to be a low estimate—as they routinely collected hundreds of millions of tax-exempt dollars.[83]

Where it gets dangerous is when you have perfectly normal sounding preachers fill the airwaves with mind-boggling assertions. One such regular expert is Dennis Avi Lipkin, also known as Victor Mordecai, a New Yorker who moved to Israel, worked for Prime Minister Yitzhak Shamir, began lecturing in Christian churches and synagogues in the U.S., studied theology, wrote six books—*Is Fanatic Islam a Global Threat?*, *Christian Revival for Israel's Survival*, *Islamic Threat Updates Almanac #1*, *Israel's Bible Bloc*, *Islam Prophesied In Genesis*, and *Return to Mecca*—and otherwise spread unadulterated loathing.[84] In *Return to Mecca*, he credits Jim and Penny Caldwell—who apparently lived in the Kingdom of Sa'udi Arabia for 14 years and shared their experiences with the fearless theologian—for enlightening him that Mount Sinai was deep inside the Arabian Peninsula, and not in the Sinai Peninsula. Islam, he claims, is "a global threat" and affirms that his faith tells him "that either the Jews and Christians hang together or [they] will hang on the gallows separately." As if this was not provocative enough, Lipkin offers the following nugget: "To terminate Islam, one must 'capture the flag', or the Ka'abah in Mecca, and either raise the Israeli flag over [it] or remove it as the vortex of Islam's evil system."[85] Terminate Islam and conquer Makkah and Madinah? Are these the results of theological studies?

This confused theologian, who believes that Allah is different from God [or at least his God], needs serious redemption though few earthlings can accommodate his extremism. What are far more serious are the political consequences of such discourses at a time when the world encounters serious security challenges. In the context of American elections, where gullible voters buy—no pun intended—into such absurdity, extremist views mobilize voters who, in turn, perceive the Muslim World in negative terms. Most ignore that Allah is merely the Arabic name for God and that millions of Arab Christians—those who were there at the beginning—have lived and maintain the most cordial ties with their Muslim neighbors. Extremist forces from all faiths naturally look for advantages in their "business models," which feeds the hate industry, but true monotheists know that they merely aspire to earn eternal grace.

Arab Majority Considers Iran a Regional Threat

If few post-1979 revolutionaries doubted that Iran could export its insurrection to the rest of the Muslim world without encumbrance, even fewer questioned the zeal with which the *wilayat-al faqih* principle would be applied among Sunnis, especially in Arab countries with significant Shi'ite populations. The Iranian phoenix, which was backed by the wily Ayatallah Ruhallah Khumayni, who fully understood his country's geo-strategic advantages, soared high.[86] A little more than four decades later, however, Iran confronted existential challenges. Will it continue to literally shake the vast realm surrounding it or, more likely, strive to secure yet another regeneration to save itself?

Like all aspiring peoples, Iranians harbored a certain idea of themselves, projecting visions of grandeur that matched their intrinsic characters. Although an established historical society, the post-1979 revolutionary era has not been kind to Iran, and it may be safe to say that 37 years after the end of the Pahlavi Dynasty that ushered into power hungry clergymen, the country's domestic conditions and foreign relations were not particularly successful. In fact, exporting the Islamic Revolution defined Iranian policy, even if regional hegemonic objectives mimicked the late Shah's ambitions. Muhammad Riza Pahlavi wished to transform Iran into the Japan of the 21st century, a goal shared by the Mullahs who, when confronted by reality, scaled back their aims to a mere domination of the Muslim World. Will Tehran now triumph?

To achieve such an objective required that Iran become the "Custodian of the Two Holy Mosques," which was easier said than done because Sa'udi Arabia was a real country, led by effective and foresightful officials who took their responsibilities seriously and, it was important to underscore, not ready to surrender to Iranian hegemony. Consequently, the Muslim World was confronted by an irreconcilable standoff, with Riyadh steadfast to honor its commitments to protect and preserve the birthplace of Islam, while Tehran actively promoted and backed Muslim revolutionaries who loathed Western values and wished to engage them in perpetual wars ostensibly because Westerners encroached themselves throughout the realm. Of course, many Muslims rejected that interpretation and, led by Sa'udi Arabia, opposed Iranian meddling in Iraq, Bahrain, Lebanon, Yemen, and especially in Syria. To put it as succinctly as possible, Sa'udi leaders, in particular, believed that Iran was not entitled to meddle in fellow Muslim countries' internal affairs. Lest one conclude that such interferences only targeted Arab entities that included significant Shi'ah populations, it may be useful to briefly return to oft-repeated Iranian declarations about Sa'udi Arabia and other Arab Gulf States, which reveal true intentions. Indeed, it was the late Ayatallah Khumayni who unveiled his anti-monarchy positions, when he challenged the very legitimacy of the Al Sa'ud ruling family as the protector of the Muslim holy cities of Makkah and Madinah. In 1987, the cleric declared that Makkah itself was in the hands of a "band of heretics" and characterized the Sa'udis as "vile and ungodly Wahhabis."[87] Little changed during the past 37 years, as the current Iranian Supreme Leader, Ayatallah 'Ali Khamane'i reemphasized Khumayni's views, as he called for "revolution against a tyrannical regime."[88]

To be sure, Western powers with global agendas opted to overlook such threats and even succumbed to the charm offensives that astute Iranians like Presidents Muhammad Khatami or Hassan Ruhani promoted, but savvy Sa'udis and other Arabs remained wary. Although Riyadh looked askance at the P5+1 [the five UN Security Council members and Germany] discussions with Iran over the latter's nuclear initiatives concluded, Sa'udi Arabia focused on core Arab developments, which revealed genuine Iranian purposes.

Nowhere was this confrontation as serious as in Syria that now included sectarian features with Iran ordering the Shi'ah militia of Hizballah to serve its interests there. Although kept out of sight, Tehran dispatched scores of officers to Syria, some of whom died in battle and received popular burials in their respective hometowns. One of the core ideological aspects of the "Battle for Syria" remained the defense of a shrine near Damascus that contains the remains of Sayyidah Zaynab, a granddaughter of the Prophet and a daughter of the Imam 'Ali. In contrast, the Grand Mufti of Sa'udi Arabia, 'Abdul 'Aziz Al al-Shaykh, issued a fatwah that banned Sa'udis from fighting in Syria on behalf of the opposition even if Riyadh provided limited financial and military assistance to the Free Syrian Army.[89] Even the hugely controversial Shaykh Yusuf al-Qaradawi, whose admonitions on behalf of the Egyptian Muslim Brotherhood—designated as a terrorist organization by Sa'udi Arabia—earned him scorn, declared that Hizballah was not the 'army of God', as its name suggests, but rather the 'army of Satan.' A rabid anti-Shi'ah cleric, Qaradawi called on "every Muslim trained to fight and capable of doing so to make himself available" for jihad in Syria, which was categorically rejected by Sa'udi officials.[90]

These illustrations highlighted a small aspect of the Iranian-Arab struggle for Syria, where Iran weighed-in heavily on the side of its client in Damascus. Few ought to be surprised that the mullahs in Tehran would do everything in their capabilities to protect their perceived interests even if their involvement threatened to literally ruin the country. For its part, Sa'udi Arabia may also be expected to defend its core interests, which included a gradual Iranian retreat from the Arab World. From Syria, as well as Lebanon, Bahrain, Yemen and Iraq, all of which were caught in the whirlwind of tectonic transformations that would probably take decades to resolve. Naturally, while the current standoff between Iran and Sa'udi Arabia could possible escalate—as Tehran repeatedly showcased its military achievements, allegedly producing satellites, fighter jets, helicopters, unmanned aerial vehicles, submarines, destroyers, and a slew of other equipment—Riyadh was not willing to rollover and play dead. It held its largest military maneuvers in February 2016 to signal a readiness to defend itself, its legitimacy, as well as the Holy Cities of Makkah and Madinah. Although few doubted that Iranians viewed Sa'udi Arabia as their primary enemy because the later stood in the way of Tehran's abilities to actually become *the* regional power, even fewer should misinterpret Saudi policies, which seldom fell to charm offensives. Rather, Riyadh adopted pragmatic steps to honor well-established commitments, precisely to protect and preserve core Arab and Muslim values.

Iranian Sectarianism Run Amok

When supreme leaders speak, as "supreme leaders" usually do, they offer superlative nuggets of wisdom that, to say the least, mobilize public opinion. This was what Ayatallah 'Ali Khamane'i, the Iranian "supreme leader" engaged in when he launched a blistering attack on Sa'udi Arabia, urging Muslims to "reconsider" the latter's custodianship of Makkah and Madinah.[91] Khamane'i accused Riyadh of "murder" no less. According to the Iranian's version, Sa'udi authorities "murdered" pilgrims who were caught up in a deadly stampede during the 2015 Hajj. As the Muslim world prepared for 'Id al-Adhah in 2016, and Makkah readied itself to welcome over two million pilgrims, these accusations were fresh fuel added to the sectarian fires consuming the Muslim World. Characteristically, Khamane'i relied on choice words to make his case: "The heartless and murderous Saudis locked up the injured with the dead in containers—instead of providing medical treatment and helping them or at least quenching their thirst. They murdered them," he wrote in a statement posted on his website to mark the anniversary of the tragedy that killed many.

In the chaotic 2015 stampede that saw thousands in a frenzied rush, 769 died according to Sa'udi authorities, though an Associated Press tally listed casualties at 2,426 dead. Naturally, Riyadh rejected criticisms that the incident was the result of poor management, which was understandable as authorities went out of their way to look after unprecedented crowds on a yearly basis. None of that mattered to Khamane'i who, buoyed by his own ego, insisted that the Kingdom's rulers were "satans," which was not very original since no one really knows what *satan* looks like. It was worth quoting the full sentence in which the Ayatollah accused the Al Sa'ud of transforming the annual pilgrimage into a "religious-tourist trip and have hidden their enmity and malevolence towards the faithful and revolutionary people of Iran under the name of 'politicising hajj'," since they, the Sa'udis, "are themselves small and puny satans who tremble for fear of jeopardizing the interests of the Great Satan, the U.S."[92]

Heir Apparent and interior minister Prince Muhammad bin Nayif told the Sa'udi Press Agency that the Kingdom was committed to safe and non-political pilgrimage celebrations. For his part, 'Abdul Muhsin Alyas, the Sa'udi undersecretary for international communications and media at the Ministry of Culture and Information, declared that the Iranian's accusations reflected "a new low" since such accusations were not only unfounded, but "timed to only serve their unethical, failing propaganda." Beyond the commemoration of the 2015 tragedy, what Iran wanted was far more ominous, and was ready to use every scare tactic, including a full-fledged effort to stoke sectarian fires, to accomplish its objectives. This quest, which preceded the last stampede, was to place pilgrimage in the hands of a committee—presumably led by Iranian experts—which was a naïve proposition since Sa'udi authorities, representing 90% of Muslims around the world, were not—now or ever—ready to surrender their custodianship responsibilities.

Still, what irks Khamane'i and Iranians in general, is the simple fact that the Al Sa'ud reject the Islamic revolution and its sectarian preferences. There is no denying that sectarianism has gained mythical proportions to disguise geostrategic objectives, though Iran relies on its religious identity to advance various causes, as it hopes to enhance its power on some kind of puritanical agenda. It carefully mobilizes followers along sectarian lines to impose political objectives, promotes ideological preferences under the leadership of a religious figure who, and this must be recognized, controls a government in which most officials espouse notorious zealotry.

Targeting Sunnis

A few days after President-elect Donald Trump defeated former Secretary of State Hillary Clinton, he met with Henry Kissinger, ostensibly to discuss "events and issues around the world." This was the second encounter between the two men in recent months, after a controversial mid-May 2016 gathering at Kissinger's home when the billionaire businessman sought support from members of the Republican establishment, ostensibly to shore up his poor foreign policy credentials. To be sure, Trump eschewed Republican foreign policy orthodoxy throughout the campaign—rejecting the 2003 War for Iraq, calling into question America's military alliances, dismissing the benefits of international trade, and planning to call for a temporary ban on Muslims to enter the U.S. (which Kissinger urged him to abandon)—going so far as to declare, at least then, that he would be more comfortable with another nominee. According to a press statement issued by Trump, the "President-elect and Dr. Kissinger discussed China, Russia, Iran, the EU and other events", which was to be expected though few know what the strategist told the novice leader. Interestingly, Kissinger spoke about his meeting on CNN on 20 November 2016, opining that "Not enough attention was paid to the fact that [Globalization] was bound to have winners and losers, and that the losers were bound to try to express themselves in some kind of political reaction." Flattering the president-elect, Kissinger orated that Trump was "the most unique [winner] that I have experienced in one respect", adding that the man had "No baggage."

Globalization is an important topic of course but it is significantly weakened, now that protectionism preoccupies everyone, everywhere. Yet, by focusing on it, Kissinger avoided comments on the three key concerns that the two men probably discussed in great detail, with the 93-year old strategist coaching, yes coaching, his newest apprentice. Given Trump's penchant to work with Vladimir Putin, the Kissinger caution vis-à-vis Russia was probably topic number one. Competition between the two countries, which struggled during the Cold War to delegitimize each other, reached dangerous levels in recent years as Moscow abolished the Warsaw Treaty Pact but Western powers retained the North Atlantic Treaty Organization (NATO). Putin is still livid about this and does not plan to forgive Washington for pushing NATO closer to Russia. He vociferously objects to any and all Western involvement in his backyards, including Ukraine, most of the countries in what was the former East European arena, the Caucasus and elsewhere.

For his part, Trump repeatedly criticized NATO countries and plans to send everyone a bill, oblivious to treaty obligations that are followed to the letter. Irrespective of any changing long-term perspectives in Europe, Kissinger most probably cautioned Trump to be wary of Putin, whose strategic skills are far superior to anything the New York billionaire can field. Kissinger knows that the Russian is anxious to restore his empire, and prevent a third break-up after the 1917 and 1991 revolutions, even if how modern Russia confronts serious economic challenges will determine its fate. What Trump can do about these Russian problems is peripheral though he can lower tensions between Washington and Moscow.

The second grave topic is China and, in the words of the Chinese President Xi Jinping, U.S.–Chinese ties are now at a "hinge moment", something that does not bode well as Trump is likely to walk away from the Trans-Pacific Partnership (TPP) "from day one." Trump declared that he planned to issue a note of intent to withdraw from the TPP trade deal on 20 January 2017, calling it "a potential disaster for our country." Instead he said he would "negotiate fair bilateral trade deals that bring jobs and industry back." Of course, TPP would be "meaningless" without U.S. participation and, if Trump goes through with his ideas, chances are great that fresh tensions would be added to the mix. Kissinger, the father of the U.S.–Chinese rapprochement that allowed President Nixon to go to Beijing in 1972 and who masterfully used China against the then USSR, probably cautioned Trump not to surrender this critical card. In fact, every head-of-state, including the largely negligent Obama Administration, opted for close cooperation with China on key issues such as North Korea's nuclear development and climate change, even if Washington's putative "pivot to Asia" was meant to check Beijing's expansion. Trump cast China as a foe throughout the campaign, threatened to impose new tariffs, and declared that the country was a currency manipulator. Irrespective of such bombastic declarations, the two sides will now work together to focus on cooperation, manage differences, and usher in mutually beneficial policies, something that financial necessities will impose on both. Pragmatism, which Kissinger undoubtedly counseled Trump, must prevail and few should be surprised if and when the president-elect decides to work closely with Xi.

The most critical area that most likely preoccupied Kissinger and Trump was the Middle East, as the two men prepared to further strengthen Israel and, commensurately, weaken Arab States. In fact, while the nonagenarian devoted most of his adult life to ensure the integration of Israel in the area, he most likely reminded his host that the wars in Iraq, Syria, Yemen and elsewhere were/are all meant to guarantee the inclusion of minority regimes in the area as "natural entities." The concern over Iran was most likely touched upon too with Trump confronting challenges from his ultra-conservative advisors—and potential secretaries of defense and national security counsel personnel—versus Kissinger who always opted for "divide-and-rule" tactics. Of course, time will tell whether Trump listened to Kissinger, but chances were great that the apprentice displayed awe in the presence of a strategist whose undeniable expertise for gloom and doom remained unparalleled.

Whether Arab leaders will also listen, albeit to such thinkers as Nabil Khalifé, was the crux of the matter. As the author reminds his readers, complacency is not something they should practice, and while it may be easy to dismiss his warnings, Arab leaders may wish to reassess his counsel, or those of the renowned Kuwaiti geo-political analyst, 'Abdallah al-Nafisi. Like Khalifé, and for years, al-Nafisi forcefully argued that Iran is embarked on a massive effort to conquer the Arab and Muslim worlds, whose strategic dilemmas, he concluded, were similar to those of Israel. "Both," he posited, shared "a superiority complex that causes their leaders to make wrong considerations," and "while Israel is occupying Palestine, Iran is occupying the Ahwaz [Khuzestan in Persian] region, which is 16 times bigger than Palestine," he recently chimed. "Like Israel," al-Nafisi added: "Iran feels culturally isolated since the dominant language in its region is Arabic," and not Persian (or Hebrew), which is certainly the case even if Iranian revolutionary leaders tried to blur the issue.[93]

Khalifé, al-Nafisi, and many others fear that Iranian leaders use Shi'ism in their zeal to conquer what is clearly non-Persian, and are dumbfounded that calls to occupy Makkah and Madinah, which will necessitate the overthrow of the Al Sa'ud and probably every single Arab Gulf monarchy, elicit no Western condemnation. They wonder why Americans, Russians, Europeans and others do not speak against such blatant aggression, asking themselves whether that is, in fact, the desired outcome. They are bewildered by Western perceptions of Sunni Arabs, most of whom look favorably on Western cultures and believe that their destinies are tied together, incredulous that epochal challenges that ascend from friendly sources equal those that arise from their adversaries. They nevertheless draw succor from their faith, cultures and traditional values to survive and prosper, aware that those who remain true to their norms prevail.

Notes to the Translator's Introduction

1 Adam Roberts, "The Arab Spring: Why Did Things Go So Badly Wrong?," *The Guardian*, 15 January 2016, at https://www.theguardian.com/commentisfree/2016/jan/15/arab-spring-badly-wrong-five-years-on-people-power.

2 Adam Roberts, Michael J. Willis, Rory McCarthy & Timothy Garton Ash, eds., *Civil Resistance in the Arab Spring: Triumphs and Disasters*, New York: Oxford University Press, 2016.

3 As quoted in Osmo Jussila, Seppo Hentilä, and Jukka Nevakivi, *From Grand Duchy to Modern State: Political History of Finland Since 1809*, London: C. Hurst & Co Publishers Ltd, 1999, p. 42.

4 Dean Nicholas, "Zhou Enlai's Famous Saying Debunked," *History Today*, 15 June 2011, at http://www.historytoday.com/blog/news-blog/dean-nicholas/zhou-enlais-famous-saying-debunked.

5 Woolsey spoke in clear and specific terms, as he emphasized that the West [he used the term *we*] had "a problem with a Jihad inspired set of terrorist activities and national activities that are for all practical purposes engaging us in something that you might call the third world war although there is probably some better formulation for it . . . but we are never going to win this just by arguing with the hardline Wahhabis or Shiite Muslims in Iran. We have got to get some leverage over their behavior and, as far as I am concerned, the only way to do that is to undercut—for essentially all of them—their source of income. We need to *bankrupt them* [emphasis added] and then we can start working nicely." IDC Herzliya, 2013 Conference on *Time For New National and Regional Agendas*. In addition to Woolsey, Lt. Gen. (Ret.) Francis H. (Frank) Kearney, the former Deputy Director for Strategic Operational Planning, U.S. National Counter-Terrorism Center; Ambassador Wolfgang Ischinger, the Chairman of Munich Security Conference; Jane Harman, a former U.S. Congresswoman and Director, President & CEO of the Woodrow Wilson International Center for Scholars; and Boaz Ganor, the Deputy Dean of the Lauder School of Government, Diplomacy and Strategy, IDC Herzliya, spoke on the panel "Emerging Security Challenges in the Middle East: The Proliferation of Terror and Jihad," 13 March 2013. See also Barry Shaw, "Soundbites from a Conference—Day 3," *The View from Israel*, 14 March 2013, at http://israeltheviewfromhere.blogspot.com/2013/03/soundbites-from-conference-day-3.html.

6 Julian Borger, Angelique Chrisafis and Chris Stephe, "Tunisian National Dialogue Quartet Wins 2015 Nobel Peace Prize," *The Guardian*, 9 October 2015, at https://www.theguardian.com/world/2015/oct/09/tunisian-national-dialogue-quartet-wins-2015-nobel-peace-prize.

7 Seymour Martin Lipset, "Some Social Requisites of Democracy: Economic Development and Political Legitimacy," *The American Political Science Review* 53:1, March 1959, pp. 69–105.

8 Giang Dang and Low Sui Pheng, *Infrastructure Investments in Developing*

Economies: The Case of Vietnam, Singapore: Springer, 2015 [Chapter 2, "Theories of Economic Development," provides numerous details, pp. 11–26]. For the data that follows, see World Bank. Indicators, 2011 at http://data.worldbank.org/indicator/ NY.GNP.PCAP.PP.CD.

9   "Tunisia Signs New Constitution," *The Guardian*, 27 January 2014, at https://www.theguardian.com/world/2014/jan/27/tunisia-signs-new-constitution-progressive.

10 In mid-2016, a new government was ushered in after Habib al-Sayd [Essid], who served as Prime Minister between 6 February 2015 and 27 August 2016 lost a parliamentary vote of confidence and was succeeded on 30 July 2016 by Yusif al-Shahid [Chahed], a trained agricultural engineer and university professor. The peaceful transfer confirmed that Tunisians were eminently capable of changing governments as necessary. See Marwan Muasher, Marc Pierini, and Alexander Djerassi, *Between Peril and Promise: A New Framework for Partnership With Tunisia*, Washington, DC: Carnegie Endowment for International Peace, April 2016, at http://carnegieendowment.org/2016/04/14/between-peril-and-promise-new-framework-for-partnership-with-tunisia-pub-63269.

11 "Tunisia to Broadcast Victims' Testimony at Truth Commission," *Reuters*, 17 November 2016, at https://www.theguardian.com/world/2016/nov/17/ tunisia-to-broadcast-victims-testimony-at-truth-commission-into-authoritarian-rule.

12 Tom Finn, "How Arab States Helped the CIA with its Torture-Linked Rendition Program," *Middle East Eye*, 13 February 2015, at http://www.middleeasteye.net/news/how-did-arab-states-involved-cia-torture-330269922.

13 Samer Soliman, *The Autumn of Dictatorship: Fiscal Crisis and Political Change in Egypt under Mubarak*, Stanford, California: Stanford University Press, 2011.

14 Hesham Al-Awadi, *The Muslim Brothers in Pursuit of Legitimacy: Power and Political Islam in Egypt under Mubarak*, London: I.B. Tauris, 2014. See also Emile Hokayem, *Egypt After the Spring: Revolt and Reaction*, London: The International Institute for Strategic Studies, 2016.

15 For a colorful rendition in his own voice, see "Gaddafi: 'Don't Leave Tripoli Ever to Those Rats . . . Destroy Them'—Video," *Reuters*, 25 August 2011, reproduced by *The Guardian*, at https://www.theguardian.com/world/video/2011/aug/25/muammar-gaddafi-libya-audio-speech-august-25-2011. See also Tim Gaynor and Taha Zargoun, "Gaddafi Caught Like 'Rat' in a Drain, Humiliated and Shot," *Reuters*, 21 October 2011, at http://www.reuters.com/article/us-libya-gaddafi-finalhours-idUSTRE79K43S20111021.

16 Muammar Al Qaddafi, *The Green Book*, Tripoli, Libya: Revolutionary Committees Movement, 1975, available online at http://www.bgf.nu/greenbook.pdf.

17 Assad referred to Syrians as "jarasim" [plural of jarsum] on several occa-

sions. For an illustration, see Haytham Khoury, "Bashar al-Assad and the Mounting Pressure," *The Global Free Press*, 27 November 2011, at http://www.globalfreepress.org/contributors/canada/haytham-khoury/3148-bashar-al-assad-and-the-mounting-pressure.

18 Erik Stier, "Gulf Council Presents Yemen's Saleh with Exit Plan," *The Christian Science Monitor*, 21 April 2011, at http://www.csmonitor.com/World/Middle-East/2011/0421/Gulf-Council-presents-Yemen-s-Saleh-with-exit-plan. See also Robert F. Worth, "Yemen: The Houthi Enigma," *The New York Review of Books*, 30 March 2015, at http://www.nybooks.com/daily/2015/03/30/yemen-houthi-enigma/; and Sarah Phillips, *Yemen and the Politics of Permanent Crisis*, New York: Routledge, 2011.

19 Stier, *op. cit.*

20 In the course of an hour-long interview a few years ago, the Yemeni head of state brazenly told me that I knew nothing of the Arab World, but needed to learn how things worked here in Yemen. To my polite but firm questions on his ties with various Sa'udi officials, Salih shouted, wishing to intimidate. Needless to say that among rulers who granted me audiences over the years, Salih stood out as a true brute, which confirmed the notion that a man who disrespects a guest cannot possibly be kind to his own.

21 Tanya Basu, "Who Are the Houthis?, *The Atlantic*, 9 April 2015, at http://www.theatlantic.com/international/archive/2015/04/who-are-yemen-houthis/390111/. See also Zachary Laub, "Yemen in Crisis," New York: Council on Foreign Relations, 19 April 2016, at http://www.cfr.org/yemen/yemen-crisis/p36488; and Middle East Report, *The Huthis: From Saada to Sanaa*, Number 154, 10 June 2014, Brussels: International Crisis Group, at https://d2071andvip0wj.cloudfront.net/the-huthis-from-saada-to-sanaa.pdf.

22 Robin Abcarian, "Sarah Palin on Syria: 'Let Allah Sort it Out'," *Los Angeles Times*, 31 August 2013, at http://articles.latimes.com/2013/aug/31/local/la-me-ln-sarah-palin-on-syria-let-allah-work-it-out-20130831. See also James Arkin, "Palin: 'Let Allah Sort it Out'," *POLITICO*, 31 August 2013, at http://www.politico.com/story/2013/08/sarah-palin-let-allah-sort-it-out-096128.

23 "Kurdish PM Nechirvan Barzani Sets Out Priorities Post-Oil Deal," *BBC News*, 8 December 2014, at http://www.bbc.com/news/world-middle-east-30379243. See also Judit Neurink, "Isis in Iraq: The Fall of Mosul to the Jihadists Was Less of a Surprise to Baghdad than Many Were Led to Believe—Key figures involved say Nouri al-Maliki's government brushed aside increasingly urgent calls for help in the run-up to the 'surprise' attack and reveal the frustration that detailed warnings were ignored," *The Independent*, 25 February 2016, at http://www.independent.co.uk/news/world/middle-east/isis-in-iraq-the-fall-of-mosul-to-the-jihadists-was-less-of-a-surprise-to-baghdad-than-many-were-led-a6895896.html.

24 For details on Bell's work, see Georgina Howell, *Gertrude Bell: Queen of*

the Desert, Shaper of Nations, New York: Farrar, Straus and Giroux, 2006.

25 For details on Joe Biden's original calls to create a federal Iraq, see Robert Farley, "Joe Biden Says he Never Called for Partition of Iraq," *PolitciFact*, 21 July 2010 at http://www.politifact.com/truth-o-meter/statements/2010/jul/21/joe-biden/joe-biden-says-he-never-called-partition-iraq/.

26 Marcus Tullius Cicero, *How to Run a Country: An Ancient Guide for Modern Leaders*, Selected, translated, and with an introduction by Philip Freeman, Princeton and Oxford: Princeton University Press, 2013.

27 John McHugo, *Syria: A Recent History*, London: Saqi Books, 2015.

28 "Interview With Syrian President Bashar al-Assad," *The Wall Street Journal*, 31 January 2011, at http://www.wsj.com/articles/SB10001424052748703833204576114712441122894.

29 John Simpson, "Who Are the Winners and Losers from the Arab Spring?," *BBC News*, 12 November 2014, at http://www.bbc.com/news/world-middle-east-30003865.

30 "Syria Debate: 'Evidence Should Precede Decision'—Ed Miliband," *BBC News*, 29 August 2013, at http://www.bbc.com/news/uk-politics-23886747. For Obama's famous red line rhetoric and his ruminations, see Jeffrey Goldberg, "The Obama Doctrine," *The Atlantic*, April 2016, at http://www.theatlantic.com/magazine/archive/2016/04/the-obama-doctrine/471525/ as well as the video on his pronouncements http://www.theatlantic.com/video/index/473025/syria-red-line-that-wasnt/.

31 Hashashin, from where the term assassins is derived, is a name used to refer to the late 11th century secret order of Nizari Isma'ilis, which split from mainstream Isma'ilism, a branch of Shi'ah Islam. The Assassins relied on asymmetric and psychological warfare, were often involved in espionage, and carried out assassinations of key enemy figures. Presumably, they also took drugs before they carried out their deeds, although most of the accounts that survived are based on biased medieval sources. See, for example, Marshall G. S. Hodgson, *The Secret Order of Assassins: The Struggle of the Early Nizari Ismai'lis Against the Islamic World*, Philadelphia: University of Pennsylvania Press, 2005.

32 Henry A. Kissinger, "Meshing Realism and Idealism in the Middle East," *The Washington Post*, 3 August 2012, at https://www.washingtonpost.com/opinions/henry-kissinger-meshing-realism-and-idealism-in-syria-middle-east/2012/08/02/gJQAFkyHTX_story.html?utm_term=.cef8b1ca3c0d.

33 Although few Western policy wonks delve on the Sykes–Picot agreement as a source of calamity—since it was reached in secret between Britain and France to divide the Arab World a century ago—many indigenous populations continue to see it as a model created to enjoy spheres of influence at the expense of local inhabitants. See James Barr, *A Line in the Sand: The Anglo-French Struggle for the Middle East, 1914–1948*, New York: W. W. Norton & Company, 2013. The 1916 agreement is available online as part

of the Avalon Project, Yale Law School, Lillian Goldman Law Library, at http://avalon.law.yale.edu/20th_century/sykes.asp. It might be useful to add here that many Arabs perceived Britain's presence in conspiratorial terms, preferring Persians over Arabs and, as necessary, arming Persians to fight Arabs (see Appendix 10).

34　The Arab American Institute maintains a web page that is periodically updated with many of these episodes. See Arab American Institute, "Anti-Arab & Anti-Muslim Bigotry," at http://www.aaiusa.org/islamophobia.

35　Bernard Lewis, *What Went Wrong?: The Clash Between Islam and Modernity in the Middle East*, New York and Oxford: Oxford University Press, 2002.

36　Just like the commercial for the investment firm E. F. Hutton, which focused on a catchy slogan: "When E. F. Hutton talks, people listen," Bernard Lewis advertised his services to the George W. Bush White House. One of his more compliant students was Vice President Dick Cheney, who may have learned much of what he knew about the Middle East from the erudite academic, including his unabashed aversion to Arabs.

37　Bari Weiss, "The Saturday Interview: The Tyrannies Are Doomed," *The Wall Street Journal*, 2 April 2011, at http://www.wsj.com/articles/SB10001424052748703712504576234601480205330.

38　Stefan Simons, "Nicolas Sarkozy's New 'Club Med'," *Der Spiegel*, 14 July 2008, at http://www.spiegel.de/international/europe/union-for-the-mediterranean-nicolas-sarkozy-s-new-club-med-a-565667.html.

39　Office of the Press Secretary, "Remarks by the President to Parliament in London, United Kingdom," Washington, D.C.: The White House, 25 May 2011, at https://www.whitehouse.gov/the-press-office/2011/05/25/remarks-president-parliament-london-united-kingdom.

40　Ian Morris, *Why the West Rules—For Now: The Patterns of History, and What they Reveal About the Future*, New York: Farrar, Strauss & Giroux, 2010, p. 619.

41　For the full poem, see Rudyard Kipling, "The Ballad of East and West," *Poetry Lovers' Page*, at http://www.poetryloverspage.com/poets/kipling/ballad_of_east_and_west.html.

42　Morris, *op. cit.*, p. 621.

43　Kanan Makiya, *Republic of Fear: The Politics of Modern Iraq*, Los Angeles and Berkeley: University of California Press, 1989 [an updated edition, which carried the author's name for the first time, appeared in 1998].

44　"Revealed: The Secrets of Israel's Nuclear Arsenal," *Sunday Times* (London), 5 October 1986, pp. 1, 4–5; see also "Vanunu: Israel's Nuclear Telltale," *BBC News*, 20 April 2004, at http://news.bbc.co.uk/2/hi/middle_east/3640613.stm.

45　Isabel Kershner and Rick Gladstone, "Netanyahu's Bomb Diagram During U.N. Speech Stirs Confusion in Israel," *The New York Times*, 28 September 2012, at http://www.nytimes.com/2012/09/29/world/middleeast/netanyahus-bomb-diagram-stirs-confusion-in-israel.html.

46 Franklin Lamb, "US Preparing for a Post-Israel Middle East?," *Foreign Policy Journal*, 28 August 2012, at http://www.foreignpolicyjournal.com/2012/08/28/us-preparing-for-a-post-israel-middle-east/.

47 The 2009 speech was not meant as a policy declaration but as a tone-setting presentation to reach wider audiences that were increasingly suspicious of the United States. See Jonathan Freedland, "Barack Obama in Cairo: The Speech no Other President Could Make," *The Guardian*, 4 June 2009, at https://www.theguardian.com/world/2009/jun/04/barack-obama-speech-islam-west.

48 Ted Belman, "New Study: 'Preparing for a Post Israel Middle East'," *Arutz Sheva*, 9 September 2012, at http://www.israelnationalnews.com/Generic/Generic/SendPrint?print=1&type=1&item=12159.

49 Quoted in Ramzy Baroud, "Britain's Real Promise to Israel; 'Symbolic' Vote on Palestine," *Foreign Policy Journal*, 25 October 2014, at http://www.foreignpolicyjournal.com/2014/10/25/britains-real-promise-to-israel-symbolic-vote-on-palestine/.

50 Michael R. Gordon, "Accord Reached With Iran to Halt Nuclear Program," *The New York Times*, 23 November 2013, at http://www.nytimes.com/2013/11/24/world/middleeast/talks-with-iran-on-nuclear-deal-hang-in-balance.html.

51 "Edward Snowden Interview: The NSA and Its Willing Helpers," *Der Spiegel*, 8 July 2013, at http://www.spiegel.de/international/world/interview-with-whistleblower-edward-snowden-on-global-spying-a-910006.html.

52 For details on Israel attempts to order the assassination of Iranian scientists, see "Israel Behind Assassinations of Iran Nuclear Scientists, Ya'alon Hints," *The Jerusalem Post*, 8 July 2015, at http://www.jpost.com/Middle-East/Iran/Israel-behind-assassinations-of-Iran-nuclear-scientists-Yaalon-hints-411473.

53 David Ignatius, "The Omani 'Back Channel' to Iran and the Secrecy Surrounding the Nuclear Deal," *The Washington Post*, 7 June 2016, at https://www.washingtonpost.com/opinions/the-omani-back-channel-to-iran-and-the-secrecy-surrounding-the-nuclear-deal/2016/06/07/0b9e27d4-2ce1-11e6-b5db-e9bc84a2c8e4_story.html?utm_term=.d3538fc02078.

54 Iran preoccupied analysts for decades and, in the aftermath of the 1979 crisis that saw Khumayni-sanctioned revolutionary elements take U.S. diplomats hostage for 444 days, rumors circulated regarding the Ayatollah's background, his affiliations and, in the context of conspiratorial/paranoidal Iranian views of the world, of the Supreme Guide's preferences for attention. For a flavor of these views, see "Khomeini—An Agent of the UK and US Governments," *hormozgan96*, 5 November 2012, at https://hormozgan96.wordpress.com/2012/11/05/british-ruholla-khomeini/. See also Appendix 12.

55 Executive Council, "Decision: Destruction of Syrian Chemical Weapons," EC-M-33/DEC.1, The Hague, Netherlands: Organization for the

Prohibition of Chemical Weapons (OPCW), 27 September 2013, at https://www.opcw.org/fileadmin/OPCW/EC/M-33/ecm33dec01_e_.pdf; see also Rick Gladstone, Claims of Chlorine-Filled Bombs Overshadow Progress by Syria on Chemical Weapons, *The New York Times*, 22 April 2014, at http://www.nytimes.com/2014/04/23/world/middleeast/syria-chemical.html.

56   See Fred Fleitz, "The Obama Administration Races to Finalize a Bad Nuclear Deal," *The National Review*, 13 January 2016, at http://www.nationalreview.com/article/429680/iran-nuclear-deal-worse-ever. For an assessment of the ballistic missile tests, see Louis Charbonneau, "Exclusive: Iran Missile Tests Were 'in Defiance of' U.N. resolution—U.S., Allies," *Reuters*, 30 March 2016, at http://www.reuters.com/article/us-iran-missiles-idUSKCN0WV2HE.

57   Ahmet Ertay, "Nuclear Negotiations Between Iran And P5+1," *AVIM* [Avrasya İncelemeleri Merkezi], Ankara, Turkey: Center for Eurasian Studies, 3 January 2015, at http://avim.org.tr/Blog/NUCLEAR-NEGOTIATIONS-BETWEEN-IRAN-AND-P5-1.

58   Daniel Twining, "Why Asia Should Fear the 'Persian Pivot'," *Foreign Policy*, 17 July 2015, at http://foreignpolicy.com/2015/07/17/iran-china-japan-nuclear/. See also Hussain Abdul-Hussain, "America hates Sunnis," *NOW*, 20 July 2015, at https://now.mmedia.me/lb/en/commentary/565606-america-hates-sunnis.

59   *Ibid.*

60   Anne Barnard, "Audio Reveals What John Kerry Told Syrians Behind Closed Doors," *The New York Times*, 30 September 2016, at http://www.nytimes.com/interactive/2016/09/30/world/middleeast/john-kerry-syria-audio.html.

61   "Tunisia Islamist Party Moves to Separate Politics from Religion," *The Arab Weekly*, 21 May 2015, at http://www.thearabweekly.com/North-Africa/5149/Tunisia-Islamist-party-moves-to-separate-politics-from-religion.

62   Cheikh Muhammad Abdel Wahab Rafiki, Nader Bakkar, Georges Fahmi, Muhammad Khawaja, Carine Lahoud, *The Future of Political Salafism in the Arab World*, Beirut: Carnegie Middle East Center, 16 April 2015, at http://carnegie-mec.org/2015/04/16/future-of-political-salafism-in-arab-world-event-4798.

63   William McCants, "The Believer: How an Introvert with a Passion for Religion and Soccer Became Leader of the Islamic State," New York: Brookings Institution, 1 September 2015, at http://csweb.brookings.edu/content/research/essays/2015/thebeliever.html.

64   Associated Press, "Islamic State Destroys Ancient Mosul Mosque, the Third in a Week," *The Guardian*, 28 July 2014, at https://www.theguardian.com/world/2014/jul/28/islamic-state-destroys-ancient-mosul-mosque.

65   Martin Chulov, "Isis Insurgents Seize Control of Iraqi City of Mosul," *The Guardian*, 10 June 2014, at https://www.theguardian.com/world/2014/

jun/10/iraq-sunni-insurgents-islamic-militants-seize-control-mosul.

66 One of the more brilliant developments, and evidence that Arabs relied on humor to denigrate pretentious Caliphs, was a Beirut cabaret performance by the band al-Rahil al-Kabir, or the Great Departed, which reduced Abu Bakr al-Baghdadi into little more than a puppet. One of the best lines reads: "Oh master Abu Bakr al-Baghdadi, you, who rule by God's rules," the group sings in the mock ode, "you will lead God's servants to an abyss like no other." See Robert Mackey, "Mocking ISIS in Beirut," *The New York Times*, 10 September 2014, at http://www.nytimes.com/2014/09/11/world/middleeast/mocking-isis-in-beirut.html. The 4-minute-long song is available online, with English subtitles, at https://www.youtube.com/watch?v=UjaSGXmUjWI&index=3&list=RDD-4Am98nSyA.

67 "OIC Condemns ISIS Threats and Forced Displacement of Christians in Iraq," Jiddah, Sa'udi Arabia: Organization of Islamic Cooperation, 21 July 2014, at http://www.oic-oci.org/oicv3/topic/?t_id=9241&t_ref=3695&lan=en

68 "LB[n] . . . LBCI Changes Logo in Solidarity with Iraq's Christians," *Naharnet*, 28 July 2014, at http://www.naharnet.com/stories/en/140899.

69 Kim Sengupta, "Israel–Gaza Conflict: Greek Orthodox Church of St Porphyrios Becomes a Small Refuge in the Heart of Gaza's Bloodletting: Desperate Palestinians have Sought Shelter in a Local Church," *The Independent*, 27 July 2014, at http://www.independent.co.uk/news/world/middle-east/israel-gaza-conflict-greek-orthodox-church-of-st-porphyrios-becomes-a-small-refuge-in-the-heart-of-9631777.html.

70 Fred M. Donner, *Muhammad and the Believers: At the Origins of Islam*, Cambridge, Massachusetts: Harvard University Press, 2012. For reasons that remain obscure, American and Iraqi intelligence analysts confirmed that al-Baghdadi earned a doctorate in Islamic Studies in Qur'anic studies, from Saddam University in Baghdad, although there is no evidence to back such assertions. Security consultants like Patrick Skinner (Soufan Group) and Patrick Johnston (RAND Corporation), alleged that the American and Iraqi Governments knew the pseudo-Caliph even if he managed to reveal little of his persona. This was little more than speculation, for established religious scholars are known and evaluated on their publications, which al-Baghdadi has few, if any. See McCants, *op. cit.*; Peter Beaumont, "Abu Bakr al-Baghdadi: The ISIS Chief with the Ambition to Overtake al-Qaida," *The Guardian*, 12 June 2014, at https://www.theguardian.com/world/2014/jun/12/baghdadi-abu-bakr-iraq-isis-mosul-jihad; and Tim Arango and Eric Schmitt, "U.S. Actions in Iraq Fueled Rise of a Rebel: Baghdadi of ISIS Pushes an Islamist Crusade," *The New York Times*, 10 August 2014, at http://www.nytimes.com/2014/08/11/world/middleeast/us-actions-in-iraq-fueled-rise-of-a-rebel.html.

71 See, William Boykin, "When Jesus Comes Back, He'll Be Carrying An AR-15 Assault Rifle," *Military Religious Freedom*, 19 February 2014, at http://www.militaryreligiousfreedom.org/press-releases/2014/Boykin_2-21-14.html.

72 *Ibid.*

73 Friedrich Nietzsche, *Beyond Good and Evil*, Aphorism 146, Temple of East Publishing available online at http://www.templeofearth.com/books/beyond%20good%20and%20evil.pdf, p. 39b.

74 Elise Harris, "Vatican, Al-Azhar to Officially Resume Dialogue," Rome: Catholic News Agency, 21 October 2016, at http://www.catholicnewsagency.com/news/vatican-al-azhar-to-officially-resume-dialogue-73515/.

75 Catholic Church, "The Profession of the Christian Faith," Chapter 3, Article 9, Paragraph 841, in *The Profession of Faith*, Rome: Vatican City, at http://www.vatican.va/archive/ccc_css/archive/catechism/p123a9p3.htm.

76 Joseph Kéchichian, *Legal and Political Reforms in Sa'udi Arabia*, Abingdon, Oxfordshire: Routledge, 2013, p. 100.

77 Helena Smith, "Pope Francis Takes Refugees to Rome after Lesbos Visit," *The Guardian*, 16 April 2016, at https://www.theguardian.com/world/2016/apr/16/pope-francis-flies-to-lesbos-to-highlight-humanitarian-crisis-in-europe.

78 Nicole Winfield, "Pope Embraces Al-Azhar Imam in Sign of Renewed Relations," *The Associated Press*, 23 May 2016, at http://www.truthand-grace.com/Catholicbias.html.

79 Holy See Press Office, "Audience with the Grand Imam of Al-Azhar: Common Commitment by Religious Authorities and Faithful for World Peace and the Rejection of Violence and Terrorism," Rome: The Vatican, 23 May 2016, at https://press.vatican.va/content/salastampa/en/bollettino/pubblico/2016/05/23/160523a.html.

80 Stephen Spector, *Evangelicals and Israel: The Story of American Christian Zionism*, New York: Oxford University Press, 2009, p. 118.

81 See Michael Crowley and Nahal Toosi, "Trump Appointees Endorsed Link Between Islam and Radicalism," *POLITICO*, 18 November 2016, at http://www.politico.com/story/2016/11/trump-appointees-islam-radicalism-231647; Steve Holland, "Trump Picks Conservative Loyalists for Top Security, Law Enforcement Jobs," *Reuters*, 18 November 2016, at https://www.yahoo.com/news/trump-taps-sessions-attorney-general-pompeo-cia-transition-130557678.html; Natasha Bertrans, "Trump's Choice for CIA Director Once Said U.S. Muslims who Don't Reject Terrorism are 'Complicit' in it," *Business Insider*, 18 November 2016, at http://www.businessinsider.com/mike-pompeo-cia-trump-muslims-2016-11; Charlie Spiering, "Senator Jeff Sessions Warns: More 'Islamic Extremism' Attacks Are Coming," *Breitbart*, 12 June 2016, at http://www.breitbart.com/2016-presidential-race/2016/06/12/sen-jeff-sessions-warns-attacks-coming/; and Paul Bremmer, "Sessions Nomination Brings Hope of Reversing Islamic 'Stealth Invasion'," *WND.com*, 19 November 2016 at http://www.wnd.com/2016/11/sessions-nomination-brings-hope-of-reversing-islamic-stealth-invasion/.

82   "Threats and Responses; Muhammad a Terrorist to Falwell," *The New York Times*, 4 October 2002, at http://www.nytimes.com/2002/10/04/us/threats-and-responses-muhammad-a-terrorist-to-falwell.html.

83   Brian J. Grim and Melissa E. Grim, "The Socio-economic Contribution of Religion to American Society: An Empirical Analysis," *Interdisciplinary Journal of Research on Religion* 12:3, 2016, at http://www.religjournal.com/pdf/ijrr12003.pdf.

84   Biography of Dennis Avi Lipkin/alias Victor Mordecai, at http://www.vicmord.com/biography.html.

85   Dennis Avi Lipkin, *Return to Mecca*, Jerusalem, Israel [via Amazon Digital Services LLC], 2012, pp. xiii–xvi.

86   Khumayni seldom hid his true feelings towards the Arabs. In 1983, he granted an interview to, graced the cover of, an independent Arabic language weekly magazine, *Al Dustur*, which quoted him saying: "This is my commandment: -When the war with Iraq ends, we need to start another one;—I dream that our flag will flutter over 'Amman, Riyadh, Damascus, Cairo and Kuwait." See Appendix 15.

87   As quoted in Martin Seth Kramer, *Arab Awakening and Islamic Revival: The Politics of Ideas in the Middle East*, New Brunswick, New Jersey: Transactions Publishers, 1996, p. 174.

88   Yvette Hovsepian-Bearce, *The Political Ideology of Ayatollah Khamenei: Out of the Mouth of the Supreme Leader of Iran*, Abingdon, Oxfordshire: Routledge, 2016, p. 7.

89   "Saudi Arabia to Jail Citizens who Fight Abroad," *Reuters*, 3 February 2014, at http://www.reuters.com/article/us-saudi-law-idUSBREA 1213O20140203.

90   Charles R. Lister, *The Syrian Jihad: Al-Qaeda, the Islamic State and the Evolution of an Insurgency*, New York: Oxford University Press, 2016, p. 136.

91   Asa Fitch and Marguerita Stancati, "Iran Urges Muslims to Challenge Saudi Arabia's Oversight of Holy Sites," *The Wall Street Journal*, 4 September 2016, at http://www.wsj.com/articles/iran-urges-muslims-to-challenge-saudi-arabias-oversight-of-holy-sites-1473081759.

92   The message, titled "Hajj Hijacked by Oppressors, Muslims Should Reconsider Management of Hajj: Ayatollah Khamenei," is on the Supreme Leader's web-page at http://english.khamenei.ir/news/4121/Hajj-hijacked-by-oppressors-Muslims-should-reconsider-management.

93   Maayan Groisman, "Iran and Israel Face the Same Strategic Dilemma, Kuwaiti Political Analyst Says," *The Jerusalem Post*, 27 March 2016, at http://www.jpost.com/Middle-East/Iran-and-Israel-face-the-same-strategic-dilemma-Kuwaiti-political-analyst-says-449291.

Nabil Khalifé's Essay was first published in Arabic under the title *Istihdaf Ahl al-Sunnah: Man Yataza'am al-'Alam al-'Arabi-al-Islami— Al Sa'udiyyah am Iran? Al-Mukhattat al-Istratijih lil-Gharb wa Isra'il wa Iran lil-Saytarah 'ala al-Sharq al-Awsat wa Iqtila' al-Nufuz al- 'Arabo-al-Sunni Minhuh!* [Targeting Sunnis: Who Will Lead the Arab-Islamic World, Sa'udi Arabia or Iran?—A Western–Israeli–Iranian Strategic Plan to Dominate the Middle East and to Uproot all Sunni-Arab Influences from It].

The Essay was published in Jbayl, Lebanon, by Markaz Byblus lil-Dirasat wal-Abhath [Byblos Center for Research and Studies (CBER)], in 2014.

Targeting Sunnis

Nabil Khalifé

Dedication

To my teacher . . . at a time of distinction . . . and intelligence and giving.

Shaykh 'Abdallah Al-'Alayali

AND

Martyr Shaykh Subhi al-Salih

Fidelity to History and Witness to Excellence

He sends down from the sky, rain, and valleys flow according to their capacity, and the torrent carries a rising foam. And from that [ore] which they heat in the fire, desiring adornments and utensils, is a foam like it. Thus God presents [the example of] truth and falsehood. As for the foam, it vanishes, [being] cast off; but as for that which benefits the people, it remains on the earth. [Qur'an, 13:17]

Introduction
Sunnis Confront the World

As editor of the ideas section "The Harvest of the Week" [*Hisad Al-Usbu'*] in the Paris-based Lebanese daily newspaper *al-'Amal* [Labor] through the early 1980s, I composed a lengthy four-part study under the title: "Sunni–Shi'ah Struggle Exposed between the Mediterranean and the Gulf."[1] Interestingly, the sub-title for the fourth and final essay, which advanced a few thoughts "regarding the possible changes in the regional map in terms of the battle of Tripoli [Lebanon] that will decide the identity of the Fertile Crescent and its whole destiny," revealed, in hindsight, much more than I could anticipate. As an admirer of the German geographer and ethnographer Friedrich Ratzel, whose reference work *Politische Geographie* [Political Geography] transformed him into the undisputed father of contemporary geopolitics, and in which he advanced the notion that "politics was foresight," what took place in Tripoli canalized my interest.[2] As an analyst called upon to objectively ascertain facts and evaluate political developments, I concentrated my studies on geo-strategy to improve whatever analysis I could offer as well as present studies in a way that allowed for the formulation of a vision for the future, if for no other reason than to initiate steps that decision-makers could reach.

During my presence in Paris in the second half of the 1970s and early 1980s, when I earned a doctorate in Arab-Muslim Civilization at the Sorbonne, I also accepted the position of assistant editor at *Future* [Al-Mustaqbal] Magazine, which was run by the late Nabil Khoury. Moreover, I was in charge of the Arab Center for International Studies, and served as a news broadcaster on Radio Monte Carlo, all of which allowed me to gain insights into the nascent Iranian Revolution. At the time, the leader of the Islamic Revolution, Imam Ruhallah Khumayni [Rouhollah Khomeini], resided on the outskirts of Paris in the Neauphle-le-Château commune. When the Imam Khumayni flew back from Paris to Tehran on 1 February 1979 to assume the reigns of power, I wrote a lengthy essay for *Future* entitled: "Imam Khumayni's Revolution in Light of Iran's Contemporary History and the Political Philosophy of Islam."[3] At the time, and after Professor Jacques Ferrier found merit in the assessment, it was presented to political science students attending a Sorbonne seminar. The essay earned praise from the renowned Egyptian columnist Muhammad Hasanayn Haykal, who contacted the editorial secretary at *Future*, Shukri Nasrallah, to request several copies of the magazine, as he was writing a book about the Iranian Revolution.

In hindsight, and because of ongoing disputes, it was not too difficult to foresee a Sunni–Shi'ah struggle for power in the 1990s. As my interest grew in the subject, Eastern Catholic Patriarchs gathered in Rabwah, Lebanon in 1994 invited me to deliver a lecture on "The Status of Christians in the Middle," when I offered the following observations:

> "The strategies of Western powers and that of Israel in the Middle East today are based on a construction of a new regional system that respond to their interests in the area, which includes a wide range of options, including a systematic effort to dismantle parts of the Muslim World through Sunni–Shi'ah sedition." I added as a warning: "We, as Christians, are border-land churches but we are not and should not be border-guards to Israel or the West. It is our duty to work to prevent all sedition among Muslims because peace in the Muslim realm ensures concord in ours as well. It behooves the Patriarchs to consciously prevent Christians from any participation in such schemes, not only to avoid involvement in acts of sedition, but also to stay as far away as possible from any sectarian disputes since Christian communities will be their first victims. You must do everything in your power to avoid such clashes."

This presentation was followed-up with a study whose title expressed my misgivings: "The geopolitics of the Muslim World and the Strategy of Sedition."[4]

What I recalled at the beginning of this Introduction was not meant as bravado, but to highlight the importance of alertness and expectation, so that one is not surprised by the many developments occurring in the region today, ranging the gamut from acts of violence and terrorism at the hands of Da'ish [Islamic State of Iraq and Syria, or ISIS, now short-ened to Islamic State] and others, which place the people of this region in bad light.[5] Somehow, everyone is implicated, from politicians to religious figures, from secularists to indoctrinated parties, and from groups largely unaware of what is happening all around them to more active organizations, everyone faces the consequences of strategic developments that occurred during the past three decades. Arabs subjected to such vagaries may be said to have lived in the shadow of history without noticing its true countenance that targeted them in toto.

This purpose of this book, which many Arab and European friends encouraged me to compose, is to document and analyze important and proactive ideas first developed in various studies and newspaper articles during the past few decades. It is thus a modest attempt to clarify various concerns and place them in the right perspective, by analyzing geopolitical advances beyond ideological limitations or fantasies, which deplorably draw on conspiracy theories. The only criteria adopted in the analysis that follows is the formulation of perceived strategies, precisely to identify as clearly as possible what is emerging throughout the region, and beyond it. Towards that end, the book raises the following four main questions:

- Who is against whom among opposing forces in ongoing regional conflicts?
- What are the existing motivations that compel antagonists to struggle?
- What are the objectives and intentions of these conflicts?
- What are the geographical areas over which antagonists focus, including how they propose to dominate its inhabitants?

When my article "Targeting Sunnis" was first published in the Beirut daily *Al-Liwa'* on 23 October 2013, many readers were surprised because they believed that what was developing throughout the region was the exact opposite from what I composed. Before going any further, and in light of earlier remarks, it might be useful to step away from generalizations and concentrate on details, to better place this presentation under a far more realistic title that will do justice to the seriousness of the challenge. In reality, what is at stake is nothing short of "Sunnis Confronting the World" or, perhaps, a contention that Sunnis are perceived as a global threat.

In fact, it is possible to identify five clusters of nations that perceive this challenge in particular ways, to better elucidate my contention regarding solemn international confrontations that target the Sunni realm. These include:

1. Christian societies, divided into two Protestant branches in the United States and Germany; a Catholic gathering in France, Italy and the rest of Europe; and the Anglican Church in the United Kingdom; to which must be added the Orthodox portion in Russia. These societies concluded that the Sunni bloc was and is in a standoff with Western Christian civilization.

2. Perception of challenges from the Jewish world, led by Israel with its political, security, military and economic institutions . . . and with the Zionist ideology that extends beyond its borders.

3. Perception of challenges from the Iranian-Shi'ah world, with all the goals, aspirations, and ambitions to lead the Islamic world, as well as impose full control over the Eastern Mediterranean.

4. Perception of challenges from the Indian world, as a continuation of the Pakistan–India conflict over partition as well as the Kashmir conundrum, and around the Sunni bloc in India proper which is in the range of 150 million people.

5. Perception of challenges from the Chinese world associated with problems in Xinjiang, which spreads over a large area—1.2 million square kilometers—in Western China, and the more than 50 million Muslims who represent an unmistakable challenge to Chinese society that, in turn, fears the spread of Islam within it.[6]

If Sunnis, who account for 85% of the world's Muslims and which numbered around 1.4 billion in 2014, were in a confrontation with these various global blocs, what will remain of the world in case of major conflicts? What would remain, to say the least, is something ominous. Frequently referred to by leading Western thinkers, including the politically engrossed academic Bernard Lewis, what the world witnesses is a Sunni bloc involved in an acute competition with, and that displays an alleged hatred for, the West.[7]

After the events of 11 September 2001, Islam in general and Sunnis in particular replaced the Soviet Union in the universal struggle for power that pitted the globe into two major groups. Accordingly, it is worth emphasizing basic issues in various geostrategic developments for the region, to better understand what has happened in the past, what is currently under way, and what will be the radical and dramatic transformations in the context of a nascent global regional strategy at the macro-strategic level. In fact, three principal goals can thus be identified. The first is a shift of the Sunni influence in Eastern Mediterranean countries and its substitution by an Iranian-Shi'ah influence. The second objective is an integration of Israel as a natural entity within the region, possibly in a confederal political entity. The third is the control of Iraq's oil, which promises to be the best quality and, perhaps, the most abundant, estimated at 380 billion barrels according to the latest estimates whereas the Kingdom of Sa'udi Arabia holds reserves at 265 billion barrels.[8] It is in this context that one may possibly understand the outlines of American foreign policy in the Middle East: to secure Israel and contain oil-producing states irrespective of their Sunni or Shi'ah credentials. In other words, a control of Sa'udi Arabia and the Gulf states with the right hand must be accompanied with a restraint of Iran and its regional acolytes with the left. As the adage affirms: "Both the Arab and the Persian are best when they surrender."

Yet, because of the rise of Islamist movements, whose intentions go beyond the application of Shari'ah [Islamic] Law to include a full confrontation with Western powers, as well as an effort to abolish existing borders that Western colonial entities delineated, divided Sunni Muslims in dozens of countries are increasingly mobilizing. They, that is the Islamists, insist "they are but a single nation" and, in the words of Yves Lacoste, "believers proud in the greatness of their religion, and who perceive the unity of their nation as the instrument that will make them an oasis of progress as well as a geopolitical center that will affect all of humanity."[9] It is from this premise that many categories of strain emerge, which create contradictions between the Christian and Muslim worlds, especially in the presence of powerful dictatorial regimes that drain every effort made to improve ties. Therefore, those who wish to see tensions build and distort strategies towards Sunnis, which may be summarized in the term "demonizing Sunnis," can easily prevent Western countries from cooperating with existing regimes. Such demonization benefit Shi'ah powers in the region who further criticize the survival of various dictatorships in power as illustrations of Sunni extremism.

The Da'ish phenomenon, which is portrayed as a model of fundamentalist Sunni Islam, requires historic and sociological explanations—as well as a full condemnation of what is a barbaric terrorist fundamentalist wonder. At its basic level, it is an expression that was best clarified by the Jesuit clergyman, Father Bulus [Paul] Noya and by his renowned student, the Syrian poet Adonis, who settled on a pertinent elucidation in *The Static and the Dynamic*, which explained how "for the fundamentalist the past is perfection."[10] According to this interpretation, the past that the fundamentalist cherished was that of religion and Shari'ah Law, of a way of life, its ethics, values, history, as well as the food, the clothing, and the housing that were prevalent at the time of *jihad*.[11] For many who espoused such clarifications, insurgency was not only superior to innovation, "but a return to the beginnings of the end," because the foundation was a closet that included strength and everything that was good, every truth, and all the knowledge and valid experiences that were allocated to the first believers. When history moved away from its sources, the fundamentalists supposed, "the inexhaustible pool in which life thrives withers, while innovation prospers. For them, every innovation is originality gone amiss, and there is no escape but to go back to what the founders affirmed."[12]

Da'ish, quite simply, is thus trying to emulate this *jihadist* past in all its details, tying for the first time its plans to land (Iraq and Syria), and adjusting its quest to the so-called Islamic State in order to pave the way for a new declaration that will spread the Caliphate to all parts of the Muslim world. Shari'ah, the sword, the dagger, lashes, slavery and the veil for women, as well as stoning and dhimmitude for non-Muslims, would all be introduced to ensure this succession.[13] All public and private activities, including details of violent practices, would be carefully monitored and broadcast, which most Muslims and non-Muslims alike perceive as being barbaric. The use of primitive tools like the sword and the dagger, instead of modern weapons, affirms the identity of the contemporary Islamic fundamentalists who prefer to belong to that era. Consequently, terrorist movements smothered the historically tolerant religion that valued devoutness, and introduced in its place the spirit of violence at the expense of human life, and the believer's freedom as well as his dignity. It is this vision that pushes those moving in such a circular mode to return to the past, to their distorted and deformed past that flourished during the Middle Ages, away from the longitudinal mode that was adopted by those who sought progress. Regrettably, it was this negativity that has left an impact on Arab-Islamic civilization throughout history.

The Iranian strategic offensive, and with it that of the Syrian regime, Hizballah and other Shi'ah forces, stems from a sense of historical persecution that may legitimately be summarized as a strategy based on pain. All methods of intelligence, cunning and hypocrisy are used as required—backed by international powers whose interests to extrapolate benefits from existing schisms need no elaboration—precisely to enhance the potential and possible Shi'ah energies to tame the Fertile Crescent and dominate the Arab-Muslim world. That strategy banks on utilizing the festering Palestinian Question as a legitimizing mechanism to achieve added controls. In contrast, Sunni Muslim groups or states representing a major international bloc, do not have—at least as of now—an appropriate defense strategy to counter the Iranian onslaught. What is on offer are mere political positions and/or statements, which means that Sunnis, who rule most Muslim states, are ill-prepared for what is to come next. Sunnis, who enjoyed authority from the time of the first Caliphs to the more recent Ottoman Empire, did not suffer persecution—except under Fatimid rule.[14] It was partially for that reason that Sunni rulers did not assess the need to formulate a strategy to protect themselves from the various dangers they confronted and which exposed them to harm, amid what is now a global challenge.

Furthermore, and because there is no spiritual authority in Islam similar to the Catholic Church hierarchy that created effective institutions from the Pope down to village clerics in remote hamlets, every crisis that involves Islamic political thought easily opens doors to conflicting interpretations of jurisprudence. One of the most important perceptions deals with the spoils of war that permits contemporary caliphs, or emirs as some fanatics aspire to impose skewed religious views in the absence of a religious hierarchy that by its nature would introduce order and channel contradictory opinions. That is why fanatics bank on the authority of what they allege is the Sunni concept of historic privilege, which grants those who are victorious on the battlefield certain rights; Shi'ahs display a similar concept—the *wilayat al-faqih* [velayat-e faqih (Jurisprudence of God)]—that projects battlefield victories as entitlements.[15] This is an important truth that is often ignored and overlooked by many analysts of religious political thought among Sunnis and Shi'ahs alike. The following summary best describes the difference between the two creeds on this vital point:

> *Sunni Islam emerged from a political idea long before it assumed religious legitimacy, whereas Shi'ah Islam stemmed from a religious premise that sought political justification.*

Even if a multitude of objectives propelled the uprising movements that shook Arab and Muslim societies after 2011, one of the larger goals was and is how to develop a vision of the modern Islamic State in the twenty-first century that encourages citizenship, equality and human rights. Similarly important was the identity of the leadership that articulated this vision, which was the Al-Azhar University, in the person of its president—the enlightened Sorbonne-educated Shaykh Ahmad Al Tayyib.

He was the leader who confronted the issues and problems that pained the Arab Muslim in the twenty-first century and it was his virtuous approach that compelled Al-Azhar to issue several key documents to affirm this vision. Today, these documents are considered as nothing less than a qualitative leap in Sunni political thought, that benefitted from the wisdom of senior Muslim thinkers such as Mohammed Arkoun and others, who paved the way for their formulation.[16]

That is why I deliberately added these documents as appendices to this essay, to inform readers about the importance of Al-Azhar and the modernist ideas put forward, embraced, and defended by the institution, in the face of reactionary and fundamentalist forces both in Egypt and outside of it that rejected such enlightenment. Perhaps the first results of this qualitative advancement manifested themselves in Tunisia when parliamentary elections were held in October 2014, because they affirmed that democratization was compatible with Islam and that Muslims can indeed reconcile with, and apply, democracy even if fundamental differences remained between them.

It may be useful to close this Introduction with a few observations on Saʻudi Arabia and Iran. If the Gulf region is the least stable area around the globe and the Middle East is its epicenter where explosions can rock the entire World, is it possible to state that major Western powers aim to contain its vast oil riches and preserve regional states, perhaps even check existing complex national and religious tendencies to serve their interests? Is it farfetched to make the leap, as Yves Lacoste has written, that the eight-year long Iran–Iraq War (1980–1988) was not fought for the sake of the "ten meters width of the Shatt al-ʻArab," but to redraw the historic borders between two realms: the Arabic and the Persian? Was the struggle not about the recreation of religious boundaries between two creeds: Sunnis and Shiʻahs? Should we not add, in light of more recent realities facing the region and the world that the struggle hovers around ancient sectarian divisions?

In fact, we are witnessing a conflict that is evolving fast, taking on new dimensions, as recent developments illustrate. Sunnis, led by Saʻudi Arabia, are not in the forefront of this struggle though extremist elements transformed them into ideal targets. To meet this challenge, Western powers, led by the United States, are determined to weaken Sunni Arabs to serve first and foremost Israel and, of course, themselves. If doing so requires the assistance of Iran, albeit indirectly, this is little more than a quandary. What further confronts Saʻudi Arabia and its Gulf Cooperation Council partners is that deep down, few of their leaders trust Washington, even if they cannot replace America with an alternative power capable of protecting the Gulf region, which is the ultimate and real predicament they face.

As for the perception of Imam Khumayni and the Iranian Revolution, and as confirmed by my teacher the martyr Shaykh Subhi Salih in an interview with the French daily *Le Monde*, the 1979 coup was "not an Islamic revolution, but was, in reality, an Iranian-Shi'ah Revolution." The same explanation was provided by the *Encyclopedia Universalis*, which stated that Khumayni "is a man from the past and wants to revive the past by hiding behind the revolution which conservative mullahs and capitalists exploited. They expressed extremist views as they propagated a righteous Islam, presenting the revolution as an alternative that created a state where religion and democracy coexisted."[17] The fundamental question that remains unanswered, and that sums up most of the concerns around which revolve the struggle which preoccupies Muslims in the twenty-first century, is the following: Who will lead the Arab-Muslim world—Sa'udi Arabia or Iran?

Jbayl, 29 October 2014

CHAPTER

1

Targeting Sunnis

This study is an analysis of the current situation in the Middle East that intersects the geopolitics of religion and the geopolitics of nations; simultaneously it is an invitation to reflect on our reality and destiny, in light of uprisings and wars that are ushering in major and permanent geopolitical changes throughout the area. My main objective is to distance the reader from fantasies or, at least, out of the deceptive perceptions that envelop our societies, which damage state regulations, and condemn, for example, the people living here in Lebanon to a life of uncertainty because of the tragedy that befell on its neighbor Syria. Elsewhere, the philosophy of propaganda, which shapes the views and devices of known local, regional and international parties, would like nothing better than to mislead public opinion, to further confuse as to who is struggling with whom. What are the catalysts of these conflicts and the intentions of feuding groups? Do we know or can we determine what their goals may be? Is it not fair to ask what are their strategies and who is the primary target of these major regional contests?

Our moral, intellectual, and national duty towards the peoples of this area compel us to delve on this geopolitical vision of current events as it is, reminding ourselves that truths should not lead to intimidation or fear from anyone. Towards that end, we propose to offer, first, an accurate analysis of various issues in order to find proper resolutions and, second, to assess geopolitical goals that propel nation-states to operate under specific principles. Countries often compete and wrestle over specific geographical areas, and rely on religion to advance concrete geopolitical objectives, which also allow for competition for what would be regional and world domination. A correct analysis and a proper understanding of what is occurring in our region, therefore, must be placed in the perspective of a broader global geopolitical conflict that began to take shape in the last quarter of the twentieth century. Ignoring this fact, or overlooking it, does not help. On the contrary, it must be dissected to better understand what is currently under way.

The Religious Dimension

The great confrontation in the world today pits the Western Christian civilization in its three primary branches, composed of the Protestant (America), Catholic (Europe), and Orthodox (Russia) communities—which has a Hebrew sub-branch manifested in Israel alongside the Zionist movement—against the Islamic civilization. This clash of civilizations focuses on the Sunni creed as a source that requires utmost attention.[18] In other words, it maybe safe to argue that the space that includes the entire universe and the people that include the whole of creation, laden with the histories of every religion that offers God's final word to its followers, are the reasons for this confrontation with Islamism (or Political Sunnism). And it is this issue that we intend to articulate in some detail. Our analysis concentrates on political content and not on any religious aspect of the struggle that, in turn, is characterized by three specific core concerns: strong ideology, command over the majority of energy sources around the world, and control of the Middle World that stretches from Indonesia to Morocco. Indeed, former American statesman Henry Kissinger once opined that "whoever dominates the Middle World dominates the world."[19] Kissinger's viewpoint can be contrasted with an equally prophetic declaration made by the British historian Arnold Toynbee who reportedly said: "Islam will return to play an essential role on the stage of history."[20]

The Geopolitical Dimension

Geopolitical approaches to conditions in the Middle East, especially the region of the Gulf as well as the Fertile Crescent—in other words the crossing points between the Mediterranean and Asia—long wetted major powers' appetites, whose interests in the area were affirmed by the presence of vast oil reserves. All global forces, along with several regional states, were and are ready to do whatever it might take to control these valuable resources. This interest manifested itself long before the creation of Israel even if the region became more vital after the establishment of the Jewish state in 1948. According to Western strategists, the events of 11 September 2001 in the United States changed the geopolitical value of the region too, when Islamism replaced Communism as the openly declared ideological foe of the United States.

The Strategic Dimension

The West, in which we must include President Vladimir Putin's Russia, harbors two main preoccupations that are essential to formulate. Both carry global as well as Middle Eastern strategic dimensions, which almost always influence all superpower policies and decisions throughout the region.

The first preoccupation is the expansion of Western authority over the entire globe, including peoples, land and whatever riches may exist under their feet, which is why major powers compete with each other in so many land areas, including the Middle East. Such competition will inevitably result in conflict. The second concern is the presence, fate and security of the Jewish people, and thus the fate of the State of Israel, which is a historical and existential matter for Western countries. This latter concern has been neglected for too long; the passage of time will clearly produce a demographic war, better known as the "war of the womb."[21]

Consequently, and because these two preoccupations touch upon Islamic civilization, its demographic expansion, and its geographic spread, it behooves analysts to weigh the strategic impact that sheer population numbers will have. According to statistics published by the French daily *Le Monde*, the number of Muslims around the world in 2013 stood at 1.57 billion, of whom 1.35 billion (85%) were Sunnis and 220 million were Shi'ahs (15%). This demographic spread gained extra attention after 1978, when it became clear to the Western World and to Jews that the peace treaties signed with two Sunni states bordering Israel, Egypt and Jordan, and the peace under negotiations with the Palestinians, remained fragile. Moreover, many Westerners believed then, and as they are persuaded now, that Sunni Muslims consciously and unconsciously are not now nor will they ever be ready to recognize the legitimacy of Israel's existence in the heart of what they consider to be their nation. Accordingly, the ambitions of Western states are clear: the overriding necessity to weaken the tide of Islamism in both its Sunni and Shi'ah wings, but especially in the Sunni branch. This is so because Sunni Islam is the most dangerous to Israel on the one hand, and because Western powers aim to create a geo-strategic solution that will allow the integration of Israel into its environment by forcing neighbors to explicitly recognize the Jewish state as a normal entity in the region. Such a successful outcome will effectively mean that Israel will not remain a foreign body threatened with extinction after a period of time, even if demographic changes alter the body politic, more or less permanently.

The Regional Dimension

Western Powers and the Zionist Movement have been hard at work on a micro-strategy to achieve these goals since at least the last quarter of the twentieth century. Remarkably, it was also within this timeframe that the Imam Ruhallah Khumayni ushered in his revolution, with its Iranian identity and Shi'ah/Islamic fixture, which formed a turning point in the history of contemporary Islam. From a Shi'ah perspective, the Iranian Revolution adopted the *wilayat al-faqih* theory, which Shi'ah believers considered to be the true representative of Islam. Iranians were and are persuaded that the *wilayat al-faqih* is the concrete dimension of their faith. This was buttressed by their certainty that standing up to traditional Sunni Arab leaders advanced their nationalist interests against these same regimes. Moreover, because Shi'ahs were a demographic/geographic minority within the Muslim world, they adopted an offensive strategy, espoused propaganda methods to corroborate their presence, asserted their effectiveness as a vital community by deploying beyond their borders, and supported credible radical Islamic movements that could face traditional Sunnism, which they perceived and continue to view in negative terms. All this they did through seven specific initiatives.

1. The exploitation of the annual pilgrimage to Makkah to confront the leadership of the Al Sa'ud ruling family;
2. Manipulation of the Palestinian cause, which remained the Muslim cause par excellence, and which Shi'ah Islam raised as a historical leverage—especially by the Lebanese Hizballah militia—against Israel. This pro-liberation-of-Jerusalem banner was frequently flown as a balancer to the pro-Makkah guiding principle favored by Sunnis. As a corollary, the display of military might, including potential nuclear weapons or any number of missile programs or outright offensive arms, further represented what Iranians believed to be actual power in the hands of Muslims. These, they argued, ought to be used as bargaining chips, while engaged in political negotiations with Western countries;
3. Through verbal attacks again leading Western government, especially those that considered themselves to be allies of Israel;
4. By encouraging various breaches of laws and regulations in Sunni states through Shi'ah minority populations;
5. Via the adoption of Shi'ah principles in Sunni communities that contravened existing religious protocols;

6. By highlighting its putative geopolitical influence over the Straits of Hormuz, which it threatened to close on several occasions; and,
7. By broadcasting a strategy to establish a Shi'ah crescent between the Gulf and the Mediterranean, a project that is backed by the West and Israel, for reasons that serve common interests.

The Sectarian Dimension

It is no coincidence that the Shi'ah Crescent is the geographical equivalent of the Fertile Crescent, the concept of Greater Syria, which includes Lebanon, Syria, Iraq, Palestine and Jordan. Ironically, and contrary to the known doctrine espoused by Antun Sa'adih, founder of the Syrian Social Nationalist Party who wanted to re-establish Greater Syria and who proposed fundamental reforms that were and are ideologically opposed to most things Western and Jewish, few Arabs actually carried the banner.[22] On the contrary, Iran is now the champion of Greater Syria, which represents a concrete breach of the Sunni bloc. Remarkably, Tehran is accomplishing this feat geographically, demographically, politically, as well as religiously, and is dislodging foes ideologically as well—all to uproot the Sunni-Arab influence in an area that harbors many minority populations. Rulers, systems, identities, and fixtures are all being replaced with the confederacy of a state of minorities that might well include four core groups, Jews, Shi'ahs, Kurds and Christians, if and when the sectarian dimension of its strategy is completed. This space, where the remnants of existing institutions protect Levantine Christians, is also the heart of the Middle East where the State of Israel is located. Inasmuch as the environment allows an extension of Iran towards the Mediterranean, precisely because the region is a stronghold for the largest groups of minority communities anywhere around the world—some 59 groups—the sectarian dimension has now surfaced as this is the only available means to achieve a demographic balance between the majority Sunnis and the rest of the minority populations located therein. Therefore, and as Western analysts concluded sometime ago, this "space" constitutes a great opportunity to bring about a radical change in the geopolitical equation of the Middle East, which would serve Western interests along with those of Israel and Iran—which is nothing if not a clear exploitation of the alliance of minorities.

The Political Dimension

As important as the sectarian dimension is to specific historical facts, the political reasons are equally pertinent because the Sunni majority oppressed minority populations, excluded them from society, and otherwise imposed hardships from the time of the first Caliphates to the Ottoman period and all the way through to contemporary Arab regimes. It may thus be accurate to state that these socio-political limitations led to revenge, especially on the part of the Shi'ah. This situation was and is further encouraged by the West and Israel, to stoke the fires of sedition between Sunnis and Shi'ahs, precisely to weaken Islam and specifically its Sunni wing since the latter's capabilities pose the greatest danger to Western hegemony. Consequently, existing conflicts turned into religious disputes, which overlooked nationalist contentions, a key policy target of Israel. In reality, Shi'ahs are only "opponents" of Israel because they are, like the Israelis, a minority. Sunnis, on the other hand, are Israel's avowed "enemies" because they are the majority. This means that the wall built around the Jewish State, which Israel considers as a security barrier against terrorism while Palestinians see it as a means to segregate them, intended to prevent the Sunni Arab demographic majority from swallowing the Jewish population. Indeed, this is the imminent and direct danger in the years to come, denials notwithstanding.[23]

This political focus on minorities was accompanied by a reduction of Sunni influence in the region as prominent Sunni leaders were successfully marginalized in three leading countries. First, in Syria through the 'Alawite minority regime that ruled over 18 million Sunnis, and that was engaged in a merciless war of elimination that started in early 2011. Second, in Iraq where the regime of Saddam Husayn was removed in a Western/Israeli trap—though this was done in two installments, the first to induce him to invade and occupy Kuwait where he was duly defeated, and the second through an accusation that he possessed weapons of mass destruction or that he may have had something to do with the events of 11 September 2001. Third, in Lebanon via the Hizballah militia, and its black shirt assailants, that resulted in a siege of the Lebanese Grand Saray [or Sarail, Government House] for more than a year and a half, which brought down Prime Minister Sa'ad Hariri and his government. The Shi'ah militia imposed itself, directly as well as indirectly, and gained control over all state institutions.

Elsewhere, including in Jordan, pro-Iranian forces relied on intimidation, and in Palestine—where there are few Shi'ahs—savvy anti-Sunni forces used the pro-Iranian Hamas Party as a reliable horse to pony up. In Yemen, they trained, planned and coordinated with the Huthis, armed them as necessary, and helped them start a war that is ongoing.[24] That Shi'ah influence in the Middle East rose disproportionately was a principle Iranian minority strategy, but it did not seem to have reached the ears of Prime Minister Tammam Salam, who was tasked with the formation of a government in Lebanon. Salam is still waiting . . . waiting for the solution of those who supported him verbally, and who plan to trap him practically, to keep power in their hands. They will do so after they strip him of his authority in the context of a well-defined regional plan, one they intend to strengthen and never abandon.[25]

The Minorities Dimension

In light of these features, this Western–Israeli–Iranian project becomes clear: the establishment of Middle East of minorities free from Sunni influence and condemned to Shi'ah/Iranian rule, with full Israeli consent, as well as the support of the West and Russia. These are the mysterious paths that the Syrian crisis reveals. In fact, what is happening in the region has little to do with conspiracies that abound, which are predominantly spread to hide the errors and incapacities of the main players. It is, rather, the confluence of objectives and interests by different parties albeit that divergences are periodically displayed, precisely to allow the regional plan project to prosper with an air of objectivity. When Henry Kissinger was once asked: How do you explain that the Israelis expelled Yasir 'Arafat [the Chairman of the Palestine Liberation Organization] from Beirut, and then the Syrians expelled him from Tripoli, he replied: "There is a confluence of substantive interests between Israel and Syria in Lebanon." Indeed, each country expelled 'Arafat for its own reasons, but the common aim was to weaken the Sunni military/political influence in Lebanon, in large part what was then known as the Sunni "Army of Muslims," which was how the Palestinian resistance movement was once known in the Land of the Cedars.[26]

In short, the Sunnis of the Orient are politically, militarily, ideologically, sociologically and culturally targeted. It is possible to explain all of this by way of thesis, but one sees it being played out on the ground in various parts of the region where proactively the policies are in place to "Demonize Sunnis."

Sunni Intentions and Capabilities

Is there a Sunni scheme or response anywhere in the Arab world, be it in the Levant or in the Gulf? The answer, unfortunately, is that there is no concrete Sunni vision to defend and protect the Sunni world. Neither at the national level in specific countries nor across the region, nor even internationally. I hasten to add: There are a few ideas and perspectives, but these are not integrated into a project based on the political thought of a modern contemporary vision, which encloses an effective strategy suitable for what the Muslim World needs at the beginning of the twenty-first century. The real Muslim call is not to abbreviate one's vision to the word "jihad" or a sentence like "Islam is the solution."[27] Rather, a renewed initiative requires inspired Islamic thought based on both historic as well as contemporary ideas, including the position of Sunnis towards the modern state, towards man and society, towards pluralism and the Other, and especially towards democracy, the role of minorities, interpretations of law, and human rights. In fact, what is necessary is a clear articulation of what the Sunni-Muslim means when he refers to the nation and what the definition of power stands for, both philosophically and practically. To simply define views of the Lebanese crisis, the Palestinian Question, and Arab and global concerns or a myriad similar concerns, are not sufficient to determine the future of the Middle East.

What is necessary is to expand on the very definition of citizenship, equality, democracy and freedom of conscience, along with all its doctrinal, ethnic and linguistic components. Only such elaboration will show a way out of the ideological custodianship that exists, as Sunnis tackle pluralism in thought, power, society and culture, all of which must be distant from uniformity and conformism. It is the absence of such modernist projects that will continue to witness the rise of individuals who launch fanatical schemes in the name of Sunnis, exactly what anti-Sunni forces wish for and want, because such displays harm Sunnis far more than many assume. Moreover, it is also a perfect venue to further "demonize" Sunnis in the eyes of Western powers, under the guise of fighting terrorism. Sunni Muslim philosophy rested on two pillars—fairness and moderation—from the outset, though it is critical to remind everyone that it still needs both if it is to shine as a leading light among nations.

Finally, we must point to five facts and call upon all the peoples of the region—Sunnis, Shi'ahs and Christians—to ponder over them if we are to avoid future clashes.

First, as best described by the German thinker Theodor Hanf regarding Israeli and Syrian policies, we must be aware that every minority society wishes for and practices the politics of fear. This is a dangerous policy, because it is based on taking risks about everything, most of which can and do fall outside of rationality and objectivity.[28]

Second, because so many around the world think or believe that what is underway in Syria these days is the fate of President Bashar al-Assad and his regime, we ought to ponder in depth whether a different perspective is warranted. Does the "War for Syria" not confirm that we are dealing with events that go beyond the fate of the regime? Is it not also vitally important to determine the fate and future of Israel? In other words, should we not think whether minority regimes have the ability to resist and continue to face Sunni geostrategic confrontations? The Syrian minority regime may display strong resistance against potential Sunni-Muslim power in its geographic, demographic, and political capabilities, which would certainly include lessons for Israel in terms of what it too may face in the future.

Third, as the Arab Spring is chiefly a Sunni uprising launched by Arab youths who believe in better and more honest futures, and because they wish to determine the fate of their people for democracy and freedom, have foes not used, and still use, all of the methods and means to distort the content of these uprisings? Remarkably, anti-Arab Spring proponents succeeded to a large extent, because of the weaknesses in the Sunni body politic, which is due to a lack of a modern political project. In the absence of such a vision, every Sunni extremist group, organization, emirate or caliphate can sing his own tune. Most of these extremists were and are duly inducted to carry weapons, and target Sunni powers like Sa'udi Arabia, where Shi'ah minorities are invited to launch attacks against authorities. The Huthis in Yemen have acted similarly, as have several groups in Egypt, whose aim was to take advantage of the fragmentation in Egyptian society, preoccupied with its many internal struggles that, in turn, seriously limited Cairo's abilities to defend Arab Sunnis.

Fourth, we are living through a sensitive stage of a bloody conflict between opposing forces. It is an existential as well as ideological battle whose results cannot possibly be defined at this early stage. One of the more pertinent assessments of this reality was uttered by the British Foreign Secretary William Hague, who told the BBC on 19 August 2013: "What is happening now in the Middle East is the most important event of the twenty-first century so far. There may be years of turbulence in Egypt and other countries going through this profound debate. We have to keep our nerve in clearly supporting democracy. There will be many setbacks in doing that and we should not be surprised when those take place."[29] This evaluation means, even indirectly, that what is occurring is more than a mere war. It is the process of "uprooting" doctrines from a society, caught between mutually strong sectarian, religious, regional and international forces, determined to impose their hegemony over the Middle East. Doing so means that these forces intend to create new borders that will be "derived from our minds and hearts" and not be a new "Sykes–Picot," as President Bashar al-Assad declared.

Fifth, the right vision for this conflict between the majority and the

minority, and therefore the right solution for it, cannot be the establishment of an alliance of minorities in the face of Sunnis even if the
history of these minority populations, and their sufferings, justifies such
an alliance—at least theoretically. A resolution of this confrontation
ought to have a base that draws on philosophy and sociology, not necessarily on politics or doctrine, because "the problem of the minorities is
first and foremost a problem for the majority," as expressed by the
Syrian thinker Yassin al-Hafiz, which clearly means that minorities, all
minorities, cannot and are not able to solve their problems on their own
and with each other. As a corollary, they cannot reach a resolution by
clashing with the Sunni majority either. Had the Shi'ahs the ability to
solve their problems or the problems confronted by others—Christians,
for example—they would have begun to solve them first. The solution
can only be with the majority Sunni Arab population for a singular sociological reason, as they, the Sunnis, represent the decisive majority of
Arab-Muslims throughout the region—around 70 percent of all Arab-
Muslims. In short, they hold the solution. This does not necessarily mean
a full alignment for Sunnis, but it clearly means a sociological, objective,
and historical truth, that imposes itself on all Sunnis. Had the Shi'ahs
been the majority, one would have made the same argument, insisting
that the solution is with Shi'ah Arabs.

Yet, this affirmation does not mean that the solution is with any
Sunni majority. In reality, the Sunni solution, the one that will come to
terms with minorities, is not the Sunnism of bigotry, blasphemy, fundamentalism or the Da'ishi model, but the modernizing, avant-garde
Arab-Muslim vision represented by contemporary intellectuals—Sunnis
and Shi'ah alike—individuals whose names are recognized and whose
accomplishments, writings and opinions are valued. Among these individuals are Mohammed Arkoun, whose rationalization of Islamic
thought is peerless, and Abul-Hassan [Abolhassan] Bani Sadr. We can
add the experiences of Muslim dialogues along with the anti-authori-
tarian and anti-totalitarian gatherings as proposed by Tariq Ramadan
in the European democratic Islam arena. Leading Sunni figures proposed
new paradigms for free-liberal order in Sunni thought, including men
like the late Prime Minister Rafiq Hariri, right up to the final documents
issued under the supervision of the Al-Azhar Imam, Shaykh Ahmad Al
Tayyib, which is unprecedented in the history of contemporary Islamic
thought. This vision reassesses the relationship between Islam and the
state, democracy and public rights. To summarize the thoughts
described above, what is thus required is for proposals made by these
hardworking intellectuals—anxious to elaborate the outlines of a Sunni
project and to achieve desired objectives—to be quickly implemented.

Such efforts can only be carried out by creative strategists and scholars who are masters of the geopolitics of the region, who are familiar with its history, who can evaluate opposing and competing forces, and who can respond to contemporary Muslim intellectual currents.

At the present time various institutions and Arab-Sunni personalities are busy formulating moderate and forward-thinking ideas. What is required is just one such vision to take hold of the Arab consciousness.

2

Challenges and Confrontations

Foreign analysts correctly identified "Sunnism" as a political phenomenon and stripped the term of its religious meanings in various assessments as they interpreted recent developments that affected the Muslim World. The discussion that follows, which focuses on the political challenges and confrontations that face Sunnis as a group, or as states, or even as groups of states or associations, will neither ignore nor neglect how the creed affected the Middle East in general and the Levant in particular. Rather, and because the Middle East has historically been known as the powderkeg of the world, a theme that is revisited below, an effort will be made to separate the wheat from the chaff and measure both the veracity that Sunnism is indeed a political phenomenon and identify the types of challenges and confrontations it generates.

Inasmuch as 70% of all Arab populations are Sunnis, recent geopolitical transformations affect them primarily, both within and among Arab states, as well as at the regional level in various conflicts. These confrontations carry international implications, notwithstanding deliberate deceptions practiced by several parties to distort the nature of the disputes that, and this must be articulated as clearly as possible, aim to mislead public opinion against Sunnis. How can these matters be properly evaluated and understood without in-depth geo-political analyses? Is it possible to decipher the truth without clear identifications of the parties involved in ongoing geopolitical challenges along with the incentives that these parties may be subjected to? How can we ascertain what may be the intentions and objectives of key parties to gain footholds in certain areas, precisely to extend their influence beyond pre-determined geographical spheres, which conflicting parties seek to dominate including to better monitor inhabitants? Truth be told, this is what geopolitical analyses reveal, which is the preferred method, and perhaps the only one worth relying upon, to study these contemporary dilemmas.

Middle East Geography and Demographics

For Western, especially Anglo-Saxon sources, the Middle East is composed of eighteen countries, including thirteen within the Arab world. Twelve states, namely Sa'udi Arabia, Kuwait, the United Arab Emirates (UAE), Qatar, Iraq, Jordan, Egypt, Lebanon, Yemen, Syria, Bahrain, Palestine [+Israel], fall with the Arab spheres, whereas five others are outside the Arab world, including Iran, Turkey, Cyprus, Pakistan, and Afghanistan. According to the latest statistics for the year 2014 (see Table 1), the Middle East has an area of 8.7 million sq. km, and populations of 612 million, of whom 16.5 million are non-Muslims. A total of 595.5 million Muslims are distributed as follows: 416.85 million Sunni Muslims (70%), and 178.65 million Shi'ah Muslims (30%). As for the estimated number of Muslims around the world, the Paris-based *Le Monde* reported that in 2013, the total reached the figure of 1.57 billion Muslims, including, 1.35 billion Sunnis (85%), and 220 million Shi'ahs (15%). An equally reliable source, the *Geo-Strategic Atlas for 2014*, advanced that the projected number of Sunnis will rise to 1.46 billion in 2025, while the number of Shi'ahs will reach 280 million.

An understanding of these population figures is fundamental to our grasp of local, regional and international geo-political developments in the area, because demographic data are the key factors that determine why opposing forces are engaged in ongoing struggles.[30]

Strategic Importance of the Muslim World and the Middle East

The Middle East is the heart of the Muslim World, which stretches from Indonesia in the East to Morocco in the West, a vast region. Analysts have identified six strategic reasons that gave the sphere and its inhabitants the importance it rightly deserves.

First, the Islamic continent represents the "Middle World" on account of its location between north and south, around the equator. As long echoed by Henry Kissinger, the most senior Western strategist: "He who controls the Islamic world, the Middle World, controls the world."[31]

Second, the Middle East was a fundamental collision arena between the great powers throughout history—between land empires like Russia (then the Soviet Union, now the Russian Federation) and sea powers like Great Britain and the United States of America—and remains so today. At present, this trademark feature is most visible in both the Syrian theatre and in the Ukraine, where a classic clash is underway. Often, analysts summarize this situation using symbolic but meaningful expressions, when they affirm that "world stability is found in the Near and Middle East because of their positions and wealth."

Table 1 Middle East Population Statistics for 2014

State	Area (Sq. km.)	Population (million)
Afghanistan	652,000	30.6
Bahrain	700	1.1
Cyprus	9,000	1.1
Egypt	1,001,000	84.7
Iran	1,648,000	76.5
Iraq	438,000	35.1
Jordan	89,000	7.3
Kuwait	18,000	3.5
Lebanon	10,452	4.8
Oman	310,000	4.0
Pakistan	796,000	190.7
Palestine	22,000	8.1
Qatar	11,000	2.2
Sau'di Arabia	2,150,000	30.1
Syria	185,000	21.9
Turkey	784,000	76.1
United Arab Emirates	84,000	9.3
Yemen	528,000	25.2
Total	8,736,152	612.3
Muslims		595.5
Non Muslims		16.5
Sunni Muslims		416.85 (70%)
Shi'ah Muslims		178.65 (30%)

Source: Marie Béatrice Baudet, Pierre Julien and Antoine Reverchon, eds., *Bilan du Monde: Économie et Environnement-Édition* 2014, Paris: Le Monde, 2014.

Third, the area's high rate of demographic growth, at a time when the international balance of power is frozen between world powers, presents a conundrum as devastating weapons of mass destruction find their way the Middle East. In addition, the "demographic bomb" haunts many countries, especially Israel, which lives with the obsession of drowning in the Sunni Arab demographic sea. According to the *2011 Atlas of Religions*, the most prominent demographic growth rate will be for Muslims, at 2.2% each year between 1990 and 2050. This means that the number of Muslims will go from 962 million to 2.229 billion. While the demographic growth rate among Christians will be 1.2% during the same period. One result for such an increase will be the growth rate for youth in Muslim communities, which will exceed

50%, with undeniable social effects as well as geopolitical consequences.

Fourth, the area incorporates the most important network of international links, which includes waterways and straits, led by the Straits
of Hormuz through which 40% of the oil exported to the world passes
each day. Equally important are the Straits of the Bosphorus and the
Dardanelles, the Straits of Gibraltar, the Straits of Bab al-Mandab, as
well as the Suez Canal corridor.

Fifth, the peoples of the region own nearly two-thirds of the world's
oil wealth. This is one of the most critical reasons why the Middle East
is so strategically important, since it sits of nearly two-thirds of known
global oil reserves. Indeed, proven global oil reserves amounted to
1,688.9 trillion barrels in 2012, of which the OPEC States—which are
mostly from Middle Eastern countries—controlled 72.6% according to
the *Geo-Strategic Atlas for 2014*. The extent to which energy sources
influence the course of civilizations is now well established. In fact, for
leading powers, energy sources are the key, even the basic, element of
all other components that make-up their international strategies.

Sixth, Israel's presence in the region is also a critical feature. Since the
existence of the Jewish state matters to Western powers, especially for
the United States and several European countries, Middle Eastern
concerns, more specifically the Arab–Israeli conflict, transformed after
the 1940s into an international issue that left its impact on international
relations, which clearly affected regional entities. Major powers defined
their relationships with various countries through the prism of the Arab-
Israeli conflict, devising strategies accordingly.

Opposing Forces and the Determinants of Geopolitics

There are four regional and international forces that stand against each
other in the Middle East, including (1) Sunni forces chiefly composed of
states, regimes, or groups that have had a historical control of much of
the Muslim world, led by the primary Sunni State, the Kingdom of Sa'udi
Arabia; (2) Iran with its regional and international aspirations that were
shaped after the Iranian revolution. Indeed, Iranian ambitions were so
comprehensive in content as well as substance that the former British
Prime Minister Tony Blair defined Tehran as "a strategic threat to the
region";[32] (3) Israel and the World Zionist movement whose aims are
to confirm the state's existence and spread its influence; and, (4) Western
powers comprising in the main America, Europe, and the Russian
Federation. Each of these blocs have their separate plans as well as
regional and international strategies.[33]

Given this competition between geopolitical forces, what is the best way to raise several investigative questions? What does geopolitics mean in this context? "Geopolitics," as defined by Yves Lacoste, the French scholar who contributed substantially to the revival of the discipline in France since the 1970s, "is to analyze the competition between forces that seek to control certain geographic spaces (small or large) and over their populations in order to impose influences over them. These forces could be states or armed factions, or both. The results of this competition will be based on the balance of power among contenders."[34] Based on this superlative definition, it may thus be possible to discuss the six determinants of geopolitics, which are: motivations, intentions, goals, power, control, and room (or space) required to maneuver.

Motivations justify actions taken by certain political forces to lead the political, ideological and military struggle, in which one or more states or armed groups may be involved. These motivations can be of the self-interest or material variety, and even psychological, political, ideological or economic ones. In all instances, what is important is that they express the concerns of the political forces involved, including regional powers. For example, what preoccupies Sunnis is to retain their influence over the Muslim world, motivated by the political philosophy contained within the Holy Scriptures. Likewise, what motivates Iran is the emphasis on its ideology, and thus its revolution with a Persian nationalist agenda, as well as a religious Shi'ah-legal precept—the *Wilayat al-faqih*—to spread as widely as possible its message over the lands of Islam, especially in the Levant region between the Mediterranean and the Gulf. As for Israel, the motivation is existential and security related, as successive governments linked the fate of the Jewish people with the Jewish state. For their part, the motivations that propel major powers like the United States, European countries, and the Russian Federation, are all tied to the everlasting preoccupation to ensure international expansion despite the competition that exists between them to serve different strategic, political, military, and economic objectives. Differences aside, there is a common catalyst at this Western level, which is to preserve the existence and security of the State of Israel.

Intentions mean what these forces plan to achieve despite rivalries, both in the inner psychological sense, as well as in terms of any wishful thinking. Some aspire to extend their authority, and some seek to impose new rules in their political actions. Some seek to expand their influences over others for defensive purposes, while others plan to acquire the greatest amount of wealth, perhaps even engage in a clash of civilizations. The most prominent and dangerous is the quest to find a solution to a "reasonable" and "acceptable" solution to the State of Israel within its Arab-Muslim surroundings, where it remains an alien entity, even if the intent is to integrate it into the region before the Arab-Sunni demographic weight prevents such a quest, as duly cautioned and warned by Jewish strategists at regular Herzliya conferences.[35]

Objectives are also critical to achieve the intentions identified above, as each power draws objectives to act upon, within its own specific strategies. Among these, one may cite the creation of a political and security crisis within the region, or even in the Islamic world at large, to confuse and weaken the role of Sunnis. Another objective may be to change and modulate the role and influence of regional Sunni powers, especially those that carry certain weight within the Muslim world, particularly Sa'udi Arabia, by preoccupying it with internal challenges. For example, the Shi'ah uprising in Ahsah, or the phenomenon of the Shi'ah Shaykh Nimr al-Nimr and his secessionist calls, fit into this pattern.[36] More ominous objectives may necessitate border tensions, as is the case with the Huthis who plan to control Yemen, and impose their will on traffic that goes in and out of the strategic Bab al-Mandab Straits on the Red Sea. Other objectives may foster tensions within the Gulf Cooperation Council, as Qatar or Oman, for example, may be encouraged to adopt varying policies that do not necessarily coincide with the Sunni consensus. Even keeping Egypt busy with internal tensions ranging the gamut from the rise of the Muslim Brotherhood to various terrorist activities, can neutralize the primary Arab Sunni power with myriad problems, including bombings in the Sinai, all of which further weaken Sunni Arabs in the Levant and the Gulf.

One may cite other motivations that preoccupy Sunnis throughout the Arabian Peninsula and the Mediterranean, including accompanying and monitoring Iranian expansion (at both the political level and more ominously during intensive negotiations over Tehran's atomic projects); the creation of militia forces in parallel with regular armies in Iraq, Lebanon, Syria, and Yemen, to name just a few countries, where systematic coordination with Iran to support the latter's regional strategy is on display; the encouragement to establish an alliance of minorities in the framework of the geographical space between the Mediterranean and the Gulf for objective reasons that will, consequently, allow the integration of Israel in its surroundings because minorities will face majority Sunni Arab Muslims; and to further expand existing agitations between Sunnis and Shi'ahs precisely to weaken the Sunni bloc that confronts the West. In short, every effort is made to keep Muslims busy with their own concerns, which is how Israel and Western nations fuel this sedition.

Power, which "is the will of a decisive right, and is based on a real mandate from the people through an oath of allegiance, Shurah or elections, must be maintained at all costs. Yet, this source of power loses its legitimacy if it is not built on ability or capability. Such aptitude, therefore, is the original requirement for power as much as any other rights or privileges. It is from here that those who seek power justify the ability to control a certain geographical area, which is really the area over which various forces compete, to establish their undisputed authority so that they gain control over existing wealth and the right to exploit. This description applies demonstratively to the area known as the Fertile Crescent.

Control over a specific geographic area means supervision over it, and the ability to handle its affairs, preferably in democratic and legitimate ways. If control is achieved through the use of violence, its meaning would then be interpreted as domination, or as an act of hegemony. Irrespective of interpretations, conflicting forces seek gain over geographical areas in order to assert their will-to-power so that they can achieve specific goals within such regions and to generally use pragmatic steps to secure specific targets [as was the case in Iraq most recently].

Last but not least is the *geographical sphere* determinant that, in the Levant, is mostly a pure political interpretation of history. It will be difficult, if not impossible, to translate many historical events without returning to geography in this part of the world. Indeed, the base issue in every question raised as far as determinants of geopolitics are concerned is the issue of domain, in other words the geographic region over which competition is fierce. Struggles for power do not occur in a void , but are about specific geographic realities that motivate every aspiring power to gain full control over the geographical space. This space can be small, medium or large, and can be a territory in a state, or a state in its entirety, or even a whole region like the Near East and, in the case of the great powers, might incorporate the entire world or even the universe through competition that may rely on rockets and spacecraft. Therefore, it is necessary to determine the geographical area over which a conflict may be waged among the *four regional and international forces* identified above. While it is true that fierce competition may raise geo-strategic, religious and raw interest elsewhere, there is a specific geographical area that is the most targeted and most important region among contenders, whose major objectives are existential, political, economic and ideological. For now and for the foreseeable future, this area is the heart of the Middle East, also known as the "Arab Mashriq"; it stretches from the Eastern Mediterranean to the Arabian Gulf and includes Lebanon, Syria, Iraq, Jordan, Palestine (and Israel).

Why is the Levant such a target? Simply because regional and international powers have concrete goals in mind that can be easily explained according to, **first,** strategic considerations—the region sits in the heart of the Middle East and is the center of gravity as well as the fundamental point of intersection between the Mediterranean and the Gulf, Asia, Europe and Africa.

Second, because there are geographical imperatives, given that the Levant is caught between the central state that leads the Arab-Muslim world, namely Sa'udi Arabia, and the Islamic Republic of Iran, both of which have historical, religious and sectarian ties with the peoples and countries of the area.

Third, because the Levant presents sociological concerns as it incorporates the largest group of minorities in the world, where 59 groups thrive, 26 along sectarian lines, 17 along ethnicities, while 16 qualify for their differing linguistic capabilities.

Fourth, the Levant is a demographic cauldron because it is the only region in the Muslim world where the existing balance between the majority Sunni Arabs and the rest of the minorities, including Shi'ahs, Christians and Jews, is relatively balanced—52% Sunnis to 48% minorities (see Table 2).

Table 2 Sunni Majority vs. Arab Mashriq Minorities (2011)

State	Sunnis (million)	Shi'ahs (million)	Other Minorities (million)	Total (million)
Iraq	13.0	18.158	1.842	33.0
Syria	17.0	3.68	2.32	23.0
Lebanon	1.20	1.20	1.885	4.285
Palestine	1.155	–	6.545 (Jews)	7.700
Total	38.287	23.147	12.778	74.212
Percentage %	52	31	17	100

Sources:
1) François Thual, *Géopolitique du Chiisme*, Paris, Arléa, 2002.
2) *Al-Siyassah al-Dawliyyah*, Cairo: Al-Ahram, Number 193, July 2013.
3) Bertrand Clare, ed., *Atlaseco 2013: Atlas Économique et Politique Mondial*, Paris: Le Nouvel Observateur, November 2012.
4) *L'Atlas des Religions 2011*, Paris: Le Monde, January 2011.
5) "Syrie: Le regime Al-Assad en sursis," *Moyen-Orient: géopolique, géostrategie et sociétés du monde arabe*, Number 12, September–October 2011.
6) "La Syrie depuis 5,000 ans," *L'histoire*, Number 375, May 2012, pp. 42–69.
7) *L'Atlas des Minorités 2011*, Paris: Le Monde, July 2011.
8) Patrice Claude, "Les Chiites dans le monde: une carte aux mains de l'Iran?," *Le Monde*, 25 October 2006, pp. 24–25.

Fifth, because the Levant has specific economic strengths that are the envy of the planet, especially in terms of its raw energy resources. What is being touted about Iraqi oil reserve estimates, for example, constitutes a coup in the oil wealth of the Organization of the Petroleum Exporting Countries (OPEC), which ought to be a wake-up call. At a recent London conference on Iraq, held between 16 and 17 July 2008, oil experts claimed that the estimated reserves of Iraqi oil was not only 150 billion barrels, which would rank the country fourth after Saʿudi Arabia [whose proven reserves are estimated to be around 265 billion barrels], Venezuela and Iran, but closer to 380 billion barrels. In other words, Iraqi oil reserves might be the equivalent of Saʿudi and Kuwaiti holdings, combined. Moreover, Iraq may well have the capacity to produce 13 million barrels of oil per day in 2020, which would apparently make it the foremost oil power on account of both its reserves and extraction capacities.[37]

Sixth, because the Levant is politically vital too and for exceptional reasons, since the Arab Mashriq accommodates two superpower concerns, Israel with its geopolitical problems that are raised by its very presence in the area, and the Palestinian Question, which is the first and most important concern that preoccupies Muslims throughout the world.

Seventh are the Levant's ideological catalysts because regional powers like Iran can and do exploit the Palestinian Question—over Jerusalem as well as the role that the Hizballah militia can play as an Arab resistance movement—which adds specific tools in the hands of the Iranian Revolution. The latter bank on ideological catalysts to embarrass Arab Sunni regimes like Egypt, Jordan and the advocates of peace with Israel, as Iran projects the notion that it is far more anxious to defend Islamic rights in Palestine than Sunni Arab powers.

Eight, because the Levant harbors statist features that allows the three powers—Western parties, Israel and Iran—to work towards managing the outcome of international engagements in the area. Yet, existing sectarianism also means that these states are only able to overwhelm the Sunni masses, geographically as well as demographically, in the only weak spot that exists throughout the Muslim World. It is in the Levant that Israel can assert itself, and where Iran can exercise its direct or indirect presence through Shiʿah minority populations, and in particular through the armed Shiʿah militias that exert a great deal of influence or control over three key countries from where Sunni leaders were either expelled or marginalized. From Syria in the 1970s, when the ʿAlawi minority regime came to power. From Iraq, where Saddam Husayn was first cornered, trapped, and eventually executed. From Lebanon, where

Rafiq Hariri was assassinated and the country plunged into unending crises. Most recently from Yemen too, where a full-fledged war means that a political resolution is still in the distant future. These are the clear indications of the seizure of power as a prelude to control of a full geographic space that stretches from the Arab Mashriq to the Gulf. These efforts aim to change borders, as senior Shi'ah officials declared on several occasions, and the establishment of a confederation state of minorities, which would include four minority groups: Shi'ahs, Christians, Jews, and the Kurds.[38] In the case of the latter, a nation caught in an impossible dichotomy between sectarian affiliation as Sunnis and ethnic identities as non-Arab Kurds, inclusion in the confederation presents a particularly heavy burden since most Kurds aspire for unification and independence. Hence their puzzlement, perhaps even reluctance, to compete at that level since Kurds must reconcile contradictory temptations as amply displayed in the tragic events to which they are currently exposed in Syria, Iraq and Turkey.

The plan that was hatched in the 1970s, and which apparently is being implemented to control minority populations in the twenty-first century, will transform the region. What will emerge—a confederal entity—will place the region outside its historic, geographic and demographic parameters, where political influences will no longer be in the hands of the majority Sunni Arabs. It is a plan with a Zionist design, an Iranian ability to exploit opportunistic conditions, a loss of Christian Levantines, and a Kurdish bet that independence may follow. And all this under the seal of Western approval while Sunni hesitation allows outsiders to manipulate local conditions to save the State of Israel from being swallowed up by the Arab Sunni demographic juggernaut. As Israeli demographers warned in their annual conference held at Herzliya near Tel Aviv, time is short, perhaps not exceeding tens of years, to implement this plan and determine the fate of the Jewish state in the Middle East.[39] Because of the speed of demographic change that is redrawing the human Jewish–Arab map inside historic Palestine, interested parties are keenly aware that these trends will materialize sooner than the general public imagine.

In fact, and for the first time since the creation of Israel in 1948, the Sunni-Arab population residing inside Israel stands at 6.07 million, which exceeds the number of Jews (5.78 million), a difference of 290,000. The percentage of Arabs is thus 51.5% and those of Jews 48.5%, a figure that represents the largest and most serious challenge faced by the Jewish state and its Western sponsors.[40]

In summary, this chapter has set out the clear strategic features of the project prepared for the Levant, which is nominally in the geopolitical and cultural arenas that directly target Sunnis. Unmistakably, political Sunnism is the target, as its presence, influence and role in the Arab Mashriq, the Middle East and the Muslim world at large are all subject to challenges. Of course, it is natural that the Kingdom of Sa'udi Arabia, the most concerned party regarding this anti-Sunni geopolitical strategy, would object, especially for historical reasons. But it is fair to ask what are its capabilities and prospects for any meaningful counter-response? What is specifically required and who in the Sa'udi regime will embark on addressing such concerns?

15 March 2014

3

Which Country Leads Arab Muslims: Sa'udi Arabia or Iran?

A geopolitical reading is required to understand what is happening in today's world, especially what is developing in the Orient, or as it is known locally, the Mashriq. What is meant by the Mashriq is the Eastern Mediterranean region, historically the Near East, and encompassing Lebanon, Syria, Palestine, Jordan and Iraq. Who is competing with whom in the Mashriq and for what purposes? Who is quarreling with whom and why? Who is struggling with whom and to what ends? Answering these questions will allow one to understand what happened to Iraq and the Gulf region, what is currently unraveling in Syria, and what can Lebanon face in the near future. In order to decipher these questions, it is also worth repeating the basic elements of geopolitical analysis of the Middle East, to better grasp their implications.

Opposing and Competing Parties

While there are differences among competing parties, the main confrontation is between two opposing sides. First, Western powers within Judeo-Christian traditions, in which there are three divisions— Protestant (United States), Catholic (Western Europe), and Orthodox (Russia)—in addition to a Hebrew sub-branch that is consecrated in Israel and the Zionist movement. These four branches objectively converge with Mashriq minority populations to achieve common goals to which we will return below; likewise, they also converge with the minority populations in two great powers that include significant Muslim groups, namely China and India. Second, the Islamic civilization with its Sunni Arab dimension as an alternative Western foe, to replace the Soviet Union after communism collapsed, has defined much of what has passed for international relations since the Cold War. This latter element is critical because of the Sunni world's geopolitical prominence and its ability to frame an opposition to any opposing domination, especially with regard to the position of Islam and various Muslim groups.

This confrontation comes in the context of what Yves Lacoste identified as the "geopolitics of religions," as each monotheistic religion delves on its origins, inclusive features, and final concepts that seek to control populations within specific geographical spreads by preaching their cultures and faiths.[41] Hence the importance of the religious factor and/or religious revolutions in what came to be known as the politics of God's revenge as in Poland during the 1980–1981 *Solidarność* [Solidarity] independent trade union uprising or in Iran during that country's 1979 revolution.

As stated earlier, motivation ensures an expansion of the Western Christian civilization within its three branches around the world to dominate along religious, cultural, political, military and economic parameters, as well as guarantee the existence and security of the Jewish people and the Jewish state (Israel), which is a common objective among Jews and Western societies. Equally important are those intentions in the face of the Islamist tide, which is displayed as the first rival to Western civilization, especially in terms of the quest to find a solution for Israel to fit within its Sunni Arab surroundings.

To be sure, competing parties share multiple objectives, the most important of which is to weaken Islamism by creating and encouraging sedition among Sunni and Shi'ah Muslims. That, many believe, would exhaust the energies of militant Islamists, presumably because they would be engaged in perpetual intra-Muslim wars. A parallel objective is the political confusion that permeates within the Muslim world, where multiple sources of regional Sunni power—Sa'udi Arabia, Egypt, and Turkey, for example—compete along several levels. Such competition weakens each country's influence while, simultaneously, allowing for the desired Iranian expansion, so long as it too can be monitored to remain within specific boundaries. Others may be encouraged to increase activities to further empower minorities [which partition plans for Iraq, Syria and even Lebanon contemplated], thus guaranteeing the integration of Israel in the area, which is the primary objective of Western strategists.

All of these events ought to preferably occur in the Levant, a choice that is due to several considerations, including the area's strategic location as the heart of the Middle East; the location of the State of Israel within it; the area's close geographic proximity to Iran and its 1979 Revolution that, in turn, links the Mediterranean to the Gulf; its sociological composition on account of the largest group of minorities in the world (59 religious and ethnic entities); demographic pressures because of the almost total balance between minorities and the majority Sunni Arab populations; ideological criteria because of the possibility that leading powers can indeed exploit Iran as a champion of the Palestinian Question to further embarrass Sunni Arabs; and doctrinal disclosures that promote four basic minority groups—the Shi'ahs, Jews, Kurds and Christians—in order for them to allegedly control the Levant in toto. The fulfillment of such a process will mean a geo-demographic as well as political domination of Sunni Arabs in a Zionist plan that is exploited by Iranians and condoned by Western powers.

Strategies and Tactics

How can one best implement such a scheme then? Henry Kissinger was one of the first Western policymakers to formulate a strategy that promoted Western interests on the one hand with the survival of the Jewish state on the other, which needed to be "recognized by its neighbors and with defensible borders."[42] He created a system of "red lines" in Lebanon between Israel and Syria in 1976 that, perhaps, lasted until 2005 when the Cedar Revolution forced Damascus to pull its army out of that hapless country.[43] It also became clear that peace with Egypt and Jordan was of the cool variety, which prompted Israel to build its infamous wall to exclude the demographic risk posed by Sunni Arabs, after its decision-makers concluded that little more could be achieved on the Cairo–Amman axis. The erection of the Wall in the West Bank, which boxed Palestinians in the Bantustan-like Occupied Territories, was preceded by a different tactic that, for over two decades, lured Sunni nations into various traps and pitfalls to slow their growing global presence, precisely to distance Sunnis from each other and to create a chasm between them and the West. Weakening Sunnis in the Mashriq occurred in several arenas, including:

1. Overemphasizing the utility of the Iran–Iraq War between Arabs and Persians as a vitally necessary conflict (1980–1988), though the contrary was true.
2. Encouraging Saddam Husayn to invade and occupy the Shaykhdom of Kuwait before preparations were launched to defeat him, as illustrated by the role of the U.S. Ambassador to Baghdad, April Glaspie, and the resulting 1991 war of liberation.

3. Pretending that Iraq possessed weapons of mass destruction and to use that excuse to launch a war against it in 2003 to destroy the Iraqi army, defeat the Ba'ath regime, and decapitate the country's leadership because of three major transgressions, including Saddam Husayn's quest to impose oil price floors on OPEC, incorporating the Gulf and oil as key ingredients in the Arab–Israeli conflict, and intervening in the Lebanese crisis to dislodge the consensual three-way hegemony introduced by Henry Kissinger for that theatre—an exclusive arena reserved for the United States, Israel and Syria.

4. Writing-off influential Sunni leaders in the Arab Mashriq to empower minority control, ranging from Saddam Husayn in Iraq to Rafiq Hariri in Lebanon and to Yasir 'Arafat in Palestine, all to further weaken the influence of Sunni states and to masterfully target Sa'udi Arabia and Egypt as the pillars of Sunni power facing the Shi'ah Crescent.

5. Focusing on Iraq as a great geo-strategic arena not only because it is the eastern flank of the Arab world and the barrier in front of the Iranian Revolution, but also because the Levant project that begins with the overthrow of a leading Sunni power in Baghdad, namely Saddam Husayn, can usher in the majority Shi'ah population to the forefront. The result is that Iraq ceases to be a Sunni Arab entity and is thus moved to the Shi'ah domain where authority is entrusted to Shi'ahs. In the opinion of leading strategists, this is the most critical geo-strategic development that has ever occurred in the region. It has, in turn, produced three basic consequences: (1) a change in the face of the Near East from the majority Sunni Arab states into an alliance of minorities within new borders that aim to serve Shi'ahs (including 'Alawis), Jews, Kurds and Christians; (2) an alteration of the Levant's Arab identity into an Iranian one; and (3) a modification in the affiliation of the Levant from Sunnism to Shi'ism.

6. Achieving this dramatic shift by organizing and using superior strategic means by standing alongside regional minorities who, backed by international actors, can therefore break the historical, demographic, geographic, and authoritarian Sunni supremacy. This is the model applied in Syria today, as everyone can determine independently. Sunni authority thus seems to suffer from two weaknesses: (1) lack of an effective and appropriate strategy in the sensitive phase that Muslim societies are passing through; and (2) lack of modern political thought that, regrettably, surrenders the Sunni agenda to three broad slogans: the word "jihad,"

the phrase "Islam is the solution," and the anti-democratic concept that assumes the state fulfills or ought to apply the mandates of conquests instead of applying laws.

The weakening of Sunnis in the above geo-political contexts encourages anti-establishment personalities to gain in popularity, as fanatical and *takfiri* movements score points among Sunni masses, whose efforts often fail.[44] In fact, such efforts are far more harmful to Sunnis than it is useful to them, even if most dismiss it as mere coincidence.

In summary, joining the Levant of Minorities project seems a foregone conclusion for Shi'ahs and Jews for clear and objective reasons, even if the battle to tempt or persuade Christians and Kurds to join in has yet to produce desired results. The latter, namely Christians and Kurds, have special considerations that cannot be overlooked. Christians in particular must be diligent because they confront one of the toughest and most dangerous choices they ever faced throughout their long history in the Middle East. For now, the "Arab Uprisings" are demonstrating that the Sunni world is going though serious political crises, with competing powers anxiously seeking to exploit and benefit from the organized chaos. It is worth quoting Syrian President Bashar al-Assad to illustrate what may well be the ultimate goal. In 2010, al-Assad stressed during a joint press conference with his Iranian counterpart, Mahmud Ahmadinajad, "that raised projects for the division of the region will not start from the maps or borders, but will start from our minds and hearts." He continued: "Later, after this transformation is completed in our hearts and minds, we will then proceed to drop them from the maps and on the ground."[45] Speaking at a different press conference, this one in Ankara with then Turkish President 'Abdallah Gul, al-Assad clarified his thoughts when he declared that only then, that is after the transformation of hearts and minds, will the "map of the region be much better," which he estimated would occur within a decade.[46]

Transformations of maps and new boundaries ascend from "hearts and minds" and confirm the seriousness of the Levant Minorities project in the Mashriq. Should it succeed, few ought to be surprised when regional central leadership moves away from Sa'udi Arabia towards Iran. This is the first and primary objective in Tehran's religious and political strategies, and begs the question whether it will be Sa'udi Arabia or Iran who will lead the Arab Muslim world.

18 August 2013

4

The Impact of the "Arab Spring" on Lebanon

Nations experience notable transformations at every stage of their existence that affect various aspects of life for their inhabitants. Of course, these changes differ in depth and comprehensiveness, while particular criteria further distinguish one country from another. Nation-states boast social, political, economic, cultural and specific geopolitical settings, along with systems that are governed by conflicts, disputes or competitions that they have been subjected to. How these entities govern is determined by the types of control they exercise over their populations, both within their spheres of influence as well as beyond. This phenomenon is best illustrated by the history of the Arab World.

Of course, this was the situation for most of Western Europe before the Renaissance in the sixteenth century, as well as the Arab World during its first reawakening beginning in the nineteenth century, and that of Eastern Europe after the collapse of communism in the last quarter of the twentieth century. Noticeably, this is also the state of affairs today, as the Arab World witnesses infectious transformations that affect most countries stretching from Morocco to the Levant and beyond.

It is thus normal to anticipate the impacts that such transformations will inevitably leave on every society, especially in a small country like Lebanon, on account of its dramatic and checkered contemporary history. The *Land of the Cedars* is thus poised to experience positive as well as negative consequences that, in the context of the post-2010 Arab Uprisings that shook an entire region, mean both short and long-term epochal alterations. What are these changes and how can Lebanon overcome existential challenges?

To best answer this question, the chapter is divided into four sections, which first provides a brief examination of the nature of the transformations underway throughout the Arab region, before offering a preliminary assessment of the uprisings themselves. It then evaluates the implications that these rebellions will have on Lebanon since the Levantine entity sits at a point of intersection, an arena in which the reawakened Sunni–Shi'ah conflict is progressing, and whose goal is for the winner to rule the entire Muslim World. It closes with an evaluation of the first two years of the ongoing revolutions.

Section I: Transformations of the Arab Region

Analysts agree that the dramatic transformations that began in December 2010 and picked-up steam in the Spring of 2011 throughout the Arab World created a "political tsunami." From Tunisia to Egypt to Yemen to Bahrain and then to Syria, with, perhaps, other countries that may have to confront this wave in the future, few were immune. How can we best understand these rebellions?

At the outset, it may be useful to first identify several methodological items to clarify various premises. It should be self-evident but it is worth repeating that the transformations that started in late 2010 are unfinished and may be said to be a work in progress. Although many of these developments provide us with important material for analysis, research and reflection, the comprehensive and integrated vision of the "Arab Spring" will remain, at least for now, fragmented. Each society has its own conditions and specificities along with the ability to respond to change on a need to basis. The second obstacle is the limited time that has passed to judge these epochal events. Barely two years old, the magnitudes and dangers of the rebellions are still in their rudimentary stages, and we need time to evaluate them before conclusions can be drawn.[47] Naturally, whatever evidence is advanced for many of the arguments presented by analysts must include differences and contradictions that emerged, which will allow us to examine their nature and essence, as we evaluate the consequences on Arab societies and even question the very structure of the Arab state. In fact, differences in analysis and evaluation take on larger proportions as the vocabulary used to describe events evolve too. For some, we are dealing with "revolutions" or "rebellions," which are the most commonly used terminologies in French media sources. Others have used the following terms both in the singular and the plural to describe the post-2010 uprisings: defiance, revolt, agitation, insurrection, protestation, liberation, awakening, uprising (more precisely "the uprising of Arab cities"), explosion, anger, turning point, political tsunami, peaceful or quiet revolution, popular agitation, new renaissance, new birth, and even the "end of the world." Perhaps the most common characterization in Arab and European sources, and the most distant from that which is required to correctly evaluate the nature of what is happening, is the abbreviation "Arab Spring" [*al-Rabi' al-'Arabi*]. Given the multiplicity of these words and expressions, and the numerous intellectual and linguistic differences, it is thus theoretically possible to digest the phenomenon on three separate levels:

First, a radical representation of the concept of revolution as a full and comprehensive change in the social system, which transforms peoples along moral and political norms, and has a certain cultural standard (as the word revolution carries divine connotations that, in turn, means that a coup will or can lead to a complete change in the social status of those involved). Second, to offer an average representation, which is expressed in the insurgency. In other words, at this level, we are not talking about comprehensive revolts but those that simply affect some components of society. The focus here is on changes that lead to political action, transformations in the political system, or even alterations in some of the power and social bases, though none of these reconsider intrinsic values that, in the words of the thinker Adonis, "did not break with the historical contexts of our authoritarian, social and cultural values," [which Adonis lamented in his powerful essay].[48] For the Syrian poet, the uprisings were an expression of "collective action that [are] usually accompanied by acts of imposed violence—even if unintended—that [may be] self-defense against unjust political-security authorities", which evolves and encourages rebel groups to launch attacks by various means in preparation for the overthrow of a regime and the establishment of an alternative command. Third, normal representation, which is expressed through interceptions by a protest group whose goals and aspirations are those of ordinary objectors, is limited in its ability to affect the form of an existing system, and is unlikely to challenge its philosophy or ideology. In general, if authorities require such reforms, which means that the latter are inherently non-reformist and may have fundamental reasons to deny true modifications, this may inevitably lead to a loss of power. That is why, when regimes promise systemic reforms, some believe that such efforts are disingenuous—akin to throwing dust in someone's eyes—with no intentions to implement any in practice. This third scenario is quite evident within Arab dictatorships.

Therefore, the term "Arab Spring" has now divided Arab countries into four groups, which must be duly acknowledged: (1) regimes that were overthrown (Tunisia, Egypt and Libya); (2) those that experienced massive demonstrations (Algeria, Bahrain, Jordan, and Iraq); (3) countries that are still engaged in bitter struggles between authority and rebellious forces (Syria and Yemen); and (4) those that were spared "tsunamis," at least for now, led by Lebanon. Under the circumstances, what is most likely to occur is a prolonged unraveling in many Arab countries, which means that few will be immune to severe jolts to the political system and social fabric. Likewise, the transformation processes are going to have dialectical features in each country, which means that there will be no single standard to evaluate these radical shifts in a comprehensive way. Even those countries that will not face dramatic challenges may well witness their power relationships affected by nascent ruling crises. Change will not only affect authoritarianism, but far more important, will spread to a regime's ideas, prevailing traditions, and despotic cultural supremacy.

Equally important are the shifts under way from a geopolitical perspective. Arab countries, and to a certain extent some of their neighbors like Turkey and Iran, resemble communicating vessels as they sit along geopolitical junctions, as described by Yves Lacoste. According to the French scholar, geopolitics is the "analysis of disputes between societal forces, each vying to control a particular geographic area and its population."[49] This is precisely the status of Arab countries, individually and collectively that, in light of existing balance of power conditions driven by internal as well as external components, explain why each entity seeks military and political power. How forces of oppression and domination benefit from existing conditions to impose control over the state, determine their abilities to rule. A discussion of the "Arab Spring," therefore, imposes on analysts the adoption of objective criteria to properly assess geopolitical dictates that classify ideas and proposals in the context of six components that make up the basic parameters of any geopolitical analyses: motivations, intentions, objectives, power, space, and control. To further elucidate these components, it may be necessary to re-iterate several of their attributes, which will facilitate our understanding of the events that led to the Arab Spring and that are still unraveling.

Motivations. These are the factors and causes that drive an individual or a group of citizens to embark on an act of disobedience or rebellion against authorities. The following partial list for some of these causes confirms what motivates many: individual or mass persecution or repression; debauchery, which is an important feature because some rulers consider the wealth of the state as their private property to dispose of as they see fit, distributing affluence to family members and relatives; corruption within state institutions; tyranny; impoverishment; displacement; plans by leaders, family and party members that produce factionalism instead of building a state of laws; the absence of public freedoms; the use of fear, terrorism and intimidation; the creation of systems that legitimize violence; contempt by rulers of their citizens, which eliminates individual and social dignity; loss of justice and democracy; the exclusion or marginalization of women in society; poor education and illiteracy; illegal economic and financial regulations that encourage exploitation—all of which leads us to conclude that we live in societies where injustice and lawlessness prevail, and where exploitation and tyrannical behavior reign.

Intentions. What is meant by intentions are the very purposes that highlight what one means to accomplish. When an individual or a group of citizens is exposed to serious grievances as expressed by the list of motivations above, the downtrodden can imagine another situation, which quickly becomes an alternative political viewpoint. It is natural that rebel groups would then become emboldened and that such intentions gradually transform nascent agendas. In fact, the most notable purposes that aim for, or can achieve, such intentions include: freedom; democracy and the alternation of power; the establishment of the rule of law in a state where justice, equality, truth and legitimacy prevail; respect for human dignity; investment of the nation's wealth to serve the public good; a confirmation that our existence and presence in the twenty-first century as Arabs who have histories and civilizations grounding elements, even if tyrannical regimes trampled over both; the restoration of our homelands, belongings and identities; a corroboration that the rebirth of the Arab to regain his dignity and rights that will also grant women the necessary strength to play pivotal roles in future endeavors; the rebellion of people to free themselves from confused parties that are undecided as to whether revolutions can or should lead to liberty or whether liberation is fodder for chaos; an adherence to upper values, including sovereignty, freedom, and independence in recognized and final borders duly acknowledged by one's neighbors; a substantiation that the right of peoples to gain legitimacy in the face of systems has lost their legalities; and a recognition of intellectual pluralism and cultural diversity.

Objectives. These are the purposes for which one aims. Indeed, the communities of the oppressed carry heavy burdens to liberate themselves from such painful sufferings, though transitions must urgently define objectives by which one or more groups can enable themselves to move from one position to another. Some realities prevent parties from achieving their objectives, even if the central question must be: What can one do to affirm one's objectives since what is far more important and more dangerous than the legitimacy of the revolution is the direction it may follow. In other words, while rebellions may help achieve specific objectives, where they may be headed and how are equally critical to understand.

What is required is to know the nature of the change, its limits, and fate, which are rarely improvised but usually focused in historical movements built on ideological representations. Among these one can cite the following as illustrations: Jean-Jacques Rousseau and his "Social Contract" (French Revolution); Karl Marx and his "Communist Manifesto" (Bolshevik Revolution); Michel Aflaq and his Arab "national unity" manifest (Ba'ath Revolution); and Ruhallah Khumayni and his *"wilayat al-faqih"* (Iranian revolution).[50] With respect to the current Arab situation, we are living through popular movements whose prospects are open to all possibilities—from the lowest to the highest/from the least to the most radical—that encompass every possibility in between. They are movements with a concrete manifest that may be summarized with the slogan "The people want to overthrow the regime" [*al-Sha'ab Yurid Iskat al-Nizam*], accompanied by a statement addressed to the ruler that may be abridged into a single word, "Go" [*Irhal*]. Often, rebellious groups combine both when they call for the removal of a leader and the dismantlement of a particular regime.

Nevertheless, if we try to decipher rebellion objectives in light of developments on the ground rather than those associated with public declarations, it is possible to reach an approximate understanding of what it is that revolutionary movements are looking for. Beyond the removal of corrupt regimes and dictators, the objectives of revolutionary forces include: democracy, or an alternative power to authoritarianism and, at the philosophical level, a long-term bet that history will welcome rebellious ideas. The choices are either a return to the Middle Ages, and to fundamentalism, or to embark in a new direction towards modernity. At the level of geography, the objective is to look at a community based on diversity, rather than to one that monopolises land—in its theological meaning, which embraces the theology of the homeland. The aim should be for the nation's frontiers to be properly demarcated, which thus affirms its sovereignty, independence, and the attachment of its citizens to their soil. On the socio-economic level, which highlight lifestyle choices, including the adoption of liberal attitudes or coxed ones that are presented as socialism, modernizing efforts are also called for. At the political-cultural level, where the rule of law and the meaning of citizenship dominate to empower man's freedom in an open society, unhindered homeland, and where citizens are able to have candid ties with others throughout the world precisely to benefit from the *knowledge society*. Finally, on the religious-theological level, where the quest to find the extent of compatibility between tradition and innovation, and between the fixed and the variable, are all reflected in the over-arching start to Friday prayers at the mosque.

These objectives stand out for committed revolutionary movements, and were brilliantly summarized by Adonis, who wrote: "It is the people that speak with a single voice that displays adherence to freedom! . . . Being part of such a movement is part of one's pledge to life itself before one thinks of bread and work."

Power. "Power may be summarized as the right to command, whereas the commander has the right to order what must, in turn, be obeyed and executed. Power is thus determined by satisfaction and conviction, and control shall be through bullying and coercion."[51] It is further clear that power is the most prominent expression of democracy, where free and periodic elections legitimize those who exercise it legally. Inasmuch as power struggles can lead to either authoritarianism or other forms of control, depending on the balance of power, an awareness that authority always remains in flux and that it may turn to domination, should not be neglected.

Space. It is the geographical area over which opposing forces seek to exercise their influence. Any country, Lebanon for example, or territories like the Middle East, offer such spaces as the basis of this quest for strategic importance. Such space may have symbolic value in terms of its heritage, or enjoy abundant natural resources like water, oil, or gas, and even display political value as a stronghold of democracy for instance. It may also be the harbinger of successful ideologies, religious and political or both, as was the case in the Iranian Revolution. Such space may further spread as with Hizballah in Lebanon, or be part of a barrier between two states that have regional ambitions and aspirations, as seems to be the case of Lebanon caught between the "Greater Israel" and "Greater Syria" concepts.

Control. In the end, each community struggles at all levels—political, military, social or even religious—though the aim is to gain control over targeted fields. Any display of such control may either be through legitimate means or secured through domination. It is known, for example, that an authority aims to achieve security and order and, perhaps, even ensure the common good that may enhance happiness among masses. Such objectives are at the forefront of wealth and freedom, pleasure and knowledge, virtue, fame and creativity as every rule displays strength, legitimacy and authority [evident in modernizing societies when masses participate in the decision-making process]!

Section II: Assessment of the Arab Uprisings

How can we understand the pressures that led to the "Arab Spring," especially those that are shaping it, and those that may determine how it will evolve?

An objective examination of this question will compel one, in a preliminary assessment of many of the events that rocked the Arab World after 2010, to argue that profound political transformations will leave consequences on every single Arab country, and on Lebanon in particular, because of its fragility. Of course, both positive and negative repercussions may be identified with respect to the uprisings over the term, while more consequential developments may also be identified for the long haul.

In the first part of this section, an effort is made to identify the uprisings at their core levels, concentrating on thirteen complementary points that are, by and large, positive.

The choice of the word "spring" to express what is happening in the Arab world today is a suitable choice for two reasons, both etymologically as well as symbolically. Etymologically because "spring" represents rain over pasturelands, water to thirsty plants that revitalize them, and warmth to accommodate changes in stable environments. Unlike the tragedies that left permanent concerns in the Arab conscience, this uprising, for Arabs at least, translated into two springs—the months that spread light and those that result in bounties as fruits and vegetables grow in abundance. Figuratively, spring is the symbol of youth because it is synonymous with young age, as youth burst into life and reaches a stage where human hopes allow for economic growth and social progress. These hopes are realized on four principle motivations—confidence, dynamism, hope and vision, all to ensure a better future. Given that young people are driving the Arab Uprisings, their springs are bound to be far more successful than many assume. Therefore, and based on the nature of quiet climate-driven springs, many focus on the peaceful dimension of the Arab movements, labeling them "soft power revolutions."[52] In other words, spring is a shift from "bloody tournaments to the concept of peaceful revolutions," whose aims are clear—the dismantling of dictatorships and fundamentalisms to build new societies.

The second positive feature is the call for freedom, which has never run this deep in contemporary affairs. It has ushered in comprehensive transformations under the leadership of a new generation that has guided all groups and communities. This is one of the most exciting and attractive developments that these rebellions and young revolutionaries introduced.

Third is the emphasis on removing injustice, oppression and tyrannical systems that dominated the Arab World, and replace them, or prepare to replace them, with more democratic and humane governments that value freedom and human development.

Fourth is an end to authoritarian debauchery where a ruling family and its entourage exploit the state as their private property and assume that all wealth belongs to them. To replace authoritarianism with the rule of law in every sense of the word, which introduces obligations on rulers and citizens alike, and that place moral imperatives to prevent opportunism from gaining the upper hand. One can thus confirm that the character of Arab societies and the freedom movements spreading forth are the ones addressing existing moral dilemmas.

Fifth is the rise of new youthful forces in Arab societies, where individuals who did not indulge in the quagmire of corruption and opportunism gained prominence. Remarkably, the quest for transparency gave young people genuine credibility with the public, who responded to various calls in the millions, and granted revolutionaries their full confidence away from stale slogans and ideological affiliations.

Sixth is the approach that led Arab youth to create real possibilities for the renewal of political cultures, which prompted some to describe the phenomenon as being historically significant. This approach will lead to a different world, in which thinking, knowledge, sensitivities, and the very management of authority will all be altered. Thus, it may be safe to state that we are at the forefront of a period of enlightenment, "and the birth of a new Arab world."[53] Movements that are "larger than revolutions, [but that represent] a radiation of peoples and a new birth." Arabs are thus locked in "battles of destiny, as they rediscover themselves, their innate capabilities, and their inalienable rights."[54]

Seventh, these deep structural reform projects have dual objectives: liberation from foreign influences, or from existing dependencies on major powers, and internal deliverance from tyranny and corruption. That is how Arab societies will restore their national sovereignties and establish the principles of democracy throughout numerous communities.

Eighth is the adoption by Arab youths of the five slogans for change and reform, namely, freedom, dignity, democracy, justice and human rights, as well as the development and enrichment of human capital that will add value and give a new face to the Arab World.

Ninth is the participation of women in the process of change on an equal footing with men that recognizes their real influence, not only through verbal promises but through active roles, as they boldly participate in demonstrations.

Tenth is the establishment of a pluralistic system that reflects the social and cultural realities that prevail in Arab societies. Intellectuals have long stressed, for example, that "in the beginning [of the uprisings, the goal] was diversity" and not "unity." Taking into account the specificities of each insurgency in every Arab country, both could fulfill socio-cultural goals.

Eleventh is the successful use of revolutionary data and information through social media outlets that gave Arab youth tremendous potential for communication, brain-storming and networking skills that changed conditions on the ground, especially on two central issues: the dismantling of dictatorships and the loosening of fundamentalisms. These successes solidified the uprisings along multi-dimensional levels—civil, political, economic, technological, mental and moral—as revolutionary elements displayed global attributes as much as Arab ones.

Twelfth is the legitimacy of the movements that drew on five norms, including belief in their destinies, the display of signs of confidence that told rebellion leaders they were on the right track, the articulation of unabashed calls for freedom, the popular backings for genuine representation, and the confirmation that they were embarked on a major human corrective movement—all of which led many to conclude that young revolutionaries were writing the history of liberation. These legitimate steps broke the fear barrier, which existing governments mastered, turning the tables against authorities, as regimes started to fear their own peoples.

Last but not least, those who embarked on the change bandwagon drew a new map of the area, as dramatic transformations altered most geo-strategic calculations. The Arab World espoused democratization and opted to usher in prosperity for all as the peoples of the Middle East adopted universal values.

Beyond these thirteen positive repercussions of the Arab Spring, there were also various negative features, which may be summarized as follows:

The most serious threat was that of legitimacy upon which any "new state" hoped to build. Even though armies assist regimes that come to power and stay there, what concerned revolutionary forces were the roles played by military institutions that stood with established governments, or opted to remain neutral. This essential predicament placed Arab uprisings in front of clear dilemmas as nascent states needed law and order capabilities but were wary of their long-term benefits since so many leaders in uniform backed challenged regimes. In other words, revolutionary forces confronted four sources of legitimacy simultaneously, including the traditional religious establishment, charismatic officers, the legal weight of the state, as well as partisan ideological foes. How to deal with such constituencies preoccupied many who understood that what was required was harmony among various assemblies for the project to be successful. There was an awareness that no one could neglect traditional sources of religious legitimacy, which was and remains the most critical motivation for Arab and Muslim audiences confronted with nascent revolutionary initiatives, and that were asked to differentiate between "progressive" and "fundamentalist" initiatives. The militaries were an entirely different proposition.

The second negative repercussion of the uprisings was the risk of fragmentation, which threatened the revolutions because large numbers of citizens were wary of the alternatives to "the people want the fall of the regime" slogan. It was fair to ask, for example, to what extent were advocates of the Arab Spring aware of the need to accommodate the problem of minorities in the Arab social fabric? Did they know that this fabric is full of cleavages along religious, sectarian, ethnic and tribal lines? Were they wary of potential exploitation of situations to push minority groups to demand independence, or to seek foreign protection, both of which are suicidal options for everyone concerned? As the persecution of minorities is clear evidence of a lack of political awareness, were there measures taken to prevent such exploitation at the hands of radical forces, or even at the hands of prevailing regimes? Since the intellectual rule is that very often the minority problem is first and foremost a problem for the majority, addressing such concerns required awakened leaders within the majority, which was and regrettably is not always the case.

Third were the risks that arose when regimes failed to recruit energized youths that filled the public squares and engaged in political activities. These energetic citizens, embodied at the level of the civil state, encouraged the rise of democratic institutions. They demanded free elections to secure additional responsibilities and, equally important, they focused on accountability that confirmed what young achievers intended to accomplish. Regimes objected since they perceived such demands as infringements on their "constitutional" rights, which sometimes raised questions in terms of existing relationships with security forces. In Egypt, for example, the army returned to Tahrir Square to assert its position, viewpoint, and its own demands. The law and order technique, honed to perfection by democratic societies, harmed the public interest because it pitted revolutionary forces against the military.

The fourth negative consequence pertained to sectarian sanctions. If popular demonstrations represented the will to change, the overthrow of a regime generated excessive and malicious sensitivities, which allowed for a subconscious rise of rational awareness. In turn, this led in certain cases to sectarian tensions, deliberately awakened by established regimes. Such plans, or even just rumored intentions, focused on the problem of religious affiliation and even belief systems, even if the geopolitical consequences—to tie minorities to the establishment—created bitterness. This produced fresh hatred among the majority population as Cairo banked on a manipulation of sectarian strains. Such a scenario often ends in uncertain, sometimes explosive circumstances, which is what occurred in Egypt and Syria.

The fifth concern was the Spring's spatial and temporal frameworks. Each case withered in a specific location, had its own meaning in the orbit of the seasons, and displayed its own peculiarities associated with climate, soil, moisture, perfusion, verdant pastures, hazards, and fragrances. The references to nature are meant to reemphasize the fundamental issue that the Arab Springs were "natural" in the sense that they affected human beings, who measured and calculated various steps and who were willing to be judged accordingly. Unfortunately, the Arab Spring appeared to be figurative for some, even if its sources of authority remained symbolically important. A few believed that the existential premise articulated by revolutionary forces, which is the demand for freedom, was little more than ephemeral because so much was missing. In other words, researchers who failed to identify the causes and purposes of the revolutions concluded that it was not possible to talk about them without a guide, a book, or a manifesto, ostensibly to articulate a vision of the future. What many witnessed were mere invitations from Facebook sites to overthrow the regime, and simply wondered what came next? In fact, some of the problems confronted by revolutionaries forces were due to this lack of a written theoretical platform, and, in other instances, because they were leaderless in the sense that no single charismatic individual filled the void. Rather, what existed were views and opinions propagated over "Google."[55]

Three additional challenges included differences over values, and the agendas that governed Arab societies, which oscillated between what democratic forces wished for—balancing between two opposing directions that served either divine or man-made laws—and the direction that preserved local heritage that did not prevent modernization. This is what led to the popular saying: "The change wagon is driven by two horses, each in a different direction, one that drives towards the affirmations of religious communities, and the other towards civil societies.[56]

An equally important outlook that must be taken into consideration is that of "counter-revolution." A dialectic has always existed between revolution and counter-revolution, one between militarized Arab regimes equipped with unprecedented security forces, and that seldom hesitated to use violence to achieve their aims—and thus to rely on the legitimacy that the use of violence grants states against popular will—against the ultimate popular legitimacies that arise from citizens. Yet, the threat of counter-revolution remains because tyrants cannot be easily deposed even when they declare war on their own peoples, by dropping barrel-bombs from the air on helpless civilians. Under most circumstances, these tyrants fabricate excuses to cover up their actions, including the existence of alleged conspiracies against the country, the presence of armed gangs among civilian demonstrators, isolated shooting at security forces, and even the presence of "obscurantist" forces. In the case of Colonel Mu'ammar Qaddhafi of Libya, for example, the intimidation level involved a crusade to provoke religious sensitivities, and attempts to gain control over the country's oil wealth. One may add to these lists the more recent extremist inventions of *takfiri* thought and, of course, the standby classic "terrorism" model at the hands of Islamist movements (see below for a detailed discussion of the *takfiri* [apostasy] phenomenon).

Finally, it is important to list the negative consequence that arose as anti-revolutionary forces that challenged the regime, could not infiltrate the latter. New alternative authorities formed, in some cases dangerous countervailing groups though never from within the ranks of the establishment. This is due to legacies or established monopolies whose effects linger, while new realities suffer from both a lust for power and paranoia. In the words of one observer, "undisputed monopolies, exclusiveness and tyrannies are the most powerful of the principles of justice, equality and freedom, which form an existential crust on political wounds . . . for how can we otherwise explain that victims turn into torturers?"[57] A fear existed as to whether rebellious elements would turn against revolutions, in what is a classic "the revolution devours its own children" scheme, which is why the best thing that one can do with any revolution is to support rationality rather than sanctify violence and, worse, transform presumptive leaders into heroes. Any emphasis on personalities will always ensure the end of a revolution because it leads to distraction along two planes, diversion from principles and the absence of genuine leaders from their historical roles.

Hence the importance of the army and the role it plays in determining the fate of any revolution, to back the masses and not be a tool in the hands of ruling elites to kill people, as is occurring in several Arab countries.

In short, and though it is still too early to offer a comprehensive assessment of the "Arab Spring," current data confirm that the uprisings filled the hearts of people starting in the late 2010, when events placed Arabs at a crucial junction. The uprisings obligated authoritarian regimes to be on the defensive and transformed them into disintegrating regimes, even if several did not fall. Nevertheless, most lost their credibility as well as legitimacies. Yet, those who would like to see the Arab world in a perpetual spring, perhaps even move into lasting autumns or even unending winters, will try through every means possible to take advantage of all religious, psychological and political gaps to foil the positive spring experiences in order to keep Arabs on the sidelines of history. Therefore, it is the duty of uprising leaders, whoever they may be, to arm themselves with sufficient awareness and historical realism, and to stay away from erroneous perceptions or deceptive fantasies because nations are built on visions, not on illusions

Section III: Implications of Uprisings on Lebanon

Lebanon is the geographical point where the Sunni–Shi'ah conflict intersects in the Muslim world. In the post-2010 period, the transformations taking place all around it will, one way or another, touch most Arab countries and leave serious aftereffects. Nevertheless, this does not mean that everyone will be affected similarly. Rather, it means that a few will remain immune to the epochal phenomena, which the uprisings represent. Each Arab country has its geopolitical distinctiveness and, thus, it would be wise to assume that repercussions associated with individual countries would be exclusive to that entity. To be sure, there are common concerns among most states in the framework of the Arab Spring, but there are also specific issues that affect each one separately. What are the implications of the Arab Spring on Lebanon specifically?

Before embarking on this analysis, it is necessary to clarify the meaning of the key word in this question, "repercussions" [in Arabic the word *in'ikasat* must further be clarified since it is derived from the word 'Aks, which means opposite]. What is the real meaning of "repercussions"? In the lexicon of the Arabic language, the three letters 'A, K, and S (ayn, kaf, and siin) or 'Aks when combined, mean "opposite" or "reverse." In the political sense, it could therefore denote the heart of the matter, or even a coup. It could further signify that the subject is not what it seems.

Accordingly, the repercussions of the Arab Spring on Lebanon could mean what befalls it from the impact of shifts and changes throughout the region, which further affects the path of the Lebanese situation as it currently exists, or take the situation in a new direction through various pressures.

To better address nascent consequences that were identified in the previous sections, an effort is thus made to separate these consequences into four groups: specific areas of opportunity, the geopolitics of Lebanon and regional projects, Lebanon as a "buffer-state" between Israeli and Syrian ambitions, and recent activities that trapped the republic.

Specific Areas of Opportunity. The Arab Spring had serious repercussions at all levels of the Lebanese body-politic, ranging the gamut from spiritual, cultural, intellectual, political, security, social, and economic concerns.

At the spiritual and cultural levels, there is a direct impact on the legitimacy of the modern state, especially to underline the basic premise that questions whether Lebanon is a religious or a civil state. The new paradigm tests the relationship between religion and the composition of society on one hand, with the state and its religious-cultural set-up on the other. Questions raised by the Iranian Islamic Revolution and the quest for a divine Shi'ah imprimatur—with its extensions in Lebanon and the region where significant Shi'ah populations live—impact on the nation-state as defined by fundamentalist Sunni movements. Moreover, there are also additional details attached to these concepts, including treason, dialogue with foes and friends alike, and relationships through foreign parties [Syria, Iran, and Sa'udi Arabia in particular]. In a fundamental way, what these concepts produce are the challenges of modernity, which pit the perceptions of history that place Lebanon and the Lebanese at this sensitive juncture, against concrete external threats. Several basic questions are thus raised to better identify how Beirut might fare.

At the intellectual level, for example, the Arab Spring poses a direct and serious ideological challenge in all its dimensions, types and objectives, which means that there is now a need to reconsider basic ideological premises that were introduced in the first half of the twentieth century and developed in strength in its second half. These ideologies—nationalism, Arabism, Marxism, Islamism, fundamentalism, liberalism, authoritarianism, and obsessions with the nation's separate identities (whether Lebanese, Syrian, Arab or even Islamic)—created existential concerns for the Lebanese who struggled to define and confirm their identity.

On the political level, and starting from the premise of this quest, the country's democratic, semi-liberal tendencies further corroborated freedom from political dependencies. Elites further sought to protect the state from the geopolitical ambitions of regional powers, and to limit their dependency on international forces that enjoyed and exercised strategic objectives throughout the region, whether these were Western powers or Russia.

At the ethnic level, Lebanon managed to distance itself from security constraints by introducing a legal framework in which respect for laws and regulations prevailed, at least theoretically, which were supposed to be clear and transparent. In this context the Israeli attitude is relevant, as it exploits chauvinistic slogans that threaten stability, especially those that pertain to minorities [especially with respect to Shi'ahs and Christians].

On the social level, the Arab Spring launched a new spirit of liberty throughout the area, a tendency that aims to work towards the establishment of the state of justice, liberty, equality and dignity. In practice, this means an end to the state of debauchery that further denies what an authority [meaning Lebanese or Arab elites] has hitherto assumed that it owned—the state, its wealth, and the right to distribute the latter to family members and close associates. Such violation of the concept of the rule of law and human dignity was no longer tolerated.

On the economic front, the Arab Spring contributed to a break in the exploitation loop within the state, and even abroad, which gained advantages at the expense of citizens. In fact, security services funded from outside regular budgets or the prevalence of militias that exploited loopholes and that were/are backed by foreign powers, all tested their mettle and scored undeniable economic gains. Additional incomes that lined the pockets of officials did not benefit formal treasuries, as these masters awarded projects [to their cronies] without oversight and accountability, which further encouraged corruption. If these methods were used in exchange for "speedy extraordinary growths, such financial deals weakened the state and the public sector, hit the dignity of the citizen," though what was needed in the Arab world was first and foremost the necessity to build "a state of law."[58]

It is thus safe to write that Arab economies will be exposed during this time of political turmoil to rigidities and perhaps setbacks, including fears of smuggling, lack of investment and even the flight of financial experts and capital. But these will be temporary developments during a period of transition, before a return to a period that will record growth. Clear and comprehensive options will arise, including liberal options that were first developed by Michel Chiha whose political and economic vision was introduced in the 1940s, and whose philosophical conclusions hover around "a free man in a free society with free thoughts and a free economy for free people."[59]

The Geopolitics of Lebanon and Regional Projects. If the simplified definition of geopolitics is the competition between political and military forces to control specific geographic areas, it is here in Lebanon—within its geographical setting—where the Land of the Cedars captures all of the components, elements, and justifications that drive regional and international powers to compete for control of the Middle East in general and of Lebanon in particular. The importance and seriousness of global strategic initiatives in place for this purpose cannot be neglected as numerous projects intersect and interfere with each other to the severe detriment of society at large.

There are at least ten projects that crisscross and face off in the region, and which are reflected in the situation of every actor, along religious, ideological and political dimensions, which developed over nearly a century, starting with the outbreak of the First World War. These comprise (1) the traditional Arab system that was assembled with the League of Arab States [the so-called Tarbush regimes];[60] (2) the "Greater Syria" project as designed by Antun Sa'adih, which seems to be the preferred option of the current regime in Damascus;[61] (3) the "Greater Israel" project that was fathomed by the Zionist movement, and which rests on Biblical representation, that foresees Israel's northern border along the Litani River;[62] (4) the great Arab homeland project that stretches from the Atlantic Ocean to the Arabian Gulf, according to Ba'athist and Nasirist ideologies; (5) the Islamic Middle East Project (or the Shi'ah Project) as contemplated by the Shi'ah Islamic Revolution of Iran with its extensions to the Mediterranean through the Hizballah Party; (6) the Islamic Nation project, as imagined by Sunni fundamentalist movements from Hassan al-Banna to al-Qa'idah, and which is a jihadist (*takfiri*) project based on the principle of governance that presumably combines Shari'ah [Islamic] Law with a Muslim ruler (Caliph);[63] (7) the Greater Middle East project as proposed by the United States with its democracy goal, which President George W. Bush and the neocons embarked upon in the aftermath of the 11 September 2001 events of as well as the occupation of Iraq; (8) the Great Lebanon project as proposed by Christian nationalists like Yusuf al-Sawdah and Maronite Patriarch Elias Huwayk, which was translated in the proclamation of "Greater Lebanon" in 1920;[64] (9), the Turkish Islamic Reform project, which saw light through the Justice and Development Party [Adalet ve Kalkınma Partisi or AKP] that grouped Islamism and modernization through the conciliation tactic, and which meant saving the Arab Islamic movements from their ideological legacies to access power democratically as well as pay attention to economic development that would, presumably, be more realistic, even more pragmatic, as far as dealing with regional and global powers are concerned.[65] (In the words of a leading Arab intellectual, Sadiq Jalal al-'Azm, "The Turkish model saves the Islamic movements from their historical embarrass-ments," which speaks volumes);[66] and (10) the Arab Spring project with its Sunni character and stated militant objectives to reach truth, freedom, justice and dignity within the framework of the rule of Shari'ah Law in all Arab countries. This is much more than a political movement. It is an existential undertaking that aims to create a new Arab human being, in a new Arab society, and to allocate Arabs a global presence within the civilized world and within human civilization.

The geopolitical advantages of these ten projects are many, led by the notion that all aim to create geographic/political entities at the national, regional or even international levels. Some saw the light of day, some failed, and a few were only partially operational. Despite hurdles, all strove to create ideological representations of their movement. Their philosophical constructs remained present, or are still active, in the minds of advocates and believers. By all accounts, all of these projects are still the source of militant thought to various past and current polit-ical forces, with the most important and dangerous consequence being the Sunni–Shi'ah conflict, which is to say the struggle between the Shi'ah Crescent represented by Iran, Iraq, Syria and Lebanon (Hizballah) on one hand, and between the Sunni Arc, composed of Turkey, Egypt, Sa'udi Arabia, the Arab Gulf States and Pakistan on the other. In fact, the very purpose of this conflict is first to dominate the area between the Arabian Gulf and the Mediterranean before moving on to the entire Muslim World. This explains the recent call made by the Gulf Cooperation Council (GCC) to Jordan and Morocco to join the Riyadh-based alliance, precisely to strengthen the Sunni presence and resolve matters in favor of the Sunni Arc in the region, by creating a military balance on both sides of the Gulf to counter Iran's human, military and geostrategic capabilities.[67] Inasmuch as this vacuum was until very recently filled by Egypt at the political level and by the United States at the military one, this is no longer necessarily the case.

What is happening in Syria is of the utmost gravity, as events on the ground confirm the presence of Sunni forces, especially from the Arab Gulf States, that seem to have decided they had little choice but to respond to the Iranian military presence there. The two sides have now entered into a decisive battle in which the Sunni Arc attempts, through Sunni media outlets like *Al-Jazeera* and *Al-Arabiya* as well as Syria's Sunni masses, to confront the Shi'ah Crescent. Syria boasts a majority Sunni population of over 17 million, which represents 75% of citizens in the face of the 'Alawi ruling minority, which represents 12% of Syrians. It is from this perspective that we can truly appreciate the violent nature of the confrontation.

Finally, we should underline that this confrontation between Sunnis and Shi'ahs can help the former achieve four critical goals: to settle the matter once and for all to the benefit of Sunnis between the Mediterranean and the Arabian Gulf; place a key impediment to counter the influence of Iran in the region or, at least, separate Syria from Iran; weaken the Iranian role in general and that of Hizballah in particular, especially in terms of the latter's financial and media skills to leave an impact on the Sunni scene (for example, using the Palestinian cause to boost the historic role of Shi'ahs as defenders of the cause while Sunni regimes allegedly failed to deliver, even if there are no Shi'ahs in Palestine and even if Shi'ahs, including Hizballah, champion a cause that is Sunni par excellence); and work to end ongoing financial investments and inducements by Shi'ahs to influence Sunni Arabs to strengthen rigid attitudes toward Israel, which Hizballah and Iranians champion.

Lebanon as a Buffer-State between Israeli and Syrian Ambitions. The concept of the buffer-state is a well established part of the science of political geography, just as much as the idea of the "aspirations of regional powers" constitutes a part of the science of geopolitics.[68] A buffer-state is thus a state caught between two regional entities (Lebanon between Syria and Israel; or between international forces, Afghanistan between the British and Russian empires; or Switzerland between France and Germany) that transform these median bodies into barriers, which prevent direct contact between opposing forces. Jean Gottmann perceived this formula as an "English Method" applied in Asia and Europe to secure the borders of the Empire.[69] Earlier, Friedrich Ratzel, the father of modern geopolitics, confirmed that buffer-states came under pressure from neighboring countries with expansionist ambitions, threatening the fate of these countries either in whole or in part. Therefore, their only salvation, according to Ratzel, was to espouse neutrality or resort to the protection of international law. For Ratzel, "it was not desirable for one's neighborhood to include a strong country."[70]

In the current circumstances, there are powers with regional aspirations that are seeking to intervene in various conflicts to confirm their influence in the region, which means that regional hegemony of any particular state is based on building three integrated and complimentary goals to retain power and to develop it. These grandiose schemes necessitate economic, political and military initiatives, sometimes with the addition of a cultural dimension too.[71] It is no historical coincidence, but a matter of geographical and political reality, that Britain, for example, demanded the "neutralization of Lebanon" back in 1919, on the eve of the declaration of the State of Greater Lebanon in 1920.

In fact, the Syrian and Israeli quests to dominate Lebanon were not limited to its "political borders," since there are several kinds of borders. In addition to political boundaries, there are national and ideological frontiers, as well as strategic interest confines and even limits of influence. In every one of these groundbreaking border quests, Lebanon remains a large stage and, more important to regional conflicts, a geopolitical arena between opposing forces. It is a space where different representations with contradictory ideologies clash, and where religious, national and geopolitical contradictions surface. The Lebanese entity as a state is thus at the intersection of regional projects that encompass socio-religious features because it is a laboratory of minority populations, a unique geographical spot in the middle of the Eastern side of the Mediterranean, one that also boasts an intellectual dimension as many of its citizens contributed to global civilization.

In the words of Michel Chiha, Israel "was a state project realized by Zionism with the soul of an empire."[72] Such a project inevitably carries a heavy weight on the fate of Lebanon, which is why Chiha warned: "We Lebanese are invited to see this growth on our borders and to bear the burden of this overwhelming presence," which will only occur once we overcome three widely spread ills in our societies, the failure of the mind, the absence of opinion, and the bankruptcy of justice."[73]

It is true that Israel ostensibly welcomes the Arab Spring, though it actually suffers from deep anxiety about the changes underway in Arab countries, especially the instability that these transformations are creating. Yet, as Israel moves towards the consecration of a purely Jewish state to ensure its religious serenity, it confronts four reservations regarding the Lebanese experiment: (1) Beirut's founding roles in Arab, Syrian and Lebanese nationalist ideologies that present direct risks to Israel; (2) its model of coexistence between several ethnic and religious groups, especially among Muslims and Christians; (3) its mandate as a nexus between the Arab World and Western societies, especially through its Christian populations; and (4) its modest democratizing model in the Arab world. It is in Israel's interest, but also among its goals, to remove the forces of moderation in Arab societies, and transform the conflict of identity from a nationalist one into a religious confrontation among Jews, Muslims and Christians—all to feed extremist forces among Sunnis and Shi'ahs to further ignite sedition.

In addition to Israeli designs over it, Lebanon suffers from Syrian ambitions too, as Damascus continues to refuse a demarcation of its borders with Beirut. In effect, this means that Syria does not recognize common borders between the two neighboring states and, therefore, does not recognize the sovereignty of the Lebanese state.

Equally important, Syria perceives itself as a central regional power, where leaders are not only concerned with their own fate but must also determine the fate of the entire area. It decides conditions of war and peace in Lebanon, Palestine, Iraq—what can be summed up as "Natural Syria"—and, in the words of Yves Lacoste, displays a "feeling of superior geopolitical leadership, [which becomes a] duty for the entire Near East." Damascus thus becomes the capital of the "Arab State" and Syria the interlocutor par excellence for major countries, as it stands in opposition to Israel. Yet, Syria does not have the four practical elements that can give it superior advantages in this putative role: the economic, political, military, and cultural attributes that are necessary to define the role of a regional power. Nevertheless, it has the inherent advantage in the efficient use of various security services to penetrate into the heart of political and religious fundamentalist movements throughout the region, and the Islamic world at large, which allows it to control the level of stability that can exist in any given arena, by manipulating or creating instability. It is through such a stratagem that it can present itself as the party capable to offer solutions to problems it helped create in the first place. In exchange for this prowess, Syria can exact political prices from many. Ironically, it managed to provide valuable information for successive American administrations for nearly half a century, which ensured the survival of the regime. This appears to have been a successful strategy that endured as the Syrian regime faced real challenges in the fateful Arab Spring. In the words of Philippe Droz Vincent, "Syria is a weak state, and does not always have the potential to achieve large aspirations as a vital entity, though the skills to generate regional turmoil compensate for its weaknesses."[74] If this is the case under normal circumstances, what would it be like when Damascus becomes vulnerable to disorder and instability due to numerous uprisings reaching into its political fabric at boiling point?

The Syrian dynamic is one of the most significant factors affecting Lebanon, although it is not the only one. Beirut represents strategic wealth for Damascus as best described by Elizabeth Picard in her extensive writings on the subject.[75] It is also a model site to create problems for geopolitical purposes, as Damascus believes Lebanon remains a favorite spot to open a dialogue with the Christian West, especially France, through the Christian presence in the Land of the Cedars. Beirut is thus a susceptible field for influence because of the multiplicity of conflicting interests in its society, which makes Syrian control a matter of great progressive value that, if possible, could end up with the country easily falling into its laps. It is an ideal geographical area, which Damascus can and does use to fine tune its ties with Israel, along the lines of what Henry Kissinger did in 1976, when the American official placed his "red lines system" in place. Those red lines were between the two larger countries—Syria and Israel—that went *through* Lebanon!

It is also a financial well from which Syria draws significant economic aid. Lebanon thus represents a strategic depth for Syria, which is why its leaders always speak about the security thread that runs between the two countries. In the words of Syrian President Hafiz Al-Assad, "It is hard to separate the security of Lebanon from the security of Syria."[76] On another occasion, Hafez al-Assad declared: "The nature of geographical, historical and human [ties] between Syria and Lebanon impose distinctive and special relations."[77] In his opinion "Lebanon and the Biqa' Valley as a whole are necessary for the defense of Syria."[78] In fact, "Soviet military experts confirmed to Syrian officials that all possible Israeli wars against Syria in the future will require trying to get around Damascus through the Biqa' Valley."[79] Even Henry Kissinger offered similar analyses when he concluded that Hafiz al-Assad "saw in [Yasir] 'Arafat and the PLO [Palestine Liberation Organization] an obstacle to the creation of the 'Greater Syria' embracing Lebanon, Jordan, and Palestine." According to the American official, Assad was determined to see this geopolitical plank through "even if he [himself] could not achieve it in his lifetime." In Kissinger's inimitable words, Hafiz al-Assad "hoped to leave [that objective] as a mission to his successors."[80] In other words, the Syrian President's aim was clear; it necessitated the absorption of several independent states.

Recent Activities that Trapped the Republic of Lebanon. Lebanon is not just an excited participant in the Arab Spring but, in some respects, it is one of its pioneers. For historical reasons, the people of this country opted for human freedom and democracy since antiquity, and practiced their freedoms. Those who follow the history of Lebanon understand that democracy is an authentic wealth of the country, and a uniting thread among citizens who live and implement it to the best of their abilities. It is worth noting that in the past, democratic governments emerged in Phoenician cities, where tribal councils were elected that limited the power of kings, electoral colleges were established among elites, and constitutions or collegial power systems adopted, as described by Phillip Hitti in his opus on the *History of Lebanon*.[81] All of these Phoenician institutions affected political organizations that eventually saw light in Athens and Rome as Greece and Italy emerged from their doldrums and created civilizations that brought about the Western world as we know it today.

Remarkably, it was the Amir Fakhr-al-Din Al Ma'ani, often considered as the founding father of the nation, who established a Consultative

Council [*Majlis al-Shurah*] in the early 1600s and whose members shared their views and opinions with the Druze prince that lived in Italy and was eventually executed by the Ottomans. After this came the critical roles played by Maronite civilian docents who participated in the election of patriarchs and bishops. In 1695, Maronite Church leaders at the Aleppo Monastery introduced a new concept of power sharing within their royal monastic traditions, which allowed the rise of new centers of religious authority. It was this nascent mechanism that led to the adoption of Boards of Overseers who gradually elected representatives of various communities. Lastly, the spirit of democracy entered the contemporary body politic in the 1926 Lebanese Constitution, as described by Michel Chiha, who declared that the "Republic of Lebanon was the first democracy established in the Arab World."[82] For the erudite Philip Hitti: "The Lebanese personality failed to become a force of liberation and war, though it did not fail to become a force for civilization with conquests of the mind, whose source was diversity and whose strength stemmed from the confrontations of ideas and doctrines."[83]

It is this democratic heritage of Lebanon that made it the cradle of the first Arab uprising. There is no exaggeration here, as confirmed by the thinker 'Ali Harb, who opined "that Lebanon was the first Arab country that witnessed an uprising represented in the demonstration of millions on 14 March 2005, a month after the martyrdom of former Prime Minister Rafiq Hariri."[84] Hariri's assassination proved to be much more than a mere event that made the impossible possible; it resulted in the withdrawal of Syrian troops, and the end of the security umbrella imposed over Lebanon. Unlike earlier or even subsequent rallies that were carefully programmed, the 14 March protests saw large crowds that gathered spontaneously. Citizens nauseated by the pro-Syria March 8 demonstrations—which occurred less than a month after the 14 February 2005 Hariri assassination—filled the streets. Many Hariri opponents marched too because they perceived the assassination as having targeted them as Lebanese citizens. Towards that end, the 14 March 2005 demonstration became a universal and meaningful show of principles as people from all walks-of-life, religions, sects or creeds participated. More importantly, they were peaceful as marchers clamored for nationalist goals. These broad audiences, led by a younger generation, displayed acute awareness of rapidly changing norms and, in that respect, preceded leaders who tried to spearhead opposition and nullify the impact of the rally.

This extraordinary event's vitality to civil society drew attention to key items including its large size. In fact, a third of the Lebanese population gathered in Martyrs' Square—a million out of three million—that, at least through a mathematical comparison, represented the equivalent of 28 million Egyptians in Tahrir Square (out of 85 million Egyptians), or 100 million Americans meeting in New York out of 306 million citizens of the United States.[85] From here to say that in terms of sheer numbers, spontaneity, peacefulness and civic awareness as well as democratic vision, nothing like it occurred and might not happen again in any country of the world! The Lebanese uprising can thus be regarded as a precursor of Arab and global uprisings.[86]

To be sure, all Arab societies are affected by what occurs in their vicinities, which then spills over, as was the case with the martyrdom of Prime Minister Hariri. Lebanon will surely be affected by what is occurring throughout the Arab world too, starting with Egypt and especially in Syria. As of this writing [July 2013], few know exactly where events in the Levant will lead, as matters get complicated and predications of a full-fledged tragic and devastating civil war abound. Yet, whatever experiences the Syrian regime might encounter, there can be little doubt that they will leave their mark, directly and indirectly, on Lebanon, which should brace itself for the worse.

In fact, every loss by the regime in Syria will lead to a Damascus effort to compensate for it in Lebanon at the hands of Syria's allies, led by Hizballah. What the regime might lose at home will be balanced through the establishment of the Shi'ah Crescent against the Sunni Arc. In turn, this raises the sensitive subject of the role various branches of Shi'ism, including that of the 'Alawis, will play in Lebanon, which may become a historical predicament as factions navigate between idealism and realism. Indeed, Shi'ahs are the makers of revolutions in Arab-Muslim history, even if they were and are its first victims.

Sadly, the bloody experiences in Syria illustrate the current dilemmas, which may be traced back to geopolitical clashes between the Sunni Arc (Turkey, Egypt, Sa'udi Arabia and its Arab Gulf allies, with the potential additions of Jordan and Morocco), and the Shi'ah Crescent in its midst (Iran, Iraq, Syria and Hizballah in Lebanon). Few can deny short-terms gains to the Shi'ah Crescent across the Syrian corridor, irrespective of the predominant Sunni demographic numbers in Syria, or about 75% of the total population. Therefore, it may be safe to speculate that the post-First World War Sunni Arab-based system, which has sought to regain power and control territories between the Gulf and the Mediterranean, now stands in jeopardy in the face of an unprecedented Iranian extension.

Given these realities that will surely usher in democratization, the transformations occurring in the Eastern Mediterranean will make

Israel reconsider its calculations, because it will no longer be the only democratic country in the region—as it always markets itself as such in front of Western, especially American, audiences. It is increasingly clear that there will be new democratic forces across the Arab World and, in the case of Lebanon, recent efforts will update its image to affirm that it "is not a geographical and historical mistake," as Moshe Arens once concluded.[87] Rather, that it is a "geographical and historical reality" as nationalists led by Patriarch Elias Huwayk, the father of the 1920 Greater Lebanon concept, perceived it. It is not a weak and vulnerable state but a nation that derives its strengths from its defense of human freedom first, and from the possession of energies and important wealth topped by water, oil and gas in its territorial waters in the Eastern Mediterranean. Lebanon can become an oil and gas producer par excellence.

Of course, Lebanon's well-known commitment to freedom suffers from structural problems, which create confrontations galore. Few seem aware of these hurdles but they ought to be spelled out in detail to further acculturate the reader with what is at stake.

Lebanon is, first and foremost, a pluralistic society that is not homogeneous because there are multiple religions, sects, and doctrines that live within its boundaries. Its geographic location grants it certain advantages, especially cultural and economic prosperity, since its peoples are in contact with, and open to, the world. Simultaneously, they suffer from political anxiety and military weakness as surrounding regional forces "mine" the state by backing indigenous as well as non-Lebanese armed militias that challenge its legitimacy, and work to topple the state precisely to eliminate it as an independent entity. As Patrick Seale told an *Al-Nahar* daily correspondent in 2009, Lebanon is "the battlefield where neighbors conduct their conflicts" because it falls "in a central point within the region that presents the world's crisis center."[88] Moreover, and given that the Lebanese are caught, like most Arabs, between a double-edged sword—somewhat authoritarian or unjust rule versus fundamentalist reactionary discourses—they are trapped in the March 8 and March 14 impasses. These two movements, named for 2005 demonstrations held on those dates, grouped pro- and anti-Syrian forces. One of these promotes the interests of the state (March 14), is unarmed but enjoys modest Arab and international support, even if its institutions are "fragile." The other, March 8, is led by Hizballah, a heavily armed militia that uses its military might to impose various demands on the Lebanese population. It also disrupts the interests of the state at large. Critically, Hizballah is linked with Syria politically, financially and militarily, and is in an ideological and mili-

tary alliance with Iran. In 'Ali Harb's words, Hizballah's "transformation into a mere agent working for a master that tasks it to perform direct
and indirect" services, highlights "loss of independence."[89] This difficult and complicated position makes Lebanon spearhead the
confrontation vis-à-vis Israel, which means that its own fate is linked to
a resolution of the Arab–Israeli conflict. It is in this sense that Lebanon
is an arena, or a tool, or even a hostage—it is a country deprived of
stability, which must await the resolution of all regional conflicts before
it too can enjoy genuine liberty.

The 14 March 2005 uprising (*intifadah*), which also came to be
known as the Cedar Revolution, inaugurated the "Arab Uprisings," as
it articulated some of the same existential, intellectual and political calls
for reform that emerged after 2010. Yet, and even if the impact of these
uprisings will largely be negative on Hizballah—because what is unraveling now is a Sunni Arab awakening that will mobilize Arab majority
populations—70% of whom are Sunnis—against it—the immediate
consequence of this awakening will translate in a concerted effort to
stem the Shi'ah religious-political tide as envisaged by the Iranian Islamic
revolution. Therefore, few should be surprised by the containment of
Shi'ah revolutions throughout the region. Such calls will also focus on
fossilized Sunni regimes that were overthrown, which will further
awaken Sunnis regarding their freedoms, rights and other concerns.
Equally important will be the awakening's efforts to highlight how
Iranian and Hizballah influences threaten peace and stability. Again, few
should be surprised by fresh restrictions on the latter, to stop arms
supplies through Syria and minimize its role in Lebanon. We might even
witness a refocus on the Palestinian Question, precisely to narrow the
margin of exploitation that Hizballah excels in as it promotes the cause
for its own interests. Such an inevitable awakening will open minds, raise
cultural sensitivities, and confront proposals that intend to drag the
region into the Middle Ages—as envisaged by fundamentalists. Finally,
it will diminish the influence of Hizballah's political/military capabilities throughout the region that transformed the militia into a mercenary
force.

In light of the War for Syria, such vagaries are bound to contribute
to Hizballah's geopolitical isolation, and an eventual political re-shuffle.
Whether the party will carry out its military adventures in the neighborhood or return to the Lebanese scene or even turn towards Israel, or
do both, will determine if such dangerous escapades may alter its leadership status in the Arab and Muslim street. Bearing in mind that what
preoccupies many is the fate of all minorities in the region, including in
Israel, how Lebanon will be used becomes vital. For all minorities are

potential Israeli allies, while the Sunni Arab demography stands as the ultimate foe. It is worth repeating that Arab Sunnis stand as the decisive challenger because they, and only they, refuse to integrate the people and the State of Israel as an entity in the fabric of the region. In effect, this means that Israel will continue to remain a foreign body, although policies that favor minorities—Shi'ahs, Christians, 'Alawis, Druzes and others—could break that ironclad vision.

Moreover, the direct consequences of the events in Syria on Lebanon are not limited to what is occurring on the northern and eastern borders, but are also directly related to the impact that Hizballah's presence has on the government in Beirut. Syrians and their allies perceive the Arab uprisings negatively, and do not rejoice when calls for liberty spread. They thought that they could turn the tide around as they did with the Cedar Revolution, but that was not to be. In fact, what the War for Syria demonstrates is that the confrontations are far more unsettling than anything hitherto. Amazingly, Damascus confronted an Arab/Turkish media offensive on *Al-Jazeera* and *Al-Arabiya*, which telegraphed to one and all that the time for appeasements, concessions and submissions to dictates had ended.

In Beirut, the government crisis that overthrew Prime Minister Sa'ad Hariri in June 2011, and that weakened the Hariri family in general, became a borderline hindrance in dealing with the Syrian regime. President Bashar al-Assad settled on Najib Mikati to head the Lebanese government, though the combined Arab/Turkish/American/European decision not to allow Lebanon to fall into the Iranian/Syrian/Hizballah orbit froze interference. The new Prime Minister, Mikati, was unable to overcome the latest refugee pressures imposed on him. It was remarkable and meaningful that the loyalty of an important segment of Syrian Sunnis went to Hariri, as illustrated by the reception Syrian refugees received in Lebanese Sunni communities. In turn, that awareness raised new questions, including the drawing of fresh parameters in a battle that attempts to establish a balance of power inside Syria, which is directly reflected on the balance of forces within Lebanon too. In the event, the Lebanese arena remains a cauldron though it is unlikely to fall to pro-Iranian and/or pro-Syrian forces, even if these elements continue to exercise their "divinely" inspired prerogatives.[90]

It is useful to recall that while the House of al-Assad persuaded itself of the veracity that Syria had the upper hand, and that Damascus was the first and last party to determine every issue that concerned Greater Syria—stretching from Lebanon to Palestine—post-2011 events changed this equation. In fact, the Syrian regime sabotaged the February 2007 Makkah Accords between Fatah and Hamas, which were reached under the auspices of King 'Abdallah bin 'Abdul 'Aziz, and prevented the immediate signing of the Cairo reconciliation accord to deny Egypt a role in the Palestinian Question.[91] In time, however, the escalation of tensions embarrassed Hamas, and as Syria's weakened position vis-à-vis Hamas became more pronounced, Damascus lost its grip. Largely because of internal preoccupations, Khalid Misha'al [Meshaal], Chairman of the Hamas Political Bureau, went to Cairo and signed the 2012 agreement with Fatah to mark the opening of a new page in inter-Palestinian relations, which spoke volumes. If we add to this the deployment of the Peninsula Shield forces that entered Bahrain in March 2011, and Turkey's June 2011 permission to the Syrian opposition to hold a major conference in Antalya (the Conference for Change in Syria), it might be possible to say that there is a comprehensive Arab–Turkish–Sunni assault between the Mediterranean and the Gulf, all to check the Iranian/Syrian front in the region.

Such a riposte may not achieve results or have any effect if it were not for the surges associated with Arab revolutionary movements in various countries, backed by the Turkish experience regarding reformed Islam, which is articulated by the Justice and Development Party.[92] Notwithstanding Iranian, Syrian and Hizballah accomplishments, it is too early for these forces to claim victory, even in Bahrain.[93]

Indeed, as the goal of the uprising in the small kingdom of Bahrain was nothing less than a full-scale insurrection to topple the monarchy and extend the Shi'ah crescent, regional powers prevented the creation of an important pro-Iranian base in the heart of the Arabian/Persian Gulf. The international community would not allow such a coup to occur in a strategic spot and took a firm and decisive initiative when it favored the Gulf Cooperation Council deployments. GCC declarations against Iranian plans were clear too and rejected Tehran's ambitions over the Gulf. This demonstrates once again that opposition to Shi'ah expansion in the region was encouraged by multiple parties.[94] Regrettably, the Sunni–Shi'ah struggle exists, and it is the key question even if various other tensions preoccupy elites.

Section IV: Appraisal of the First Two Years of the Uprisings

After more than two years, what are some of the preliminary observations one may draw about the Arab Spring, notwithstanding daily changes that will surely call for reappraisals?[95]

Starting from Tunisia and going through Libya and Egypt, the Arab Spring was a human cry that rose from the heart of communities that were personified by Bu 'Azizi, even if the cry for emancipation was in the making for decades.[96] Its premise and logic were not factional, neither were these uprisings partisan or physical, but humane and holistic, whose causes and struggles intended to end oppression and secure freedom. What was remarkable was how quickly Islamic movements, ranging the gamut from the al-Nahdah Party in Tunisia to the Muslim Brotherhood in Egypt to other fundamentalist movements like al-Qaʻidah and others, absconded youthful, liberal and visionary waves, and stole the very soul of the revolution. In fact, the domination of revolutionary movements under stringent religious criteria was relatively easy to do because fundamentalist organizations boasted a history of opposition—what they termed political struggle against authorities in their respective countries—and could garner public support with relative straightforwardness, which allowed them to promote their organizations.

This new image, but one that was merely a renewal for Islamic movements, was a warning for many to be vigilant. Questions arose as to whether Islamists were genuinely practicing openness or whether they simply gave lip service to the modernization process. It was not long before young revolutionaries discovered they confronted another form of dictatorship, except that this one boasted a religious cover. Several Islamic movements experienced difficulties in adapting to the new situation, especially when they confronted doctrinal, intellectual, political, and constitutional hurdles. Events in Egypt, where fierce opposition to the Muslim Brotherhood illustrated what nascent social forces expressed, rose to the surface as masses rejected puritanism that many perceived to be little more than a challenge for society anxious to turn the page, encourage socio-political ideas, artistic expression, and free media coverage, especially the unprecedented predicament of respecting other opinions.

Elsewhere in the Arab World, and led by the Gulf Cooperation Council, Saʻudi Arabia placed its political and military weight towards Yemen and Bahrain. Arab and international pressure managed to push President ʻAli ʻAbdallah Salih to step down in Sana'a, and for the Peninsula Shield forces to enter Manama to reduce tensions there. These steps were followed by gradual shifts to move from confrontation to dialogue in Bahrain and Yemen with the convocation of peace talks. In Libya and Syria, socio-sectarian vulnerabilities surfaced not only because of the political structures in those countries, but also because Iranian strategic interests compelled Tehran to intervene there, and for Moscow to offer its protection to Libya. Colonel Mu'ammar al-Qaddhafi, who lived in a utopian leadership world of his own-making, or as Henry Kissinger defined it in his memoirs, practiced a "prophetic leadership," fell on 20 October 2011. In Iraq, and as expressed by Prime Minister Nuri al-Maliki, the Shi'ah religious dimension played a great role too. Ironically, al-Maliki first accused the Syrian regime of supporting terrorism inside his country, though Iranian coercion forced him to back Damascus and facilitate the transfer of weapons and fighters from Iran to Syria through Iraq.

Events in Syria escalated too, and headed towards scary and dangerous levels for both the country as well as its neighbors, even for revolutionaries and supporters of the opposition. Let there be no doubts that the regime in Syria is ready to play all of its cards because this is the only available option it has on account of its minority-led philosophy. Damascus does not believe in a political solution to the war, because that would end the current security system in place which favors the 'Alawi minority community. When France and Britain announced their desire to arm opposition groups, followed by similar offers made by the League of Arab States, itself followed by the decision to declare the creation of a Government of Syria in liberated areas, all of these measures expanded the circle of violence, including a spillover of the fighting into Eastern Lebanon. Regrettably, weak and vulnerable areas in Northern Lebanon were unprepared for the war's spillover, as inhabitants did not estimate how the situation in Syria would dramatically reflect on them. This explains the evolution of the tragic situation in Arsal, for example, a predominantly Sunni town surrounded by Shi'ah villages along the border, where the liberal use of weapons transformed the confrontation from a mere conventional clash to one where bombers and rockets were relied upon. What followed was death and destruction, trapping inhabitants in impossible situation, caught between extremists and the Lebanese Army.

It is important to note the position of the United States on events in Syria, which seemed to be "subdued," at least in its early phases. According to Secretary of State John Kerry, Washington was ready to put pressure on the Syrian President to modify his position, and work with rebel groups towards a permanent solution. Nevertheless, it was clear from the onset that Israel shaped the American position in the area, which explained Washington's hesitation. First, because Israel is the natural leader of minority regimes throughout the region and, second, because Israel considers itself to be facing a complex of opponents—the Syrian regime and the Shi'ah, as well as its main enemy, Sunni Arabs. Clashes between Sunnis and Shi'ahs are in Israel's interests, because quarrels and collisions between its adversaries and enemies, which would exhaust both, is the ultimate objective. The Israeli position on Syria is not new, with the most accurate commentary offered by Ze'ev

Schiff, whose views echo loud and clear within political and military circles in Israel. In 2007, Schiff stated: "Despite everything, it is preferable to have Bashar al-Assad sitting in Damascus—rather than the Muslim Brotherhood."[97]

Every development in the Arab World leaves an echo in Lebanon. So how about if the events were uprisings, epochal changes, or a new Arab Spring with far reaching consequences that a small and vulnerable country can barely handle? Although Michel Chiha warned the Lebanese that their neighbors will not make them rest whether they enter the country or withdraw from it, Lebanon is a gallery for regional and international fretting, which becomes stronger when two profound issues collide: democratic gains that allow the Lebanese to confirm and sustain their historically expressed objectives throughout time, and an awareness of its natural affluence that transformed the country from having a functional role to one that enjoys "vital interests."

Whatever commitments exist to protect it, as expressed by the major powers led by the United States, the geographical proximity of various conflicts to the Land of the Cedars will continue to mean that efforts must be made to contain spillover effects. Lebanon will remain a central crisis point threatening regional and international peace and stability. It would be for supporters of Lebanon and those who believe in it, especially those who are working for peace and freedom within it, to save it from the clutches of neighbors and from some of its own utopian sons. The only solution to lingering Lebanese crises, which are a prime international affairs example concerning buffer-states, is to aim for a neutral status along the Austrian model. Proceeding from its geographical location, social pluralism, intellectual contributions, role in regional balance of power schemes, and place in defending international interests, all of these required awareness and action. In fact, British diplomacy foresaw these challenges nearly a century ago and developed a project to protect Lebanon as far back as 1919, proposing that the country become a nonaligned entity. That recommendation came on the eve of the declaration of the State of Greater Lebanon in 1920, though few heeded the call, which made repeated attention to the matter long overdue. This British diplomatic vision affirmed a credible option, and was even echoed by the historian Arnold Toynbee. At a 1957 Cenacle symposium in Beirut, Toynbee delivered a lecture titled "Lebanon: The Expression of History," during which he referred to an English poet [William Wordsworth] who lauded European resistance against Napoleon and his domination. The poet reflected that "Freedom around the World can have two voices: the voice of the mountain [meaning Switzerland], and the sound of the sea [meaning Britain]. Toynbee added: "In Lebanon, these two voices are challenged, because the history of Lebanon is the history of the people in the mountains alongside navigators . . . it is the history of liberty."[98]

Yes, the Lebanese mountain and its sea are not mere arenas, but represent the space of freedom. If such a country is to survive and endure, it needs to be governed by ideas, not illusions.

Jbayl, 2013.

5

A Major Strategic Project for Two Contenders in the Middle East: Iran and Sa'udi Arabia

According to Henry Kissinger, the power "that dominates the Middle Continent [which is the Muslim belt that stretches from Indonesia to Morocco], controls the world" and whoever rules over the Middle East controls the Middle Continent. In turn, the power that sways influence over the Arabian Gulf leads the Middle East.

This tri-dimensional equation makes the Arabian Gulf region the hottest location in ongoing political, economic, ideological, religious, financial and oil-related conflicts anywhere in the world. Hence the need, even the duty, to carry out a geopolitical and strategic survey, to identify the fundamental regional and international forces that matter in the area, in particular focusing on two leading actors: Iran and its geopolitical Shi'ah axis, and Sa'udi Arabia as the central power that aims to adopt a strategy of moderation to lead the Arab-Muslim World.

There are many reasons why it is necessary to embark on such an analysis, including the obligation to identify national Arab and Muslim interests. For in today's world it is no longer permissible for a leader with governance duties to adopt emotional, impulsive or even utopian standards to determine political choices to reach national security decisions. Moreover, it is no longer acceptable to simply talk about politics and diplomacy in isolation, away from strategy. This means that there is a requirement to rationalize political actions in terms of features, options, strategies and tactics based on rationality, logic, and the ability to lead the course of history towards a specific goal, all done within a clear vision. The ultimate goal of these political battles is the supreme interest of the state, to achieve internal as well as external stability, protect national sovereignty, develop the country's resources, increase its economic wealth, defend its religious and ideological beliefs, maintain and enhance national culture, and commit to the principles of peace.

Therefore, and no matter the degree of political awareness, no official in any country can achieve strategic goals along the seven constituents identified above—all for the ultimate objective of defending the nation's supreme interests—without devising specific mechanisms that would facilitate various initiatives and steps. Hence the reliance on research centers, which in developed countries conduct dispassionate studies and formulate national visions, precisely to handle such complex tasks. Their findings may be different from what leaders believe, or even wish for, though sound analyses allow one to design and achieve the best ways to reach clearly identified goals. In short, states that lack strategic visions will be more prone than others to fall into errors, which will impose heavy economic burdens and, far more important, create security dilemmas.

The Middle East region in general, and the Gulf area in particular, are in dire need for a geopolitical study of rivalries, disputes, and conflicts between competing forces that aim "to control this geographical region, its populations and wealth," as a prelude to determine its security and the destiny of its inhabitants. It is now increasingly clear that Iran has aspirations and ambitions of an ideological and religious nature, whose dimensions include a Shi'ah expression of a specific strategy to gain full control of the Gulf and the Middle East, perhaps to even extend its reach over the entire Muslim World. Tehran uses all ways and tactical means to reach these objectives, at the forefront of which is the incredible tool of the Shi'ah Crescent, which stretches from Iran through Iraq and the alliance with the Syrian regime all the way to link-up to Hizballah in Lebanon, which is a faction of the Iranian Revolution. Recently the Huthis have been exploited in Yemen and the Shi'ahs in Bahrain.

Against this reality, the Kingdom of Sa'udi Arabia has a key role to play in terms of the best way to address Tehran's aspirations and ambitions, if for no other reason than to preserve the faith of true Sunnis first, and in defense of the interests, wealth and the sovereignties of Arab countries second. Moreover, Riyadh is called upon to preserve the security of the Gulf States, ward off the exploitation of their Shi'ah minority populations, enhance commitments to achieve prosperity and stability for the peoples of the region, and establish regional security and international peace.

Inasmuch as the convergence of these geopolitical confrontations impose two indivisible commands on Iran and Sa'udi Arabia, it is fair to ask what are the most pressing concerns? To better answer this question, an analyst is bound to observe two general rules. First, to provide a complete and accurate study of the two opposing sides across the Gulf in all arenas of confrontation, including current geographical, historical, religious, ideological, political, sociological and cultural features, as well as an examinations of economic issues, the creation of wealth, existing and putative alliances both of the political and military varieties, without neglecting the conditions that affect minorities and partisan ties along various axes. Second, there is a need to logically explain Iranian approaches, both at the strategic and tactical levels, because Tehran is the initiator of multi-pronged attacks, playing a multi-faceted game. For against the strategic vision of the Kingdom of Sa'udi Arabia, Iran routinely supports contrary initiatives, while it simultaneously works to guarantee their failures. It does this as a prelude to victory throughout the entire region, which remains an unabashed goal, notwithstanding its relatively weak diplomatic prowess.

It is thus possible to summarize the ongoing conflict between Ruhallah Khumayni's Iran, with its *wilayat al-faqih* mandate, and Sa'udi Arabia's farsightedness, whose nearly symbolic demonstration of endurance says it all, in the following way. That Iran, which relies on its imperial heritage and Shi'ah revolution, is engaged in an effort to remove Sa'udi Arabia from its position as a central power in Islam, in the Gulf region, and the Arab and Muslim worlds. By doing so, Tehran hopes to replace Riyadh as the central entity in the faith; this aim is not a mere idea and should be taken seriously. That is why it is necessary for Sa'udi Arabia to offer an appropriate response to this serious and fateful challenge. Indeed, recent activities justify diligent attempts regarding the "Grand Strategy on the Middle East" project, because it will be the strongest and most effective Sa'udi weapon in the inevitable future confrontation. That effort is the embodiment of the motto: "To prevail, one must persuade."[99]

═══ ❖ ═══

The Geopolitics of Iran: A Strategic Reference Point in the Shi'ah Axis

In this précis, it is important to once again ask what is geopolitics, and why it is critical to understand the concept before we proceed. As discussed above, geopolitics is the modern political thought process in the study of international relations, including differences amongst nations, which is based on effective strategies. The Middle East is important because of its location and the types of regimes that rule there. In the Arabian Gulf region, geopolitics gains value because of its global position and because the Gulf is no longer exclusively Persian when that empire ruled with impunity. Naturally, the area's geography stands out as it sits along vital resources for most of the world, which also means that its security, in terms of who guards the interests of the world, are crucial.

For the Islamic Republic of Iran, an enhanced geopolitical reading is at play too, including the fact that Tehran applies a geographical justification (in terms of its physical presence through the entire northern part of the Gulf), along with an ideological emphasis that highlights geography and history, and which is best illustrated by its insistence that the body of water that separates it from the Arabian Peninsula is the "Persian Gulf," and not the "Arabian Gulf." There is also a wealth factor that oils the Shi'ah engine through demography, money, and strategic location. In addition, Tehran relies on its heritage and its dynamic, radical ideology, especially against Israel—and the West in general—as points of strength. Towards that end, the country focuses on militarization and the acquisition of advanced weapons, including a nuclear capability with effective delivery systems ranging from missiles to bombers. In short, Iran's geopolitical reading may be best summarized by its ambitions to emerge as an effective regional power, capable of demanding and receiving global deference.

Under the circumstances, what then is Iranian strategy? At least four components may be identified to better answer this question: First, Tehran harbors an overall objective, which is to control the Gulf and the Middle East in general as a preamble to dominate the entire Muslim World. This logic must be understood in the context of a dual stratagem based on (1) the establishment of a "rejectionist front" against Israel, the United States and the West that, in reality and for objective historical reasons, is a mere feud rather than an avowed enmity, and (2) on the establishment of a "Shi'ah Axis" that proposes to defend the rights, interests and aspirations of Shi'ah minority populations throughout the region, ranging from governments and systems, as in Iraq and Syria, to parties like Hizballah in Lebanon. Second, Iranian strategy is based on a specific religious dimension, which combines Shi'ism with Iranization. Third, the regime's outlook has a political dimension too, which has several sub-divisions, including a key oil policy, a tendency for opposition figures to define independence, and a view to secure a dominant position within the international community. Fourth is the country's search for a sound military capability composed of a strike force as well as an ideologically motivated army that aims to handle nuclear weapons, missile delivery systems, and the capacity to take advantage of its strategic location near the Straits of Hormuz, which can be blocked at will if Iran so decides. It further aims to deploy troops on the three occupied islands of Abu Musa, the Greater Tunb, and the Lesser Tunb at the entrance to the Straits, ostensibly to protect its perceived national security interests.

How would Iran go about to apply its strategies and what kind of tactics would it adopt? At least seven separate options are available to Iranian leaders, led by a continued orientation that started with imperial Iran under the reign of Shah Muhammad Riza Pahlavi, and that persisted with the Islamic Republic under the Imam Khumayni. Iran can also rely on the direct use of violence, as was the case with the attack on the Makkah Grand Mosque in 1987, events that were repeated in both the Kingdom of Sa'udi Arabia and elsewhere on several occasions since then.[100] A third option is to exploit Shi'ah minority populations throughout the Middle East and the world at large, today visible in the alliance between Iran and the Syrian 'Alawi regime; the establishment of an Iranian faction known as Hizballah along Israel's border in Lebanon; the aspiration to gain control and, if possible, grab power in Bahrain; a mobilization of supporters in the Hasah region in eastern Sa'udi Arabia to occupy and weaken the Kingdom from within because Riyadh stands as Iran's principal challenger in the Gulf, the Middle East, and the Muslim world, all under the guise of protecting its "holy cities"; and elsewhere among the Arab Gulf countries, in the United Arab Emirates and Kuwait in particular, through the mobilization of fifth columnists as well as in Yemen by backing the Huthi movement. A fourth available tool to Tehran is the exploitation of the Palestinian cause by celebrating "Jerusalem Day," creating the Quds [Qods] Force, a refusal to recognize Israel, even going so far as propagating the slogan that "Israel must be wiped off the map."[101] A fifth capability is its readiness to use financial resources to advance political goals. A sixth is to rely on the carrot and stick approach to promote religious/political Shi'ah doctrines in mosques and husayniyyahs.[102] Finally, Iran can also direct various media outlets, like the *Al-Manar* and *Al-Mayadin* television stations in Lebanon or *Al-'Alam* beaming out of Iran, to reach audiences beyond its local constituencies.[103]

Khumayni's revolution must also be assessed in light of the history of Iran and Islam. In fact, the Islamic government maintains/gives the impression that it is an exemplar of divine judgment, while its ideology is Iranian-Shi'ah. Of course, this means that the mullahs are in power, which makes Iran a Mullah-state. How it addresses the fate of minorities, especially minority Sunnis inside Iran, becomes important too, especially since Iranian society has a legacy of anguish over this matter, which dates back to the time of the Safavids, and was sharpened under the Pahlavis, fearful of outside interference or invasions.[104] Iranian intentions expanded under the Pahlavis, again with the goal of regional domination, best illustrated in the crises over Bahrain, the Shatt al-Arab, the three Emirati islands, the Dhuffar War in Oman, and the fate that befell the Huthis in Yemen, all of which confirm that these policies have not changed but expanded over time. In fact, it is fair to say that Iranian objectives extended dramatically after Tehran became the "Policeman of the Gulf," which imperial and revolutionary leaders alike used to spring the country to become the Middle East and global reference point as the Shi'ah center of authority. Iran nurtured its nationalist agenda and transformed it into a religious-political-global phenomenon.[105]

The seventh component of Iranian strategy hovers around the country's determinants and borders. These can also be separated into several modules. There is, first, the perception of geographic vulnerability, since 15 countries ring Iran.[106] Second is the demographic impasse, because only 15% of all Muslims worldwide are Shi'ahs whereas 85% are Sunnis, even if the percentages are 30–70% in the Middle East (demographics play a prominent role in the destinies of peoples and nations especially in the Middle East.) Third is the ideological difference which must reconcile the irreconcilable. In other words, the Iranian/Islamist/Shi'ah/revolutionary/fundamentalist/demographic factor, which is presented in the framework of the will of God and not through the will of the people, must justify the guardianship of the Iranian Revolution. Fourth are the historical risks involved given that the Iranian Shi'ah experience lurches between violence and responsibility, and because there is a tendency to rely on prophetic dimensions among leaders who develop and espouse Shi'ah ideology. Fifth, Iran must come to terms with four border determinants, including transcending international frontiers, expanding its strategic boundaries, confirming the limits of its influence, and improving the parameters of its interests. Sixth, Iranian policy must also balance between facts and fantasies, as best illustrated by former President Mahmud Ahmadinajad whose numerous threats and childish calls for violence were in the end not taken seriously by international players. This must be weighed alongside the defense of freedom and responsibility, not just the resort to violence to right wrongs, precisely to save human dignity and see to it that the philosophy of resistance has a purpose. Finally, if Iran is to be a reference point, it is fair to ask, for whom? Is it only to affiliate the sectarian Shi'ah agenda in the Shi'ite Crescent or does it also serve the geopolitical interests of other peoples in the Middle East? In other words, is Iran interested in the legitimate interests of Shi'ah minorities, and not those of others, including other states? Is the strategy based on sectarian factionalism, away from either a national, or even a human affiliation?

In short, Iran has been, still plans, and continues to hope through its various extensions in the Shi'ah Crescent from Iran to Southern Lebanon and across Shi'ah minorities around the world, to rewrite history. It hopes to play a role similar to what Saladin enjoyed against the Shi'ah Fatimid Empire in the twelfth century, which aimed to upset the existing parity in the Muslim world and transfer control from Sunnism to Shi'ism and from a state of defeat for Sunnis to the *wilayat al-faqih*.[107] As the historic Saladin victory over the Fatimids demonstrated, Sunni regimes returned to power in various parts of the Muslim world. Iran today is trying by all means possible, and on the basis of a new historical leverage, namely the Palestinian Question, to do the impossible. By absconding the emotional Jerusalem issue more specifically, and by directly sponsoring Hizballah and the Huthis as advance units of the Islamic Revolutionary Guard, it hopes to create a new balance of power within the Muslim World. It works to take advantage of the existence of Israel and the tragic Palestinian Question as an Islamic issue par excellence. It wishes to thus build on existing anti-Western sentiments among many Muslim societies, including in Sa'udi Arabia, for that end. Still, the lesson taught by the history of Islam has been and continues to be the following: While "Shi'ahs were and are the most revolutionary in the history of Islam, they also were and are the first victims."[108]

The Geopolitics of the Kingdom of Sa'udi Arabia: A Centrist Strategy of Moderation to Lead the Arab-Muslim World

This précis looks at Sa'udi Arabia, which is caught between polarization and various geopolitical targets within the Great Game that is under way in the Middle East and around the world.

How can we determine the geopolitics of the Kingdom of Sa'udi Arabia? Naturally, by first examining its geographical configuration, a large country with vast open borders located in a sensitive part of the globe. We must also take into account its demographic evolution and we must assess its importance, which includes a unique religious heritage as it hosts the key holy cities of Makkah and Madinah. In addition, the Kingdom is endowed with material wealth through oil and gas; vast financial resources through its petro-dollars; a significant geo-regional fortune due to its access to both the Arabian Gulf and the Red Sea; and a hugely valuable geo-strategic capital due to its central location between Asia and the Arab World.

Equally important is Sa'udi Arabia's centralism in the sense that the country must address tensions that arise from the key role it plays as the largest and most important regional power to lead the Arab-Muslim World. To be sure, its location grants it undeniable influence, and while it is protected by vast desert stretches of sands and vibrant oases, it must come to term with certain realities that concentrate on decentralized centers of authority in the Sunni world. Moreover, and even when backed by a unique tribal composition, empowered by family loyalties and with relatively limited sectarian problems, the Kingdom was in the past beholden to large powers like Britain, and more recently the United States, and must deal with worldwide fundamentalist forces between Sunnis and Shi'ahs that upset internal harmony.

Despite all of this, the pioneering role that the founder of the Kingdom, 'Abdul 'Aziz bin 'Abdul Rahman Al Sa'ud played, ushered in unparalleled prosperity for its people, boosted the ruling family, strengthened the power of the state, and equipped the country with political and security institutions. It also focused on the nation as a nation-state, and balanced that with the centrality of the *Ummah*, which is the Muslim concept of nation par excellence.

Sa'udi Arabia further enjoys being the power that promotes the central notion that Islam equals moderation, in the full meaning of the word, and that temperance stands against radical Islamic movements, both Sunni and Shi'ah. This "centralism" is a vital component of intermediate religious, cultural, political, social and economic stability, which encourages moderation and dialogue among religions and cultures. Sa'udi Arabia is precisely that intermediate state because of where it is located, its protection and promotion of religion, as well as various policies and practices that concentrate on the welfare of the nation. The Kingdom is thus the entity that opens the door of moderate jurisprudence along the model of the al-Azhar religious institution that issues vital opinions, something that successive rulers emphasized, and which can no longer be in doubt even if foes point to strict interpretations issued by clerics anxious to impose local cultural norms on a rapidly evolving society.

Under the circumstances, Sa'udi–Iranian relations offer unique geo-strategic perspectives which may include eight different aspects over which the two sides differ and will continue to struggle: a comprehensive and fateful conflict over religion and ideology with the geo-strategic goal to lead the entire Muslim world; a direct confrontation zone in the Arabian Gulf where the Cooperation Council for the Arab States of the Gulf (GCC) plays a key role; a symbolic clash over Jerusalem as a catalyst to provoke Muslim sentiments; the means to mobilize Shi'ah minorities especially in the eastern Hasah region of the Kingdom and with the Huthis in Yemen; the security of the Gulf region in terms of which party threatens the other and which one preserves it to fulfill global security obligations; over Iraq as a "buffer" or "barrier-state" between Sa'udi Arabia and Iran, which witnessed a bloody war between 1980 and 1988; over the repercussions of the Syrian–Iranian axis on Sa'udi Arabia, its ties with both countries and, by extension, on Lebanon; and on Egypt as a strategic depth to Sa'udi Arabia, in terms of religiosity and, geopolitically, as part of the Sunni Arc framework to counter the Shi'ah Crescent.

There are three other critical components to Saudi strategy that need elaboration, including ties with the United States, its principled responses when challenged, and its historical destiny. Each of these merits detailed attention to further illustrate the direction followed by the Al Sa'ud.

While relations with the United States began in earnest in the 1940s and grew exponentially ever since, and no matter how many unpalatable some of the concerns that preoccupied both sides appeared to be, higher strategic interests—oil for security—brought the two sides together. Naturally, relations included determinants and limits, though the Kingdom represented vital strategic interests for the major powers, especially the United States. Towards that end, large companies like Aramco and critical organizations like OPEC reached major decisions over oil production and prices, which meant that the country confronted a permanent test of independence. In fact, the Kingdom's energy resources and the fate of civilizations and nations in the twenty-first century, depended on it, even if Sa'udi-American ties had a negative aspect because of the U.S. commitments to Israel.[109]

According to the British historian Arnold Toynbee, the Kingdom's principled responses when challenged demonstrated a great deal of responsibility. Toynbee highlighted how the State of Israel and the Zionist movement affected Sa'udi Arabia, though he also pointed to other concerns, including the role of Shi'ah minorities, the repercussions of foreign fundamentalist organizations, the presence of foreign labor, the role that OPEC played to manage the international balance of energy resources, desertification, water scarcity, the dangers associated with mass lethal weaponry, the demographic problem, democracy and political reforms. How the proliferation of these principled responses fit in

Sa'udi Arabia's historical destiny is critical to understanding its current standing. In fact, there is a correlation between centralism and moderation even if many dismiss the consequences of various positions taken by Riyadh. Sa'udi officials are required to possess the highest level of political awareness at all levels and in all public institutions that affect family affiliations, psychological and cultural affinities, ideological obligations, and their authoritarian positions to advance the Kingdom's interests. They are obligated to promote the transition from restricted Arabism to civilized Arabism in the twenty-first century. They are called upon to address the role of women in society, moving from a position of weakness to one of strength, which links Islam with life. Equally important, the rationalized spending and commitments to the future need to be analyzed within existing and projected economic conditions, all to better serve the nation.

Far more critical is the necessary renewal of Sunni Islam, especially Wahhabi interpretations in light of the moderation espoused by Al-Azhar in the person of Shaykh Ahmad Al Tayyib. Independent reasoning [*ijtihad*] must also evolve for a thorough exertion of a jurist's mental faculties to find solutions to legal questions and to encourage religious authorities to perform due diligence responsibilities. Indeed, the necessity for religious coordination with Al-Azhar authorities has never been this important, both to approach issues of concern to the Muslim World from a relatively sound position, and to deal with contemporary challenges upfront. For Islam and modernity, the renewal of human society, and the development of a pluralistic democratic society, can no longer be separated and must all be tackled in unison.

It is also important to touch upon the Kingdom's historical and cultural legacies as decision levers to determine the fate that may befall the country. This requires fresh attention to higher education as confirmed by a recent UNESCO report, which declared that access to higher education will decide the fate of countries in the twenty-first century.[110] In other words, Sa'udi Arabia will require universities and advanced research centers, not only intelligence services, to survive and prosper.

In short, there is no country in the world except Sa'udi Arabia where core global interests are connected with local strategies. Any threat to these strategies will have the gravest of consequences to international security and the interests of many countries. Riyadh is the leading oil power and holds one of the world's largest reserves; at the present time (2016) Sa'udi Arabia is the leader in production and exports, and this is likely to last for some time. This means that the Kingdom will remain vulnerable to regional and international interactions, if for no other reason than for being the proprietor of this most expensive strategic wealth. In fact, such a delicate, difficult, and dangerous situation demands from Sa'udi officials, and the Sa'udi people, to remain permanently vigilant and to possess the adequate awareness and appropriate means to respond to all of the threats, risks and challenges that the Kingdom faces. This will not happen unless a comprehensive strategy is developed, stemming from the country's geopolitical position based on facts, not on perceptions or fallacies. To achieve its higher national interests, Riyadh must take into account the interests of the international community in development matters, stability and peace concerns too. Regrettably, such a strategy does not exist today, not at the required level or indeed at any level for that matter. Yet, it is only through such an approach that the country will be able to confront various challenges, and introduce practical strategic formulations.

8 May 2012

CHAPTER

6

Concluding Remarks

Whether being a former secondary school teacher, university professor, journalist, writer, as well as a geopolitical analyst equips one with the skills to deliver or share original and clear ideas, are best determined by others. In this study, and away from tangential narratives, the reader is presented with specific interpretations though this Conclusion offers eight key observations.

First, many will be surprised by the book's title since they believe that the opposite is true. Sunnis, in their view, judging from some of the practices fundamentalist movements engage in, are the aggressors and not the targeted parties. Those who think that Sunnis are the belligerents do not realize that what is underway around us is the result of what Sunnis face worldwide on several fronts: religious, cultural, social and political assaults against Sunni Muslims. Simply stated, Sunnis are in a confrontation with America and all of Europe, with Shi'ah Iran and its acolytes, even with Buddhist China and Hindu India. In other words, more than two-thirds of the world's population harbors ill-will towards them, because Sunnis make up the largest compact bloc, and have, like other major religious forces, a geopolitical project to assert themselves.

Second, and after the collapse of Marxism and other nationalist ideologies, the major global crisis today is how to best rationalize, actualize, and update religiously motivated thoughts in both Islam and Christianity. It may appear odd to advance such a claim but the rise of Muslim and Christian fundamentalisms are accurate truths, even if these experiences are difficult to identify and accept. Indeed, we are all confronted by cultural, religious and political challenges, which require commitments to logic and authentic history, not to basic instincts or depressing emotions that every "fundamentalism" promotes.

Third, a revolution that is supported by those who seek change is an existential cause, because what is at stake today is a matter of life and death for millions if not billions. Moreover, what is important in any revolution is not the violence that it frequently generates but responsibility, both towards oneself and towards others. For in the end, responsibility means freedom that, in the words of the Jesuit clergyman Bulus [Paul] Noya, must be weighed between the "violence that is a manifestation of juvenile behavior, which rests deep in our souls," and liberty.[111]

Fourth, the revival or updating process required for thoughtful conversations about religion, culture, and other concerns that preoccupy many, fall under the broad headline of modernization. According to Mohammed Arkoun, "Modernization is an expression of holistic strategy that is followed by logic to control all areas of existence, knowledge and practice by subjecting them to valid or invalid standards. It is understood that these standards increase in rigidity, accuracy and flexibility to understand matching and accurate realities. Therefore, we cannot take only a part of modernization and leave the rest."[112]

Fifth, we will take from Mohammed Arkoun, a model of modernization that is the most accurate and, perhaps, the most important, in Islamic ideology. That is the concept of unity, the state's centers of power, and citizenship. This conceptual understanding of unity in Islam is based on the historical idea around the oneness of God, the revelation of the ruling power, state authorities, their values, systems and lifestyles. In fact, unity is the moral peak in Islam, whereas freedom is the equivalent pinnacle within Christianity. Arkoun says: "Arabs and Muslims have always thought about the issue of the state through central monotheism [unity]. No Arab or Muslim political leader considered [or considers] the view that the state could be a political solution to the problems of multiculturalism in civil society. Even if one acknowledges that diversity and pluralism are not opposed to solidarity and unity, but act as their tonic, there is no denying that they make unity look more realistic and more humane."[113]

Sixth, the worst option is the option of the alliance of minorities in the face of the Sunni Arab majority, since that is little more than a project for future massacres. The best option is the option that tames conflicts and works towards the establishment of historical understandings between minorities and the majority. Under such a scheme, solutions would benefit both sides, which will appeal to reason, ensure the exclusion of violence, and affirm the commitment to the interests of the community, not the interests of those foreign powers seeking to weaken Muslims by fomenting discord amongst them. For while the interests of international entities could benefit from Sunni–Shi'ah clashes, perhaps even to distort their respective images and ruin existing reputations (because—this logic assumes—fundamentalist movements can only be involved in barbaric practices), such efforts do not advance the cause of peace.

Seventh, extremist and separatist movements who defend what they believe are the freedoms of the community and its identity, are often led by fanatics who embark on religious and doctrinal adventures that imperil the nation. To be sure, radical currents that are led by leaders who consider their dependency and loss of identity as the worst things that could befall them, confront a double-edged sword. In light of the historical experiences that everyone in the Muslim World endured for decades, and which many are experiencing today, it is clear that practical, historical, relevant, and purposeful steps are required to support an alternative. The time is long overdue for a third movement, one that backs the stream of moderation, which will be the sole guarantor that can ensure freedom and protect genuine interests.

Finally, and as espoused as early as the 1990s, I was one of the first who called for the establishment of an international organization along the lines of a "World Foundation for Muslim–Christian Dialogue," headquartered in Lebanon. This must now be expanded to include "Muslim–Muslim dialogue on account of Sunni–Shi'ah clashes. Such an institution would invite Christian and Muslim intellectuals, perhaps with permanent links to the Al-Azhar University in Egypt and to Qom seminaries in Iran and elsewhere, to pre-empt any crises that might affect Christian–Muslim and Sunni–Shi'ah relations. Its basic mandate would be to leave an effective impact on the region and the world by lowering tensions. It would function according to the messages incorporated in the Azhar documents reproduced in the appendices of this book, to fight against sectarian tendencies and fanaticisms, highlight the spirit of civility, create permanent dialogue between Muslims and Christians, and disseminate updated visions in the two religions and their various sects. It could embark on countless endeavors by unleashing the talents of diligent scholars of Islam and Christianity. All this within the context of deep respect because what unites the two religions are far greater than what separates them. Tomorrow will not be secure except through the dialogue of civilizations, and the dialogue of civilizations will not succeed save for interchanges between and among religions. Al-Azhar, Qom, and the Vatican are thus invited to carry out this historic mission, to confront the most dangerous crises that Christians and Muslims face today.

Islam and Democracy[114]

Islam has five reservations about democracy:
1. Its laws are divine not human-made.
2. The ruler is God and not humanity.
3. Citizenship does not enable equality among all citizens in an Islamic state because non-Muslims are only "protected people" [*dhimmis*]. This is why Islamist movements oppose civil right bills.
4. The power of the ruler (or the authority who prevailed through conquest) imposes obedience even if the ruler is a despot, from outside the realm, or whose governance goes against the majority.
5. Unity is the basis of Islamic ideology, or what Mohammed Arkoun labeled "Central Oneness" [*Le centrisme unificateur*], not the deed of any Arab or Muslim political leader who promotes pluralism associated with the majority.

The uneasiness of democracy is due to two matters:

1. Because Western colonialism is a manufacturer, holder and protector of democracy, which is a product of Western Christian civilization; and
2. Because democracy is tied to secularism, which contradicts understandings between "religion and state" in Islam, and which present real challenges to believers.

Notes to *Targeting Sunnis*

1   *Al-'Amal*, 11, 18, 25 April 1982 and 16 May 1982.
2   Friedrich Ratzel was born on 30 August 1844 in Karlsruhe, Germany, and was the first thinker to use the term *Lebensraum* [living space], which was adopted by the National Socialist Party after the First World War. Ratzel studied the classics in Switzerland and was destined to the life of an apothecary though an interest in zoology led him to publish, in 1869, an essay on Darwin under the title *Sein und Werden der organischen Welt* [Nature and Development of the Organic World]. An avid traveller, he visited several Mediterranean spots as his curiosity in geography began to form his intellect, which changed his life. Letters home to family, friends and acquaintances describing his numerous travel experiences led to a position as a roving reporter for the *Kölniösche Zeitung* [Cologne Journal], which led to fresh opportunities. Ratzel then embarked on several expeditions, the lengthiest and most important being his 1874–1875 trip to North America, Cuba, and Mexico. It was during this trip that Ratzel developed

an interest to study the influence of people of German origin in the United States and to contrast them with those of other prominent ethnic groups. He produced a written work of his account in 1876, *Städte-und Kulturbilder aus Nordamerika* [Profile of Cities and Cultures in North America], which established the field of cultural geography.

When he returned to Germany in 1875, he accepted the position of lecturer in geography at the Technical High School in Munich and, in 1880, was promoted to full professor. As an academic, he produced several more tomes, and in 1886 accepted an appointment at Leipzig where his lectures were widely attended. He published his opus *Politische Geographie* [Political Geography] in 1897, in which Ratzel introduced concepts that contributed to *Lebensraum* and Social Darwinism. He lived in Leipzig until his sudden death on 9 August 1904 in Ammerland, Germany.

Although his writings justified imperialism, it is important to note that he was mostly influenced by the West Point, New York-born American Navy admiral, Alfred Thayer Mahan, a man often called "the most important American strategist of the nineteenth century" on account of his vision for "sea power" as a game-changer in global affairs. Long before the field of geostrategy was defined, Mahan inspired Ratzel to aspire for a German naval reach not only to impose one's power but also sustain profitable trade activities. What Ratzel added to Mahan's vision was the contribution that *geopolitik* was the expansion on the biological conception of geography, without a static conception of borders. For Ratzel as for Mahan, borders represented temporary lines in the growth of powerful states, where land represented critical bonds for inhabitants who drew sustenance from it. As nations expanded their wealth, their borders shrank, though Ratzel perceived *lebensraum* as a nationalist goal not necessarily as a political objective. The concept banked on cultural superiority, where weaker nations supported stronger ones, and where the latter spread some of their culture to others. This, Ratzel believed, ought not be practiced aggressively, but simply be allowed to take root as part of a natural expansion of strong nations into areas controlled by weaker ones.

English-language readers may avail themselves to an annotated translation of several of Ratzel's works in Ellen Churchill Semple, *Influences of Geographic Environment, on the Basis of Ratzel's System of Anthropo-Geography*, Los Angeles: HardPress Publishing, 2013. For a translation in French, see Friedrich Ratzel, *La geographie politique: Les concepts fondamentaux*, translated by Francois Ewald, Paris: Fayard, 1987.

3 Nabil Khalifé, "Thawrat al-Imam Khumayni 'ala Daw' Tarikh Iran al-Mu'asir wal-Falsafat al-Siyasiyyah lil-Islam" [Imam Khumayni's Revolution in Light of Iran's Contemporary History and the Political Philosophy of Islam], *Al-Mustaqbal* (Paris), Number 108, 17 March 1979, pp. 57–68.

4 Nabil Khalifé, "Geopolitik al-'Alam al-Islami wa-Strategiyyat al-Fitna"

[The Geopolitics of the Muslim World and the Strategy of Sedition," *Yawmiyyat*, Volume 2, 1995, pp. 11–21.

5 Da'ish [Daesh] is the Arabic acronym for *Al-Dawlah al-Islamiyyah fil-Iraq wal-Sham* or Islamic State for Iraq and Syria (ISIS), sometimes also referred to as ISIL, or the Islamic State for Iraq and the Levant. It rebranded itself into the Islamic State (IS) in June 2014, even if it is neither. See Faisal Irshaid, "ISIS, ISIL, IS or Daesh? One Group, Many Names," *BBC*, 2 December 2015, at http://www.bbc.com/news/world-middle-east-27994277.

Prince Turki al-Faisal, the former head of Saudi intelligence and the former ambassador to the United Kingdom and the United States, who became the chairman of the King Faisal Centre for Research and Islamic Studies in Riyadh, proposed the name Da'ish be changed to *Fa'ish* [or Faesh] as the word is derived from an Arabic name meaning obscene. The editorial appeared in both Arabic and English and was widely distributed. See Turki al-Faisal, "Opinion: A New Name for ISIS," *Al-Sharq Al-Awsat*, 15 January 2015, at http://english.aawsat.com/2015/01/article55340407/opinion-a-new-name-for-isis [the Arabic version was published on 13 January 2015].

6 Yves Lacoste, *Géopolitique: La longue histoire d'aujourd'hui*, Paris: Larousse, 2012, p. 183. In 1970, Lacoste published a critical volume that earned him both scorn as well as admiration, even if academicians were shocked by its contents. See Yves Lacoste, *La géographie, ça sert d'abord à faire la guerre* [Geography is First Used to Make War], Paris: Maspero, 1976.

7 Bernard Lewis, *What Went Wrong?: Western Impact and Middle Eastern Response*, New York: Oxford University Press, 2001. See also Lewis' equally polemical *The Crisis of Islam: Holy War and Unholy Terror*, New York: Modern Library, 2003.

8 According to the U.S. Energy Information Administration, Iraqi proven reserves stood at 144 billion barrels in 2015, although there are many rumors that actual holdings may be far larger. A 2010 publication raised the ante considerably, claiming that actual holdings were probably higher than any other country. Newspaper accounts advanced huge figures, ranging the gamut from 200 to 380 billion barrels. Several authors speculated that the holdings topped the 300 billion figure. See U.S. Energy Information Administration, *International Energy Statistics 2015*, at http://www.eia.gov/cfapps/ipdbproject/iedindex3.cfm?tid=5&pid=57&aid=6&cid=r5,&syid=2011&eyid=2015&unit=BB; Fadhil J. Chalabi and Thamir Iqaili, *Hydrocarbon Exploration and Field Development in Iraq*, London: Centre for Global Energy Studies, 2010; and "Iraq has 'more crude oil' than Saudi Arabia," Emirates 24/7, 29 February 2008, as reproduced by Free Republic at http://www.freerepublic.com/focus/f-news/1978413/posts. See also Iain A. Boal, T. J. Clark, Joseph Matthews, and Michael Watts, *Afflicted Powers: Capital and Spectacle in a New Age of War*, London and New York: Verso, 2005, p. 46.

9   Lacoste, *Géopolitique: La longue histoire d'aujourd'hui*, p. 312. The original quote in French reads as follows: "Avec, de surcroît, la richesse du pétrole, ce don de Dieu, et avec une telle masse de croyants convaincus de la supériorité de leur religion, comment l'*umma*, proclament-ils, ne deviendrait-elle pas, si les fidèles sont unis, le foyer des progrès et le centre géopolitique qui influencera l'humanité tour entière?"

10   First published in 1973, *The Static and the Dynamic* is a four-volume study that describes creativity in Arabic poetry that, Adonis maintains, includes both conservative and innovative trends. The history of Arabic poetry, he posits, "has been that of the conservative vision of literature and society (*al-thabit*), quelling poetic experimentation and philosophical and religious ideas (*al-mutahawil*)." The static (*al-thabit*) manifests itself in the triumph of conveyance (*naql*) over original or independent thought (*'aql*), in the attempt to make literature a servant of religion, and in the reverence accorded to the past whereby language and poetics are essentially Qur'anic in their sources, and therefore not subject to change. In his reevaluation of Arabic literature, Adonis concluded that writers preferred the static and unmoving, arguing for particularity (*khususiyyah*) because each nation and region opted to valorize separate cultural attributes instead of concentrating on Arab unity. For details, see Adonis, *Al-Thabit wal-Mutahawil* [The Static and the Dynamic], Beirut: Dar al-Saqi, 1978.

11   Time of *jihad* usually refers to the period when Islam was first revealed and spread throughout Arabia and the surrounding region, roughly from AD 622 to AD 1258, when the 'Abbasid Empire dissolved. *Jihad*, which is frequently used without a clear understanding of what it represented is, first and foremost, religious duty to maintain and spread the faith. The word *jihad* is a noun meaning the act of "striving, applying one-self, struggling, or persevering," while a *mujahid*, a person engaged in *jihad*, ought to "strive in the way of God (*al-jihad fi sabil Allah*). There allegedly are disagreements over the very definition of the term but this is largely overblown for political reasons. It is of course accurate to state that the term has several meanings, though the Qur'anic interpretation is the accurate one, which concentrates on the inner spiritual struggle, even if Muslims are also called upon to repel those to besmirch the faith or its believers. *Jihad* is often translated as "Holy War" but this view is attributed to Orientalists like Bernard Lewis who claims that "the overwhelming majority of classical theologians, jurists," and other specialists in the *hadith* "understood the obligation of *jihad* in a military sense." Since *hadith* sayings included many controversial topics at times of great turmoil, the more honest, and far more accurate interpretation was the one available in the Holy Scriptures. Moreover, even in classical Islam, the military form of *jihad* was carefully regulated to protect civilians, which contemporary terrorists disdain. See Bernard Lewis, *The Political Language of Islam*, Chicago: The University of Chicago Press, 1991, p. 72. See also John L. Esposito, *Unholy War: Terror in the Name of Islam*, New York: Oxford University Press, 2002, p. 26.

12 Bulus Noya, "Al-Thawrah Bayna Diyanat al-Ab wa Diyanat al-Ibn" [The Revolution Between the Religion of the Father and the Religion of the Son], *Mawaqif* [Lebanon] 1:3, June 1969, pp. 149–159, the quotation is on page 151.

13 Dhimmitude is a neologism borrowed from the French and popularized as a polemical term by writer Bat Ye'or [Gisèle Littman], an author of the history of religious minorities in the Muslim world. It was formed from *dhimmi*, by analogy with *servitude*, to draw an implicit comparison and describes the "specific social condition that resulted from *jihad*," as a "state of fear and insecurity" of "infidels" who are required to "accept a condition of humiliation." Of course, the term is both misleading and Islamophobic, which is not surprising. See Bat Ye'or, *The Decline of Eastern Christianity under Islam: From Jihad to Dhimmitude, Seventh-Twentieth Century*, Madison and Teaneck, New Jersey: Fairleigh Dickinson University Press, 1996. See also an excellent review of the book by Sidney H. Griffith in the *International Journal of Middle East Studies* 30: 4, November 1998, pp. 619–221.

14 The Fatimid Caliphate was a Shi'ah empire that spanned large parts of North Africa and ruled from Cairo between 909 and 1171. Khalifé also refers to the Rashidun Caliphate, which was the Islamic center of power in the earliest period of Islam, and which covered the first four caliphs— the "Rightly Guided" one, or the Rashidun. See Jamel A. Velji, *An Apocalyptic History of the Early Fatimid Empire*, Edinburgh, UK: Edinburgh University Press, 2016; and Hugh Kennedy, *The Prophet and the Age of the Caliphates: The Islamic Near East from the Sixth to the Eleventh Century*, New York: Longman, 2004.

15 Much has been written on the *wilayat al-faqih* [velayat-e faqih in Persian], which translates as the Guardianship of the Islamic Jurist, or the Governance of the Jurist or Jurisprudence of God. The *Encyclopedia Britannica* provides the following explanation: "The justification for Iran's mixed system of government can be found in the concept of velayet-e faqih, as expounded by Ayatollah Ruhollah Khomeini, the first leader of postrev-olutionary Iran. Khomeini's method gives political leadership—in the absence of the divinely inspired imam—to the faqih, or jurist in Islamic canon law, whose characteristics best qualify him to lead the community. Khomeini, the leader of the revolution (rahbar-e enqelab), was widely believed to be such a man, and through his authority the position of leader was enshrined in the Iranian constitution. The Assembly of Experts (Majles-e Khobregan), an institution composed of 'ulama', chooses the leader from among qualified Shiite clergy on the basis of the candidate's personal piety, expertise in Islamic law, and political acumen. The powers of the leader are extensive; he appoints the senior officers of the military and Revolutionary Guards (Pasdaran-e Enqelab), as well as the clerical members of the Council of Guardians (Shara-ye Negahban) and members of the judiciary. The leader is also exclusively responsible for declarations

of war and is the commander in chief of Iran's armed forces. Most important, the leader sets the general direction of the nation's policy. There are no limits on the leader's term in office, but the Assembly of Experts may remove the leader from office if they find that he is unable to execute his duties." See Encyclopedia Britannica, "Iran: Government and Society," at https://www.britannica.com/place/Iran/Government-and-society# ref783951.

16 Mohammed Arkoun was born on 1 February 1928 in Taurirt [Taourirt] Mimoum, Algeria, to a Berber family. After he earned a degree in literature in Algiers, Arkoun moved to France and graduated from the Sorbonne, earning a degree in Arabic language in 1956, followed by a doctorate in literature in 1968. One of the most influential secular scholars of Islamic studies in the twentieth century, Arkoun called for dramatic reforms, as he criticized those who rejected modernization, secularism and humanism. Although he wrote mostly in French and occasionally in English and Arabic, students and readers alike admired sharp insights that invited believers to rethink Islam in the contemporary world, to balance faith with theology and practice, in rapidly developing environments. Arkoun taught at several universities, including Lyon and Paris in France, and accepted visiting fellowships at Louvain, Belgium in 1977–1979, Los Angeles (UCLA in 1969), Princeton (1985, 1992–1993), Berlin (1986–1987 and 1990), Amsterdam (1991–1993), and the Vatican-sponsored Pontifical Institute of Arabic Studies in Rome in 1995–1996. He died in Paris on 14 September 2010 at the age of 82. Among his numerous books are, *Rethinking Islam: Common Questions, Uncommon Answers*, Boulder, Colorado: Westview Press, 1994; *L'immigration: défis et richesses*, Paris: Bayard, 1998, and *The Unthought in Contemporary Islamic Thought*, London: Saqi Books, 2002.

17 *Encyclopedia Universalis*, 1990 Supplement, p. 600.

18 Khalifé does not comment of the debate unleashed by Samuel Huntington in his Summer 1993 *Foreign Affairs* essay, which was expanded into a book, nor does he provide any insights on the debate that followed among various intellectuals. He assumes that the reader is broadly familiar with the concept and discussions that followed, although his focus is on the larger implications that a clash of civilizations may actually introduce. He is interested in Huntington's most famous statement, that "Islam has bloody borders," which confirms Khalifé's fears. See Samuel Huntington, "The Clash of Civilizations?," *Foreign Affairs* 72:3, Summer 1993, pp. 22–49, the quotation is on p. 35. See also, Samuel Huntington, *The Clash of Civilizations and the Remaking of World Order*, New York: Simon and Schuster, 1998. For several pertinent critics of the thesis, see Edward W. Said, "The Clash of Ignorance," *The Nation*, 4 October 2001, at https://www.thenation.com/article/clash-ignorance/; Nicolas Richter, "The Clash of Civilisations: Where Huntington Got It Wrong," *Qantara*, 10 October 2013, at https://en.qantara.de/print/17072; and James North,

"The Clash of Civilizations Theory is Absolutely and Completely Dead," *Mondoweiss: The World of Ideas in the Middle East*, 29 March 2014, at http://mondoweiss.net/2014/03/civilizations-absolutely-completely/.

19   Henry Kissinger drafted a highly controversial National Security Council Memorandum in 1974, NSSM-200, under the title "The Foundational Document on Population Control Issued by the United States Government," which famously claimed that food control was one of Washington's objectives. Although he is credited for declaring in 1970 that "control oil and you control nations; control food and you control the people," it is actually difficult to verify this attribution. See Barbara Peterson, "America's Silent Killing Fields," 24 March 2009, at https://survivingthemiddleclasscrash.wordpress.com/tag/kissinger/.

20   Arnold J. Toynbee is also a frequently quoted thinker, with his most famous saying regarding Islam being: "The extinction of race conscious-ness as between Muslims is one of the outstanding achievements of Islam, and in the contemporary world there is, as it happens, a crying need for the propagation of this Islamic virtue." See http://www. brainyquote. com/quotes/ quotes/a/arnoldjto201061.html. In a major book that includes a chapter titled "Islam, the West, and the future," the Englishman wrote that "Islam's creative gift to mankind is monotheism, and we surely dare not throw this gift away." He continued his discussion on Islam with the affirmation that the faith has "a mighty spiritual mission still to carry out," even if in the longer chapter devoted to the future, he underscores that "nationalism, and not Pan-Islamism, is the formation into which the Islamic peoples are falling; and [that] for the majority of Muslims an inevitable, though undesired, outcome of nationalism will be submergence in the cosmopolitan proletariat of the Western world." See Arnold J. Toynbee, *Civilization on Trial*, New York: Oxford University Press, 1948, pp. 87–88.

21   This is a very controversial topic that dates back decades but is always in the news. See, for example, Rhoda Ann Kanaaneh, *Birthing the Nation: Strategies of Palestinian Women in Israel*, Berkeley, California Series in Public Anthropology, 2002. See also Rebecca Steinfeld, "Wars of the Wombs: Struggles Over Abortion Policies in Israel," *Israel Studies* 20:2, Summer 2015, pp. 1–26; and "Israel's Villa in the Jungle: Israel's foes have weakened, but Palestinians are winning the battle of the womb," *The Economist*, 14 May 2016 [Special Report on The Arab World: The War Within], p. 14, also available at http://www.economist.com/news/special-report/21698439-israels-foes-have-weakened-palestinians-are-winning-battle-womb-israels.

22   Antun Sa'adih [Antoun Sa'adeh] opposed the Franco-British division of the region (determined in the infamous 1916 Sykes–Picot Agreement), prefer-ring unity. He emigrated to Brazil to avoid jail terms, but returned to Beirut in 1947, a few years after the country gained its independence from France on 22 November 1943. A professor at the American University of Beirut,

Sa'adih founded the Syrian Social Nationalist Party (SSNP) and, on 4 July 1949, became involved in a contentious gathering in Jimayzih [Gemayzeh], a Beirut district, which authorities interpreted as a "revolution." In the event, the "revolt" was suppressed and Sa'adih sought refuge in Damascus where Husni al-Za'im, then president following that country's first post-independence coup d'état, betrayed him. He was arrested and handed to Lebanese military authorities on 8 July 1949, speedily tried and executed, as he cried out "Tahiyah Suriyyah" [long live Syria]. In fact, because Lebanon prided itself for its freedoms and liberties, the secretive trial and hasty execution, which skirted due process, were so controversial that successive governments refused to come to terms with the political and moral consequences of his death. To be sure, Bisharah al-Khuri and Riad al-Sulh, the country's first president and prime minister, concluded that Sa'adih was dangerous, and that the SSNP threatened Lebanon's confessionally-based National Charter by advocating union with Syria. For details on Sa'adih, his life, message, trial, and execution, see Adel Beshara, *Outright Assassination: The Trial and Execution of Antun Sa'adeh, 1949*, Reading, UK: Ithaca Press, 2010.

23   According to a prominent Palestinian source, the number of Palestinians in historic Palestine reached 51.5% of the total population in recent years whereas the number of Jews fell to 48.5%. See *Palestinian Affairs* (Shu'un Filastinyyah), September 2014. *Shu'un Filastinyyah* is a quarterly magazine issued by the Palestine Liberation Organization's Palestine Research Center (PRC). The magazine publishes articles in Arabic related to Palestinian politics, culture, economics, international relations, and other subjects. Issues 1 (1971) through 135–136 (March–April 1983) were published in Beirut. The publication moved to Nicosia, Cyprus after a car bomb attack on the Center in February 1983 killed eight staff members. It resumed publication in the summer of 1985. Publication stopped with Issue 244–245 (July–August 1993) for financial reasons, but resumed again in Ramallah in November 2011. The long-time director of the PRC was Sabri Jiryis and editors of *Shu'un Filastiniyyah* included Anis Sayigh and Mahmud Darwish; others involved included Faysal Hurani, Bilal al-Hassan, and Mahmud al-Khatib.

24   The Huthis [Houthis], officially known as the Ansar Allah, are Za'idi Shi'ahs who grouped in a political movement that emerged from Sa'adah, in Northern Yemen in the 1990s; they are engaged in military clashes against the Yemeni central government. For a useful précis, see Zacharay Laub, *Yemen in Crisis*, New York: Council on Foreign Relations, at http://www.cfr.org/yemen/yemen-crisis/p36488.

25   Khalifé is referring here to the long period of time it took Prime Minister Tammam Salam, who was appointed to his post by President Michel Sulayman on 6 April 2013, to form a new government. It was only formed on 15 February 2014 and, with the completion of Sulayman's term in office on 24 May 2014, Salam assumed the position of acting president—

although the constitution requires all cabinet members (currently 24 individuals, two of whom resigned but are serving as caretakers) must approve decrees unanimously. Hizballah managed to impose its views in the cabinet by relying on the Free Patriotic Movement Christian component. For details, see Chapter 4 below.

26 As an interesting aparté, it is useful to note that Kissinger perceived the Middle East through the U.S.–Soviet prism, and told the journalist Leslie Gelb that he was trying "to create a foreign policy based on permanent values and interests." In fact, what he wished to do, as he explained in his memoirs, was "to frustrate the radicals—who were in any event hostile to us—by demonstrating that in the Middle East friendship with the United States was the precondition to diplomatic progress." Moreover, Kissinger was willing to pressure Israel, but only if "the Arabs showed their willingness to reciprocate." See Leslie H. Gelb, "The Kissinger Legacy," *The New York Times Magazine*, 31 October 1976, p. 85. See also Henry Kissinger, *White House Years*, New York: Simon & Schuster, 2011, pp. 354, 361.

27 Khalifé is referring to the Muslim Brotherhood slogan "Islam is the solution." See Shadi Hamid, *Islamic Exceptionalism: How the Struggle over Islam is Reshaping the World*, New York: St. Martin's Press, 2016, p. 89.

28 Theodor Hanf, *Co-Existence in Wartime Lebanon: Decline of a State and Rise of a Nation*, London: Center for Lebanese Studies and I.B. Tauris, 1994.

29 "William Hague: Situation in Egypt 'Very Bleak'," *BBC News*, 19 August 2013, at http://www.bbc.com/news/uk-23753320.

30 According to a new Pew Research Center report, the number of Muslims around the world will nearly equal those of Christians by 2050 before eclipsing it around 2070 as per current trends. "The main reason Muslims are growing not only in number but in share worldwide is because of where they live," Pew's director of religion research, Alan Cooperman, told news sources in April 2015. "Muslim populations are concentrated in some of the fastest-growing parts of the world," confirmed Pew, whose interest in this subject is long-standing. "As of 2010, Christianity was by far the world's largest religion, with an estimated 2.2 billion adherents, nearly a third (31 percent) of all 6.9 billion people on Earth," the Pew report affirmed, with "Islam [standing as a] second, with 1.6 billion adherents, or 23 percent of the global population." See *The Future of World Religions: Population Growth Projections, 2010–2050: Why Muslims Are Rising Fastest and the Unaffiliated Are Shrinking as a Share of the World's Population*, New York: Pew Research Center, 2 April 2015, at http://www.pewforum.org/files/2015/03/PF_15.04.02_ProjectionsFullReport.pdf. For updates on more recent demographic figures, see *The 2016 World Population Data Sheet*, Washington, D.C.: Population Reference Bureau, August 2016, at http://www.prb.org/pdf16/prb-wpds2016-web-2016.pdf

31 Henry Kissinger may well have said this but it is difficult to pinpoint a quotable source; the concept is usually attributed to Halford John Mackinder who developed a *"World Island Theory"* that included several precepts, including "Who Controls the Heartland, Controls the World," which in 1919—when the English geographer first wrote these words—consisted of the Soviet Union, East Europe, Arabia and North Africa. See Pascal Venier, "The Geographical Pivot of History and Early Twentieth Century Geopolitical Culture," *The Geographical Journal* 170:4, December 2004, pp. 330–336; and Geoffrey R. Sloan, "Sir Halford Mackinder: The Heartland Theory Then and Now," in Colin S. Gray and Geoffrey R. Sloan, eds., *Geopolitics, Geography and Strategy*, London: Frank Cass, 1999, pp. 15–38. More recently, one of America's leading strategists, former National Security Council Advisor Zbigniew Brzezinski, wrote in one of his seminal works that "Eurasia [was] the center of the world and that he who controls Eurasia controls the world" in reference to what Adolf Hitler and Joseph Stalin envisaged for the globe before asking, a half century later, whether "America's primacy in Eurasia [would] endure, and to what ends might it be applied?" See, Zbigniew Brzezinski, *The Grand Chessboard: American Primacy and Its Geostrategic Imperatives*, New York: Basic Books, 1997, p. xiv. Finally, it may also be worth recording that Iranian President Mahmud Ahmadinajad uttered similar words at a Tehran conference on 30 January 2010. See "Ahmadinejad: Whoever controls the ME controls the world," *The Jerusalem Post*, 30 January 2010, at http://www.jpost.com/Breaking-News/Ahmadinejad-Whoever-controls-the-ME-controls-the-world.

32 The Khalifé quote is from the daily *Al-Nahar*, 13 December 2006. For details, see Matthew Tempest, "Blair: Iran is Major Threat," *The Guardian*, 12 December 2006, at http://www.theguardian.com/politics/2006/dec/12/foreignpolicy.uk

33 It may be useful to repeat that Khalifé considers all Western Christians to fall into his three categories divided among Catholics in Europe, Orthodox in Russia, and Protestants in America.

34 Yves Lacoste, *Géopolitique: La longue histoire d'aujourd'hui*, Paris: Larousse, 2006, p. 8. The French text reads as follows: "Le terme de géopolitique, dont on fait de nos jours de multiples usages, désigne en fait tout ce qui concerne les rivalités de pouvoirs ou d'influence sur des territoires et les populations qui y vivent: rivalités entre des pouvoirs politiques de toutes sortes—et pas seulement entre des États, mais aussi entre des mouvements politiques ou des groupes armés plus ou moins clandestins—rivalités pour le contrôle ou la domination de territoires de grande ou petite taille."

35 Khalifé is referring here to the annual Herzliya Conference that draws together senior Israeli and international participants from government, business and academia to address pressing national, regional and global

issues. The conferences are organized by the Interdisciplinary Center (IDC) Herzliya. See the English language site at http://www.herzliya conference.org/eng/.

36   For details on the Shi'ah uprisings in Ahsah and the case of Shaykh Nimr al-Nimr, Toby Matthiesen, *The Other Saudis: Shiism, Dissent and Sectarianism*, Cambridge, UK: Cambridge University Press, 2015, pp. 114–139 and 160–165.

37   "Géopolitique de l'Irak: Histoire, société, politique, économie, stratégie [Geopolitics of Iraq: History, Society, Politics, Economics and Strategy], *Diplomatie: Affaires Stratégiques et Relations Internationales*, Number 19, February–March 2014, p. 58.

38   Khalifé is referring here to declarations attributed to the Iranian General Qasem Soleimani, Commander of the Iranian Revolutionary Guard Corps Qods Force deployed his infamous militia alongside the Nuri al-Maliki and Bashar al-Assad regimes in Iraq and Syria, while 'Ali Riza Zakani, a member of the Iranian Majlis [parliament] declared in late 2014 that "three Arab capitals [Baghdad, Beirut, and Damascus], have already fallen into Iran's hands and belong to the Iranian Islamic Revolution." Zakani, not renowned for his modesty, recorded that Sana'a became the fourth Arab capital to join the Iranian Revolution after the Huthis overthrew its legitimate president. See Dexter Filkins, "The Shadow Commander," *The New Yorker*, 30 September 2013, at http://www.newyorker.com/magazine/2013/09/30/the-shadow-commander; and "Sanaa is the Fourth Arab capital to Join the Iranian Revolution," *Middle East Monitor*, 27 September 2014, at https://www.middleeastmonitor.com/20140927-sanaa-is-the-fourth-arab-capital-to-join-the-iranian-revolution/.

39   Khalifé is referring here in particular to the 2012 conference when former Foreign Minister Tzipi Livni claimed that Israel was isolated because it failed to reach key decisions. See the proceedings of the 2012 gathering, titled "In The Eye of Storms: Israel and the Middle East," at http://www.herzliyaconference.org/eng/?CategoryID=465.

40   The figures used in this paragraph are drawn from *Shu'un Falastiniyyah* [Palestinian Affairs], Issue 257, Summer 2014, p. 245.

41   Yves Lacoste, "Le Monde Musulman et les Islamistes: Le choc des Représentations idéologiques," in *Géopolitique: La longue histoire d'aujourd'hui*, pp. 302–315.

42   Ironically, Israel has yet to define its borders, and one of the more thoughtful essay on the topic is Tony Jundt, "Israel: The Alternative," *The New York Review of Books*, 23 October 2003, at http://www.nybooks.com/articles/2003/10/23/israel-the-alternative/. See also Daniel Levy, "The Role of the Border in the Israeli–Palestinian Conflict," *Harvard International Review*, 26 June 2011, at http://hir.harvard.edu/the-role-of-the-border-in-the-israeli-palestinian-conflict/.

43   Patrick Seale, *Asad of Syria: The Struggle for the Middle East*, Berkeley

and Los Angeles: University of California Press, 1989, pp. 278–280.

44 *Takfir* and *takfiri*(s) are derogatory terms that refer to the practice of excommunicating fellow Muslims. They are frequently used, inter alia, to associate al-Qa'idah and other extremist groups with violence. Frequent references to all violent Sunni extremists as *"takfiris"* highlight the practice of excommunicating other Muslims and portray Wahabism, Salafism and other Sunni movements with the same brush.

45 President Bashar al-Assad, "Mu'tamar Sahafi Mushtarak lil Sayyid al-Ra'is Bashar al-Assad wa Nazirihi al-Irani Mahmud Ahmadinajad fi Dimashk" [Joint Press Conference between President Bashar al-Assad and his Iranian Counterpart Mahmud Ahmadinajd in Damascus], 25 February 2010, at http://www.presidentassad.net/index.php?option=com_content&view=article&id=1084:25-2010&catid=302&Itemid=469.

46 President Bashar al-Assad, "Al-Assad/Press Statements In Istanbul," 8 May 2010, at http://www.presidentassad.net/index.php?option=com_content&view=article&id=364:president-al-assad-press-statements-in-istanbul-may-8-2010&catid=116&Itemid=496.

47 This section was written in 2013, though Khalifé's prognostications withstood the test of time, as discussed in the Introduction to this volume.

48 Adonis, "Madarat Yaktubuyah Adonis: Ramadu Bu-'Azizi'" [Perspectives from Adonis: Bu-'Aziz's (Bouazizi's) Ashes], *Al-Hayat* (pan-Arab daily), 27 April 2011, at http://www.alhayat.com/Details/248273. See also footnote 10 above.

49 Yves Lacoste, *Géopolitique: La longue histoire d'aujourd'hui*, Paris, *Larousse*, 2006, p. 8.

50 Jean-Jacques Rousseau, *The Social Contract*, New York: Penguin, 1968; Karl Marx and Friedrich Engels, *The Communist Manifesto*, New York: International Publishers Company, 2014; Michel Aflaq, *Choice of Texts from the Ba'th Party Founder's Thought*, 1977, available at http://www.archive.org/details/ChoiceOfTextsFromTheBathParty FoundersThought; Ayatullah Ruhullah al-Musawi al-Khomeini, *Islamic Government: Governance of the Jurist*, 2012, available at http://www.feedbooks.com/userbook/29110/islamic-government-governance-of-the-jurist.

51 Nassif Nassar, *Mantiq al-Sultah* [The Logic of Power], Beirut: Dar Amwaj, 1995, pp. 7–9.

52 'Ali Harb, *Thawrat al-Quwwah al-Na'imat fil 'Alam al-'Arabi: Nahuah Tafkik al-Dictaturiyyat wal Usuliyyat* [Soft-Power Revolutions in the Arab World: Towards the Dismantling of Dictatorships and Fundamentalisms], Beirut: Dar al-'Arabiyyah lil-'Ulum, 2011. See also Ali Galal Mouawad, "Egyptian Revolt and Soft Power Relevancy in the Middle East," a paper submitted to a collaborative project between the London School of Economics and the Faculty of Economics and Political Science, Cairo University, 27 June 2013 and available at http://www.lse.ac.uk/middleEastCentre/research/Collaboration-Projects/collaboration-2011-

2012/LSE-Collaboration-with-FEPS/AliGelal.pdf; and Sonia L. Alianak, *The Transition Towards Revolution and Reform: The Arab Spring Realised?*, Edinburgh, UK: Edinburgh University Press, 2014.

53 Burhan Ghalioun, "Al-Wiladah al-Jadidah lil-'Alam al-'Arabi" [A New Birth for the Arab World], *Majalat al-Dirasat al-Falistiniyyah* [Palestinian Studies], Volume 22, Number 86, Spring 2011, pp. 8–16, at http://www.palestine-studies.org/sites/default/files/mdf-articles/10956. pdf. The quotation is on page 16.

54 *Ibid.*, p. 8.

55 'Abdul Mun'im Sa'id, *Al-Sharq al-Awsat*, 27 April 2011.

56 Sij'an Azzi, *Al Safir*, 30 April 2011. Lebanese readers would of course be familiar with Sij'an Azzi, a long-standing member of the Phalange Party, and most recently Minister of Labor in the Government of Prime Minister Tamman Salam. In 2016, Azzi was expelled from the Phalange after he refused to resign as instructed by the party, though he held on to his political perch at the ministry. A prolific opinion-maker, Azzi hogs television news broadcasts with views on a variety of topics, and is often ensnarled in controversial positions.

57 'Ali Harb, *op. cit.*, p. 112.

58 Samir Aita, "Abattre le pouvoir pour libérer l'Etat," *Le Monde Diplomatique*, April 2011, pp. 20–21.

59 Michel Chiha (1891–1954) was the father of the Lebanese Constitution, which saw light in 1920 under the French Mandate, long before independence in 1943. A banker and writer who dabbled in journalism and, eventually, politics, Chiha was an original thinker whose ideas shaped contemporary elite views. He was born into a Christian Assyrian family that migrated from modern-day Iraq though his mother hailed from a wealthy Melkite [a leading Greek Catholic Church with roots in modern Syria] Beiruti family, the Pharaons. Chiha settled in Cairo in 1915 though he sensed that the collapse of the Ottoman Empire would create opportunities for Lebanon (and Syria) and, in preparation, developed specific political views about the future. He returned to Beirut in 1918 and worked in earnest with the French High Commissioner who proclaimed "Le Grand Liban" ["Greater Lebanon"] in August 1920. Remarkably, he was interested in setting up the country's new borders—which Damascus never acknowledged—as well as the creation of the nascent country's first institutions. In 1925, Chiha was elected as a representative in the Lebanese parliament, and though his term ended in 1929, it was he who pushed through the adoption of both the Constitution and the monetary system that transformed Beirut into a financial capital that was the envy of many, and which culminated with the foundation of the Beirut Stock Exchange in 1940. Three years earlier, Chiha acquired the French language newspaper *Le Jour*, in which he wrote a daily editorial until his death in 1954. When his brother-in-law, Bisharah al-Khuri, became the president of the newly independent Lebanese Republic in 1943, Chiha was promoted, and

became the head-of-state's advisor, a position he kept until 1952. In addition to Lebanon, Chiha wrote extensively on the Palestine Question, especially after Israel was created in 1948, and actively defended the cause. If he perceived the spillover effects of the Arab–Israeli wars on Lebanon better than most, his fears and prognostications—which surfaced during the 1975–1990 Civil War—proved to be prophetic. In December 1947, for example, Chiha wrote how Israel presented a direct menace for Lebanon, arguing: "(. . .) The decision to partition Palestine by creating the Jewish State, is one of the most serious mistakes of world politics. The most surprising consequences are going to result from an apparently small thing. Nor is it offensive to reason to state that this small thing will have its part to play in shaking the world to its foundations." He lamented how Israelis ended Palestine's confessional composition, and warned: "We have ahead of us a permanent danger, a hatred without end." In one of his column, he wrote that "a mistake of this size committed in the middle of this century, [will mean that] our grand-children will reencounter it in the middle of the next one." Chiha was admired even if few Lebanese remember him today. See, Nabil Khalifé, *Michel Chiha: Awal Anbiya' Lubnan wa Akhir Anbiya' Falastin* [Michel Chiha: Lebanon's First Prophet and Palestine's Last], Jbayl, Lebanon: Byblos Center for Studies and Research, 2013. See also Kamal S. Salibi, *A House of Many Mansions: The History of Lebanon Reconsidered*, London: I.B. Tauris, 2003, pp. 179–181; Jean Salem, *Introduction à la pensée politique de Michel Chiha*, Beirut: Librairie Samir, 1970.

60 A tarbush is a brimless cap made of felt or cloth that resembles the fez and that is usually red and often with a silk tassel, worn either alone or as part of a turban, by Muslim men—especially in the Levant. The tradition was most probably introduced to the Arab World from Spain—where men wore a traposo or trapucho. In fact, Moriscos who settled in North Africa after their expulsion from Spain in the 1600s introduced the headgear, though the item gained popularity in Egypt and spread Eastward. Khalifé uses the term in a critical sense, to refer to Arab regimes that were led by elites with the means to wear fezes or tarbushes, but who had little knowledge of, and less interest in, populations abandoned to their fate.

61 Adel Beshara, *Outright Assassination: The Trial and Execution of Antun Sa'adeh, 1949*, Reading, UK: Ithaca Press, 2010. See also Daniel Pipes, *Greater Syria: The History of an Ambition*, New York: Oxford University Press, 1990.

62 Frédéric Encel, *Atlas géopolitique d'Israël*, Paris: Autrement, 2008, p. 11.

63 As stated above, *takfir* and *takfiri*(s) are derogatory terms that refer to the practice of excommunicating fellow Muslims and are frequently used to associate al-Qa'idah and other extremist groups with violence. Hassan al-Banna was the founder of the Muslim Brotherhood. See Carrie Rosefsky Wickham, *The Muslim Brotherhood: Evolution of an Islamist Movement*, Princeton, New Jersey: Princeton University Press, 2013.

64 Gérard D. Khoury, *La France et l'Orient Arabe: Naissance du Liban Moderne 1914–1920*, Paris: Armand Colin, 1993.

65 William Hale and Ergun Özbudun, *Islamism, Democracy and Liberalism in Turkey: The Case of the AKP*, Abingdon, UK, and New York: Routledge, 2010.

66 Sadiq Jalal al-'Azm, "al-Harakat al-Islamiyyah wal-Numuzaj al-Turki" [Islamic Movements and the Turkish Model], *al-Safir*, 16 May 2011.

67 Joseph A. Kéchichian, *From Alliance to Union: Challenges Facing Gulf Cooperation Council States in the Twenty-First Century*, Brighton, Chicago, Toronto: Sussex Academic Press, July 2016, pp. 218–235.

68 For a recent theoretical overview, see Tanisha M. Fazal, "State Death in the International System," *International Organization* 58:2, April 2004, pp. 311–344.

69 Jean Gottmann, *La politique des Etats et leur géographie*, Paris: Armand Colin, 1952, pp. 138–139.

70 Frederich Ratzel, *Geographie politique,* traduction de Pierre Rusch, Paris: Economica, 1988, p. 265.

71 Patrice Gourdin, *Géopolitiques, manuel pratique*, Paris: Choiseul, 2010, p. 496.

72 Michel Chiha, *Palestine*, Beirut: Chiha Foundation and Dar Al-Nahar, 2003, p. 1. A 135-page long booklet—also titled Palestine—is available in English on the Chiha Foundation web page at http://www.michelchiha.org/international-relations/palestine/79/1/. The English version is a collection of Chiha's writings in local and international dailies and clarifies many of the points first developed in his opus. In one of the passages, on page 124, Chiha writes: "Israel's ambitions are well known. *Their aim is to over-populate the country and make further advances. The idea is to conquer the whole of Jerusalem and to re-establish something resembling the Kingdom of David and Solomon of thirty centuries ago.* Finally the idea is to build a homeland in the Near East with tentacles reaching out over a Jewish world empire."

73 Chiha, *Palestine*, pp. 126 and 239.

74 Philippe Droz Vincent, "L'Insertion régionale de la Syrie," in Baudouin Dupret, Zouhair Ghazzal, Youssef Courbage et Mohammed al-Dbiyat, eds., *La Syrie au Présent. Reflets d'une société*, Paris: Sindbad/Actes Sud & Ifpo, June 2007, pp. 779–848.

75 See, for example, Elizabeth Picard, "The Political Economy of Civil War in Lebanon," in Steven Heydemann, ed., *War, Institutions, and Social Change in the Middle East,* Berkeley: University of California Press, 2000, at http://publishing.cdlib.org/ucpressebooks/view?docId=ft6c6006x6&chunk.id=ch10&toc.depth=1&toc.id=ch10&brand=ucpress; and Elizabeth Picard, *Lebanon, a Shattered Country: Myths and Realities of the Wars in Lebanon*, New York: Holmes & Meier, 1996 [Originally published under the title *Liban: État de discorde*, Paris: Flammarion, 1988].

76 Hafez al-Assad, "Interview," *Al-Hawadith*, Number 972, 27 June 1975.

77 Hafez al-Assad, "Interview," *Al-Mustaqbal* [Paris], 8 May 1982.

78 "Lebanese–Syrian relations, Part One," Beirut: Lebanese Center for Documentation and Research [CEDRE—Centre Libanais de Documentation et de Recherche], 6 March 1982.

79 Nabil Khalifé, *Al-Istratijiyyah al-Suriyyah wal-Israiliyyah wal-Urupiyyah Hiyal Lubnan: Bahth fi Masir al-Dawlah-Al-Hajiz* [Syrian, Israeli and European Strategies Towards Lebanon: An Analysis of the Fate of a Buffer-State], Jbayl, Lebanon: Byblos Center, 2nd edition, 2008, p. 63.

80 Henry Kissinger, *Years of Renewal*, New York: Simon and Schuster, 1999, pp. 1024–1025.

81 Philip K. Hitti, *Lebanon in History from the Earliest Times to the Present*, London: The Macmillan Company, 1957.

82 Hitti, *ibid.*, p. 599.

83 Yusuf Hurani, *Lubnan fi Qaym Tarikhihi* [Lebanon in its History], Beirut: Dar al-Mashriq, n.d., p. 43.

84 Harb, *op. cit.*, p. 87.

85 Estimates on the number of people who gathered on 14 March 2005 in Beirut's Martyrs' Square varied between 1 and 2 million individuals out of the resident population of over 6 million that year. Demographic statistics are state secrets in Lebanon though the 3 million figure used by Khalifé is low. See Rudy Jaafar and Maria J. Stephan, "Lebanon's Independence Intifada: How an Unarmed Insurrection Expelled Syrian Forces," in Maria J. Stephan, ed., *Civilian Jihad: Nonviolent Struggle, Democratization, and Governance in the Middle East*, New York: Palgrave Macmillan, 2009, pp. 169–185. See also Michael Young, *The Ghosts of Martyrs Square: An Eyewitness Account of Lebanon's Life Struggle*, New York: Simon & Schuster, 2014, p. 40; and Are Knudsen and Michael Kerr, eds., *Lebanon: After the Cedar Revolution*, New York: Oxford University Press, 2014.

86 Harb, *op. cit.*, p. 87.

87 This quotation is attributed to several individuals, most notably to David Ben-Gurion, the first Prime Minister of Israel, who apparently discussed the matter on 22 October 1956 at Sèvres when he, Sir Anthony Eden, the driving force on the British plot to attack Nasir's Egypt, on the road to war, and French Foreign Minister Christian Pineau, got to know each other. Ben-Gurion apparently opened the discussion by listing his military, political and moral considerations against 'the English plan,' and presented a comprehensive alternative, which he himself called 'fantastic' because it proposed to simply reorganize the Middle East. "Jordan, he observed, was not viable as an independent state and should therefore be divided. Iraq would get the East Bank in return for a promise to settle the Palestinian refugees there and to make peace with Israel while the West Bank would be attached to Israel as a semi-autonomous region. Lebanon suffered from having a large Muslim population, which was concentrated in the south," a problem Ben-Gurion proposed to solve by Israel's expansion up to the

Litani River, which would "thereby [help] to turn Lebanon into a more compact Christian state." See Avi Shlaim, "The Protocol of Sèvres, 1956: Anatomy of a War Plot," *International Affairs* 73:3 (1997), pp. 509–530, at http://users.ox.ac.uk/~ssfc0005/The%20Protocol%20of%20Sevres %201956%20Anatomy%20of%20a%20War%20Plot.html.

88 Patrick Seale, *Al-Nahar*, 22 September 2009. See also Seale, *Asad of Syria, op. cit.*, pp. 267–289 [a chapter appropriately titled "The Lebanese Trap"]; and Eyal Zisser, *Asad's Legacy: Syria in Transition*, London: Hurst and Company, 2001, p. 13.

89 'Ali Harb, *op. cit.*, p. 89.

90 Khalifé assumes that his readers are familiar with internal political developments in Lebanon. His unsettling conclusions will upset Hizballah and its backers, though members of the elite owe him a debt of gratitude to offer cogent analyses about the destiny of the country. For two recent assessments of Lebanon, representing pro-March 8 and pro-March 14 positions, see Bassel F. Salloukh, Rabie Barakat, Jinan S. Al-Habbal, Lara W. Khattab, and Shoghig Mikaelian, *The Politics of Sectarianism in Postwar Lebanon*, London: Pluto Press, 2015; and Theodor Hanf, *Coexistence in Wartime Lebanon: Decline of a State and Rise of a Nation*, London: I.B. Tauris, 2015. For a neutral perspective, see Maximilian Felsch and Martin Wählisch, *Lebanon and the Arab Uprisings: In the Eye of the Hurricane*, Abingdon, Oxfordshire: Routledge, 2016.

91 An Accord was signed in May 2012 though inter-Palestinian tensions persisted.

92 See, for example, Thomas Patrick Carroll, "Turkey's Justice and Development Party: A Model for Democratic Islam?," *Middle East Intelligence Bulletin* 6:6–7, June/July 2004, at https://www.meforum.org/ meib/articles/0407 t1.htm. See also Bilal Sambur, "The Great Transformation of Political Islam in Turkey: The Case of Justice and Development Party and Erdogan," *European Journal of Economic and Political Studies* 2:2, April 2009, pp. 117–127.

93 For a useful primer on these accomplishments, see Gilbert Achcar, *Morbid Symptoms: Relapse in the Arab Uprising*, Stanford, California: Stanford University Press, 2016.

94 For an examination of the Bahrain uprising, see Al'a Shehabi and Marc Owen Jones, *Bahrain's Uprising*, London: Zed Books, 2015. See also Justin Gengler, *Group Conflict and Political Mobilization in Bahrain and the Arab Gulf: Rethinking the Rentier State*, Bloomington and Indianapolis: Indiana University Press, 2015); Toby Matthiesen, *Sectarian Gulf: Bahrain, Saudi Arabia, and the Arab Spring That Wasn't*, Stanford, California: Stanford University Press, 2013; and Bahrain Independent Commission of Inquiry, *Report of the Bahrain Independent Commission of Inquiry, 23 November 2011 (revised on 10 December 2011)*, available at http://files.bici.org.bh/BICIreportEN.pdf.

95 Although Khalifé presents a preliminary assessment in these pages, his first

insights are remarkably accurate, confirmed by later developments, even if it is still too early to reach any kind of conclusion on the impact that the Arab Uprisings will have on contemporary history.

96 Muhammad Bu 'Azizi immolated himself on 17 December 2010 in the central Tunisian town of Sidi Buzid [Bouzid], because of a routine infraction that prevented him from making a living as a fruit-seller. See Robert F. Worth, "How a Single Match Can Ignite a Revolution," *The New York Times*, 21 January 2011, at http://www.nytimes.com/2011/01/23/weekin-review/23worth.html?_r=0. For an insight of the civilian municipality worker who allegedly slapped him (which she denied), see Michael J. Totten, "The Woman Who Blew Up the Arab World," *World Affairs*, 17 May 2012, at http://www.worldaffairsjournal.org/blog/michael-j-totten/woman-who-blew-arab-world.

97 Ze'ev Schiff, "Some Serious Thoughts on Syria," *Haaretz*, 2 March 20017, at http://www.haaretz.com/some-serious-thoughts-on-syria-1.214463

98 Nabil Khalifé, *Madkhal ilal-Khususiyyah al-Lubnaniyyah* [An Introduction to Lebanese Particularity], Jbayl, Lebanon: Byblos Centre for Studies, 1997, p. 403.

99 Khalifé uses a popular French saying in the Arabic text to drive his point home: "Pour vaincre, il faut convaincre."

100 For an overview of these and other clashes, see Yaroslav Trofimov, *The Siege of Mecca: The Forgotten Uprising in Islam's Holiest Shrine and the Birth of Al Qaeda*, New York: Doubleday, 2007; Martin Kramer, "Khomeini's Messengers in Mecca," in Martin Kramer, *Arab Awakening and Islamic Revival*, New Brunswick: Transaction, 1996, pp. 161–87; and Yasmeen Serhan, "The Sectarian Spat Over the Hajj," *The Atlantic*, 16 September 2016, at http://www.theatlantic.com/news/archive/2016/09/hajj-saudi-arabia-iran/498938/.

101 Nazila Fathi, "Text of Mahmoud Ahmadinejad's Speech," *The New York Times*, 30 October 2005 at http://www.nytimes.com/2005/10/30/weekin-review/text-of-mahmoud-ahmadinejads-speech.html. See also James Catania, *Iran's Nuclear Program: A Presaging the Coming U.S. and Israeli Response*, American Military University 28 March 2011, at http://www.lamp-method.org/ecommons/catania2011.pdf; and Spencer Case, "Unthinking the Thinkable: Iran and the Bomb," *The National Review*, 26 September 2016, at http://www.nationalreview.com/article/440377/iran-nuclear-arms-dangerous.

102 A husayniyyah is a congregation hall for Shi'ah commemoration ceremonies that is used for propagation of the faith as well as promulgation of political ideas.

103 *Al-Manar* is a Lebanese television station affiliated with Hizballah that broadcasts from Beirut. It was labeled a "Specially Designated Global Terrorist" entity by the United States on 17 December 2004 and banned in most Western countries, where it may be accessible online, though it saw its broadcasts yanked out of Nilesat in 2015 that severely limited its access

to Arab markets. *Al-'Alam* is an Arabic news channel broadcasting from Tehran, Iran. The network's political coverage tends to be anti-Arab.

104 Khalifé does not provide demographic details on Iran. Although 99 percent of Iranians are Muslim, it is generally estimated that 90 to 95% are Shi'ahs and only 5 to 10% are Sunnis. Iranians further claim that most Sunnis in Iran are Kurds, Larestani people (from Larestan), Turkomen, and Baluchs, living in the northwest, northeast, south, and southeast. There are hardly any references to Iran's large Arab population that lives in 'Arabistan, known as Khuzestan in Persian, and whose numbers could be as high as 5 million. See David A. Graham, "Iran's Beleaguered Sunnis," *The Atlantic*, 6 January 2016, at http://www.theatlantic.com/international/archive/ 2016/01/iran-sunnis-saudi/422877/. See also Farshad Mohammadi, "Iranian Sunnis complain of discrimination," *Al-Jazeera*, 9 March 2014, at http://www.aljazeera.com/indepth/features/2014/03/ iranian-sunnis-complain-discrimination-2014397125688907.html; and Najmeh Bozergmehr, "Fears Grow Over Iran's Disgruntled Sunni Muslims," *The Financial Times*, 1 January 2015 at https://www.ft.com/content/3a246c0a-86d7-11e4-8a51-00144feabdc0.

105 For a solid examination of ties between the Arab World and Iran, see Amin Saikal, *The Arab World and Iran: A Turbulent Region in Transition*, New York: Palgrave Macmillan, 2016.

106 Starting in the East, clockwise, the following countries share borders with Iran: Iraq, Turkey, Armenia, Azerbaijan, Russia, Kazakhstan [the latter two as Caspian Sea neighbors], Turkmenistan, Afghanistan, Pakistan, Oman, the United Arab Emirates, Qatar, Bahrain, Sa'udi Arabia and Kuwait.

107 Salah al-Din Yusuf Ibn Ayyub [or *Selahedînê Eyûbî* in Kurdish] (1137/1138 – 4 March 1193), and who is better known in the Western world as Saladin, became the first Sultan of Egypt and Syria as well as the founder of the Ayyubid Dynasty. He was of Kurdish origin and earned his fame on account of his successful opposition to the European Crusades that sought to conquer the Levant. A significant leader whose sultanate included Egypt, Syria, Mesopotamia [Iraq], most of the Hijaz and the Yemen, along parts of North Africa, Saladin left his mark. For a definitive study, see Anne-Marie Eddé, *Saladin*, Cambridge, Massachusetts and London: The Belknap Press of Harvard University Press, 2011.

108 I first offered this conclusion to my Shi'ah students when I taught Arabic literature at the secondary Hassan Kamil Al Sabah School in Nabatiyyah, Southern Lebanon, in 1964. Most were incredulous.

109 See, for example Rachel Bronson *Thicker than Oil: America's Uneasy Partnership with Saudi Arabia*, New York: Oxford University Press, 2006; Anthony Cave Brown, *Oil, God, and Gold: The Story of Aramco and the Saudi Kings*, Boston and New York: Houghton Mifflin Company, 1999; Parker T. Hart, *Saudi Arabia and the United States: Birth of a Security Partnership*, Bloomington and Indianapolis: Indiana University Press,

1998; David Holden and Richard Johns, *The House of Saud: The Rise and Rule of the Most Powerful Dynasty in the Arab World*, New York: Holt, Rinehart and Winston, 1981; Joseph A. Kéchichian, *Faysal: Saudi Arabia's King for All Seasons*, Gainesville: University Press of Florida, 2008; Idem, *'Iffat Al Thunayan: An Arabian Queen*, Brighton, Chicago, Toronto: Sussex Academic Press, 2015; *Legal and Political Reforms in Saudi Arabia*, London and New York: Routledge, November 2012; Robert Vitalis, *America's Kingdom: Mythmaking on the Saudi Oil Frontie*r, London and New York: Verso, 2009. The anti-Al Sa'ud literature is rich and the following are but a small sample of the available and rapidly growing fare: Stephen Schwartz, *The Two Faces of Islam: The House of Sa'ud from Tradition to Terror*, New York: Doubleday, 2002; Dore Gold, *Hatred's Kingdom: How Saudi Arabia Supports the New Global Terrorism*, Washington, D.C.: Regnery Publishing, Inc., 2003; As'ad AbuKhalil, *The Battle for Saudi Arabia: Royalty, Fundamentalism, and Global Power*, New York: Seven Stories Press, 2004; Craig Unger, *House of Bush, House of Saud: The Secret Relationship between the World's Two Most Powerful Dynasties*, New York: Scribner, 2004; Mark Hollingsworth, *Saudi Babylon: Torture, Corruption and Cover-Up Inside the House of Saud*, Edinburgh: Mainstream Publishing, 2005; Laurent Murawiec, *Princes of Darkness: The Saudi Assault on the West*, Lanham, Maryland: Rowman & Littlefield Publishers, 2005; Gerald Posner, *Secrets of the Kingdom: The Inside Story of the Saudi–U.S. Connection*, New York: Random House, 2005; Kristin Decker, *The Unveiling: An American Teacher in a Saudi Palace*, College Station, Texas: Virtualbookworm.com Publishing, 2006; John R. Bradley, *Saudi Arabia Exposed: Inside a Kingdom in Crisis*, New York: Palgrave Macmillan, 2006; David B. Ottaway, *The King's Messenger: Prince Bandar bin Sultan and America's Tangled Relationship with Saudi Arabia*, New York: Walker & Company, 2008; and Karen Elliott House, *On Saudi Arabia: Its People, Past, Religion, Fault Lines— and Future*, New York: Alfred A. Knopf, 2012.

110 "Higher Education in the Twenty-First Century: Vision and Action," Paris, France: UNESCO, 9 October 1998, at http://www.unesco.org/education/educprog/wche/declaration_eng.htm.

111 Noya, *op. cit.*, p. 155.

112 Mohammed Arkoun, *The Unthought in Contemporary Islamic Thought*, London and Beirut: Saqi Books, 2006 (3rd edition), p. 181 [the page reference is to the Arabic version translated by Hashim Salih].

113 Mohammed Arkoun, *Islamic Thought: Common Question, Uncommon Answers*, London: Saqi Books, 1990, pp. 286–287 [reference to Arabic version].

114 Khalifé closes his book with these observations to explain what he believes are the salient points of contention between Islam and democracy. In the original, the section is enclosed in a box, and is meant as a short synopsis.

Appendices

Appendix 1
The 1978 Al-Azhar Islamic Constitution

Long before the post-2011 uprisings, the Al-Azhar Academy for Islamic Research met in Cairo in October 1977 to write an Islamic constitution that, its authors hoped, would be made available to any country wishing to model itself after the Islamic Shari'ah. The assembly recommended that, to the extent possible, the principles laid down in this constitution be compliant with all Islamic schools of law. Operating under the guidelines set by two resolutions that are included at the end of this document, and under the leadership of Dr. al-Husayni 'Abd al-Majid Hashim, Committee members (whose names appear below), submitted their results to the Grand Imam at Al-Azhar who, in turn, made it public. It was first published in the Al-Azhar University Magazine in April 1979 and reproduced in various newspapers ever since. The pan-Arab daily Al-Hayat published large excerpts on 9 November 2013. What follows is the full document.

In the name of God, the Merciful, the Compassionate

Section 1   The Islamic Nation
Article 1a: Muslims form one nation.

Article 1b: Islamic *Shari'ah Law* [hereafter *Shari'ah*] is the source of all legislation.

Article 2: The Muslim nation may include several countries even if the forms of government vary among them.

Article 3: A Muslim State can enter into a union with one or more Muslim countries under any form they agree upon.

Article 4: The people [citizens] are in charge of monitoring the Imam, his representatives, and the rest of the government. Citizens are duty-bound to hold officials accountable in accordance with the *Shari'ah*.

Section 2   The Foundation of Islamic Society
Article 5: Cooperation and integration are the foundations of society.

Article 6: Commanding good and forbidding wrong is obligatory.

Article 7: The family is the foundation of society. Religion and morality are the bases of the family. The State guarantees to support the family, to protect motherhood, to look after children, and to bring about the means to ensure this.

Article 8: The Protection of the family is the duty of the State, which must pursue this goal by encouraging marriage, providing newlyweds the material means of housing and any other aid, honoring married life, stipulating the means for the responsibility of a woman to assist her husband and her children, and considering family care as the woman's first priority.

Article 9: It is the responsibility of the State to attend to the welfare of the nation and the well being of individuals. It should provide free health care and distribute preventative and therapeutic medicines.

Article 10: Education is a religious duty. The State is responsible for education in accordance with the law.

Article 11: Religious rearing must be part of a core curriculum at every stage of the education cycle.

Article 12: The State is required to teach Muslims the fundamentals of the faith on which there is consensus. Among these are: religious obligations, the biography of the Prophet, the lives of the Rightly-Guided Caliphs, all of which should be taught comprehensively throughout the education cycle.

Article 13: The State is required to teach the memorization of the Qur'an to Muslims as appropriate to each grade level. Likewise, it must create specialized institutions for Qur'an memorization for adults. The State will print copies of the Qur'an and facilitate their circulation.

Article 14: Excessive beautification is forbidden and chastity is required. The State will issue laws and decrees to defend public sensibilities from vulgarity in accordance with *Shari'ah*.

Article 15: Arabic is the official language of the State and the *Hijri* calendar must be displayed on all official correspondence.

Article 16: Public sovereignty is based on the interests of citizens, in particular to protect religion, mind, soul, property, and honor.

Article 17: It is not sufficient for the ends to be legal, but rather and at all times the means must also be in accordance with *Shari'ah*.

Section 3 The Islamic Economy
Article 18: The economy will be based upon the principles of *Shari'ah*

that guarantees human dignity and social justice. It requires striving in life through both thought and deed and ensures lawful profit.

Article 19: Freedom of trade, industry, and agriculture are guaranteed within the framework of *Shari'ah*.

Article 20: The State will draft plans for economic growth in accordance with *Shari'ah*.

Article 21: The State will fight against monopolization and will not interfere with prices except when necessary.

Article 22: The State will fight desertification and increase arable land as necessary.

Article 23: Paying or receiving usury is not permitted nor is participating in any transaction involved with usury.

Article 24: The State has legal possession of all of the natural resources that are underground, i.e., metals, ores, etc.

Article 25: All possessions that have no owner become the property of the treasury. The law will regulate how individuals can make claims for such properties.

Article 26: The State will regulate how alms disbursements collected from individuals are channeled through public or Islamic financial institutions.

Article 27: Establishing endowments for lawful purposes are permitted and will be organized according to the law.

Section 4   Individual Rights and Freedoms

Article 28: Justice and equality are the foundation of governance. The rights to a legal defense and to file lawsuits are guaranteed. Infringing upon these rights is not permitted.

Article 29: Freedom of religion and thought, the freedom to work, the freedom to express opinions directly or indirectly, the freedom to establish trade union associations and to participate in them, personal freedoms, and the freedom of movement and congregation are all basic and natural rights that are protected within the framework of *Shari'ah*.

Article 30: The privacy of homes, correspondence, and private affairs are inviolable and spying on them is forbidden. The law can spell out ways that the State can restrict this inviolability in cases of high treason or imminent danger to others. Such restrictions can only occur with permission from the judiciary.

Article 31: The right to move within the country and abroad is recognized. Citizens will not be forbidden from traveling abroad nor will they be required to stay in one place instead of another without a court order. The judge must disclose the reasons for any restrictions. Expatriating citizens is not permissible.

Article 32: The extradition of political refugees is prohibited. The extradition of criminals is regulated by agreements with interested countries.

Article 33: Torturing is a crime. Neither the crime nor the punishment becomes void during the life of the perpetrator. Whoever committed the criminal act and any accomplice(s) are responsible for the crime monetarily. Whosoever helps in the planning, or execution, or if he remains silent about any crime is, legally, a criminal accomplice and assumes civil responsibilities. The government will hold criminals accountable.

Article 34: Any government employee who knows of a torture incident being committed in his department and does not report it to the proper authorities will be punished by *ta'zir* [which fall under the discretion of a judge].

Article 35: In Islam, blood is not shed in vain. The State must compensate: the families of homicide victims when the murderer is unknown, and the families of those rendered disabled, also if the perpetrator is unknown. The State is also responsible for compensation if the perpetrator does not have enough money to pay for the amends.

Article 36: Every individual has the right to submit a complaint about a crime committed against him, or against someone else, or about instances when public money is being embezzled or squandered.

Article 37: The right to work, earn a profit, and property ownership, are guaranteed. This cannot be infringed upon unless required by *Shari'ah* laws.

Article 38: Women have the right to work within the framework of *Shari'ah* laws.

Article 39: The State guarantees the freedom of ownership, and the inviolability of property rights. Confiscation of financial instruments is prohibited for any reason. Private confiscation can only occur through a court order.

Article 40: Expropriation of property is prohibited unless it is for the public good and the aggrieved party is fully compensated according to specific laws instituted for such purposes.

Article 41: The founding of newspapers will be allowed. Freedom of the press will be within the framework of *Shari'ah*.

Article 42: Citizens have the right to form labor organizations and trade unions according to the law. Those that go against the social system, or which secretly have a military character, or that infringe on any aspect of *Shari'ah* are not allowed.

Article 43: Rights will be practiced in accordance with the aims of *Shari'ah*.

Section 5   The Imam

Article 44: The State will have an Imam. Obedience is required even if there is disagreement with his person.

Article 45: Obedience to someone who disobeys God is unacceptable. An Imam who disobeys *Shari'ah* with his actions should not be obeyed.

Article 46: The law will clarify the path for elections to choose an Imam. Elections will be carried out under the supervision of the judiciary. The candidate with the required majority of votes will prevail.

Article 47: Candidates for the presidency of the State must be: Muslim, male, past the age of majority, of sound mind, pious, and knowledgeable about the rules of *Shari'ah*.

Article 48: The election of the Imam will be completed with a pledge of allegiance from all classes of the nation as required by law. Women have the right to demand to participate in an election when they meet set requirements and are thus able to vote.

Article 49: Expressing a negative opinion about the election of an Imam before the procedure is completed is not a crime.

Article 50: Those who hold the rights to the pledge of allegiance can dismiss the Imam when there is reason to do so in a way proscribed by the law.

Article 51: The Imam will defer to the judiciary. He has the right to have an attorney at court.

Article 52: The President of the State enjoys the same rights and responsibilities as do all citizens.

Article 53: The Imam cannot inherit the estate of any deceased individual. Endowments cannot be established for the benefit of the Imam or any of his relatives up to the fourth degree. However, it is permitted for the Imam to inherit if the deceased was a direct relative and the inheritance is according to the law. The Imam may not purchase or rent property that is owned by the State, nor can he sell or lease such property.

Article 54: Giving gifts to the Imam is calamitous; thus all gifts will be donated to the State treasury.

Article 55: The Imam is an example of justice, piety, and good deeds for his subjects. He shares the duty with other Muslim Imams in looking after everything that effects the Muslim community. Similarly, he will send a delegation every year to participate in the annual *hajj* and to participate in both official as well as private conferences.

Article 56: The Imam is responsible for guiding his army to engage in *jihad* against the enemy, protect the homeland, enforce *hudud* [punishments, which are those specifically mandated in the Holy Qur'an], and to sign treaties once they have been drawn up.

Article 57: The Imam is responsible for the empowerment of individuals and those who command good and forbid evil along with the performance of religious obligations.

Article 58: The Imam appoints government employees. It is permissible for the law to assign someone else to appoint government personnel except at the highest levels.

Article 59: Only the law can only grant amnesty for crimes other than those punished by hudud. The Imam has the power to grant pardon criminal offenses in particular circumstances with the exception of *hudud*-crimes and high treason.

Article 60: Upon necessity—if great troubles occur, or something occurs which warns of great troubles, or threatens the State, or warns of civil war, or of war with another country—the Imam has the power to take extraordinary measures. These must be presented to the Parliament within a week after they have been enacted. If a Parliament has not yet been elected, then the old Parliament will be convened. All measures are void if these steps are not followed. A law will be issued that regulates these extraordinary measures, their consequences, the reasons why they were adopted, and the way in which their effects will be adjusted in case the measures are not affirmed.

Section 6   The Judiciary
Article 61: The judiciary shall rule with impartiality according to *Shari'ah* laws.

Article 62: The people are equal before the courts. It is not permissible to discriminate against an individual, or a group, in clandestine tribunals.

Article 63: Special courts may not be established nor may any defendant be deprived of having a regular magistrate to adjudicate.

Article 64: It is not permissible to forbid the judiciary from hearing a claim against the Imam or the ruler.

Article 65: Rulings should be published and implemented in the name of "God, the Merciful, the Compassionate." Judges will only be subject to *Shari'ah* laws in their judgments.

Article 66: The implementation of rulings is the responsibility of the State, and omission or inaction in their implementation, is forbidden.

Article 67: The State guarantees the judiciary's independence, and compromising its independence is a crime.

Article 68: The State shall select the most qualified men for the judiciary and facilitate the management of their labor.

Article 69: In *hudud* crimes, the accused must be presented to the court with a counsel of his choosing. If an attorney does not represent the accused, the State must appoint one for him.

Article 70: The Judicial Council should be public. The general populace has the right to attend. It is not permissible to hold court in secret unless legally required to doing so.

Article 71: *Shari'ah* penalties for the *hudud* are applied for the crimes of fornication, false accusation of fornication, theft, banditry, drinking alcohol, and apostasy.

Article 72: The law limits judicial punishments that the judge may prescribe in non-*hudud* crimes.

Article 73: The law clarifies laws for oaths regarding pledges of innocence in murder cases. It is impermissible for civil liability to exceed blood-money amounts.

Article 74: The law clarifies the conditions of accepting repentance and its rulings.

Article 75: The death penalty is not given for a crime unless the plaintiff declines reconciliation or amnesty.

Article 76: In *qisas* (retribution) cases, reconciliation is permitted to be more than blood-money compensation.

Article 77: It is permissible for a woman to stand as equal to a man in terms of blood-money compensation.

Article 78: *Qisas* (retribution) conditions for wounds are exactly the same as in lethal cases and the judge must apply *Shari'ah* penalties.

Article 79: Flogging is the principle punishment in non-*hudud* punishments. Imprisonment is forbidden except for a few crimes and for a limited period decided by the judge.

Article 80: It is not permissible to humiliate the imprisoned, force him to work, or insult his dignity.

Article 81: A Supreme Constitutional Court shall be founded, having jurisdiction to adjudicate upon the conformity of laws and regulations according to the *Shari'ah* as well as the rulings of this Constitution. The law shall define its other spheres of authority.

Article 82: A Grievances Board [Ombudsman's Office] shall be established. The law shall delimit its form, its field of authority, and the salaries of its members.

Section 7   Shurah, Regulatory Bodies, and Legislation

Article 83: The State shall have a Consultative Assembly [Majlis al-Shurah] exercising the following specific duties:

1. Enacting laws that are harmonious with *Shari'ah*.
2. Approving the annual budget of the State and its final account.
3. Monitoring the actions of the executive branch.
4. Holding those responsible in any ministry accountable for their actions and withdrawing confidence from them whenever necessary.

Article 84: The law outlines conditions for elections, how these should occur take, and the conditions of membership. These stipulations will be reached after consultation, which determine that any sane person who has reached the age of majority, and is of good reputation, is guaranteed to participate in expressing his opinion. The law will also outline Council members' monetary compensation. The Council shall draft its internal regulations.

Section 8   The Government

Article 85: The government assumes the responsibility of governance, realizing agreed-upon legitimate interests, and is responsible before the Imam.

Article 86: The law outlines conditions for appointing ministers, the activities prohibited from them during the terms in office, and the way to hold them accountable for actions carried out while on duty.

Section 9   General and Transitional Rules

Article 87: The city of (........) shall be the capital of the country.

Article 88: The law shall clarify the flag of the nation, its motto, as well as delineate the particular rules for each of them.

Article 89: The laws apply from the date of entry into force, and will not be retroactive, unless so stated. Such a step requires the approval of a two-thirds majority in Parliament. There shall be no retrospective action in criminal matters.

Article 90: The laws shall be published in an Official Gazette within two weeks from the date of their proclamation. They will have the force of law one month after the date of their publication, unless other dates are specified.

Article 91: The Imam and Parliament may request the amendment of an Article, or Articles, of the Constitution. The article, or articles, to be amended along with the reasons calling for such revisions, must be stated in any request. Should the petition come from Parliament, the House must first approve it. In all cases, the House shall discuss the principle of the amendment, and proclaim a resolution on the matter with a two-thirds majority. If the request is refused, then a request for amending the same Article is not permitted until a year after the initial refusal. If Parliament approves the principle of revision, debate shall start at least two months from the date of the agreement, to either amend the constitutional article or not. Once two-thirds of the House approves the amendment, it must be presented to the nation in a referendum, and if it passes, it may then be considered operative from the date of the announcement of referendum results.

Article 92: All of the provisions for laws and regulations before the publication of this Constitution remain valid. However, they may repealed or amended by regulations laid out in this Constitution, and if any rule contradicts *Shari'ah* laws, it shall be repealed and replaced.

Article 93: This Constitution goes into effect from the date the nation approves it in a referendum.

This project has been prepared in accordance with the following resolution:

In the Name of God, the Merciful, the Compassionate.
Resolution #11 of the Shaykh of Al-Azhar; dated 25 Muharram 1398 H/5 January 1978.

After reviewing Law #103 of the year 1961 regarding the matter of reorganizing Al-Azhar, the agencies that comprise it, the amended laws regarding it, Presidential resolution #250 (1975) regarding the publication of the executive regulation of the law #103 (1961) mentioned above, the decisions and recommendations of the 8th meeting of the Islamic Research Academy that was held in Cairo on Dhu al-Qa'dah 1396 H/October 1977 that contained the first recommendation regarding the drafting of an Islamic Constitution to be available to any country that wishes to model itself after the Islamic *Shari'ah*, it is resolved:

Article 1: The formation of a High Committee to Draft a Plan for an Islamic Constitution to be available to any state that wishes to model itself after the *Shari'ah*. Consideration shall be made for the principles agreed upon by Muslim schools of law to the utmost extent possible. It is up to the [High] Committee to form a subcommittee made up of its members.

Article 2: The formation of the High Committee mentioned above is as follows:
1. His Eminence, the Grand Imam, Dr. 'Abdul Halim Mahmud (Presiding).
2. His Eminence Al-Husayni Hashim.
3. 'Abdul 'Aziz Hindi, Consultant.
4. His Eminence Shaykh [Hasanayn] Muhammad Makhluf.
5. His Eminence Dr. 'Abdul Jalil Shalbi.
6. His Eminence Shaykh 'Abdul Jalil 'Isa.
7. 'Abdul Halim al-Jundi (Rapporteur), Consultant.

8. 'Abdul Fattah Nasr, Consultant.
9. Minister 'Abdul Mun'im 'Amara, Consultant.
10. 'Ali 'Ali Mansur, Consultant.
11. His Eminence Dr. Muhammad Hasan Fayad.
12. His Eminence Shaykh Muhammad Khatir Muhammad al-Shaykh.
13. Muhammad 'Atiyyah Khamis, J.D.
14. His Eminence Dr. Mahmud Shawkat al-'Adawi.
15. Mustafah 'Afifi, Consultant.
16. Dr. Mustafah Kamal Wasfi, Consultant.

In case of the absence of the head of the Committee, the oldest member shall preside.

Article 3: The Executive Secretary of the Academy for Islamic Research shall undertake secretarial duties, and he may be joined by other secretaries, should the Shaykh of Al-Azhar decide so.

Article 4: Work shall proceed in accordance with this resolution from the date of its proclamation, and it shall supersede any prior resolutions. Its implementation is the duty of the relevant bodies.

<u>The Shaykh of al-Azhar: 'Abdul Halim Mahmud</u>

Then, the following was added to this resolution:
Resolution #12 of the Shaykh of Al-Azhar; dated the 25 Muharram, 1398 H/5 January 1978.

After reviewing Law #103 of the year 1961 regarding the matter of reorganizing Al-Azhar, the agencies that comprise it, the amended laws regarding it, Presidential resolution #250 (1975) regarding the publication of the executive regulation of the law #103 (1961) mentioned above, and our Resolution #11, dated 5 January 1978, regarding the issue of forming a High Committee for Drafting the Islamic Constitution following the recommendation of the conference, has so resolved:

Article 1: The formation of a subcommittee made up of members of the High Committee for Drafting the Islamic Constitution structured to include:
1. His Eminence, Dr. Al-Husayni Hashim.
2. 'Abdul 'Aziz Hindi (Rapporteur), Consultant.
3. His Eminence Shaykh Hasanayn Muhammad Makhluf.
4. 'Abdul Halim al-Jundi, Consultant.
5. 'Abdul Fattah Nasr, Consultant.

6. Minister 'Abdul Mun'im 'Amara, Consultant.
7. His Eminence Shaykh Muhammad Khatir Muhammad al-Shaykh.
8. Muhammad 'Atiyyah Khamis, J.D.
9. Mustafah 'Afifi, Consultant.
10. Yaqut al-'Ashmawi, Consultant.
11. Mustafah Kamal Wasfi, Consultant.
12. His Eminence Dr. Muhammad Shawkat al-'Adawi.

The oldest member among those in attendance shall preside over the Committee. In the case of the attendance of His Eminence, the Grand Imam, at Committee meetings, he shall preside.

Article 2: The subcommittee shall present the conclusions of its research and studies regarding the plan for the Islamic Constitution to His Eminence, the Grand Imam, the Shaykh Al-Azhar.

Article 3: It is the duty of the relevant bodies to implement this resolution according to how it applies to them.

<u>Shaykh of Al-Azhar: 'Abdil Halim Mahmud</u>

Source: Al-Husayni 'Abdul Majid Hashim, *Mashru' al-Dustur al-Islami* [Islamic Constitution Project], Cairo, Egypt: Al-Azhar Academy for Islamic Research, 1978.

Appendix 2
The Al-Azhar Document on the Future of Egypt

21 June 2011

Shaykh Ahmad Al Tayyib, Egypt's highest Muslim religious figure presiding over the world's most important seat of Sunni learning, issued the "Al-Azhar Document" on 21 June 2011—or five months after the 25 January 2011 Revolution—which outlined the institution's vision on key political, social, and economic issues.

The main articles that follow confirm the institution's support for "the establishment of a modern, democratic and constitutional state" in Egypt, which will observe the separation of powers and guarantee equal rights to all citizens. As such, this was the first time in a century and a half that Al-Azhar introduced a comprehensive statement on Egyptian identity and Islamic culture.

Equally important was the document's focus on ties between "state and church" or, more accurately, between state and religion since the notion of "church" as an organized body of all believers is less formalized in Islam. Though the declaration upheld the principles of Shari'ah Law as "the basic source of legislation," it nevertheless added that non-Muslim Egyptian citizens were entitled to their own religious traditions in deciding personal status matters. In other words, the document affirmed the rights of non-Muslims concerning their places of worship, as it called for respect to be shown to the three monotheistic religions as well as for the protection of their places of worship. Sectarian rifts, it underscored, were to be considered as nothing short of "national crime[s]".

Seldom read outside of the Arab World, the document further emphasized that Al-Azhar embraced democracy based on free elections, which represented the modern formula of the Islamic precept of "Shurah" (consultation) and, in what can only described as a revolutionary goal in its own right was the call for the re-establishment of the Board of Senior 'Ulamah (scholars). The latter body would thus be responsible for the nomination and election of the Grand Imam of Al-Azhar. In other words, the "Al-Azhar Document" in Clause 10 envisaged independence from the Government of Egypt, as Article 3 of Law Number 103 (1961), which governed Al-Azhar and that placed the institution under the jurisdiction of the Ministry of Endowments would, henceforth, be changed. Law 103 (1961) further granted—in Articles 5, 18 and 41—unique privileges to the President of the Republic, as the latter appointed the Grand Shaykh, members of the Islamic Research Academy, and even the Chancellor of the Al-Azhar University. It was a rare call for the separation of "church from state" that went unnoticed but that promised to shake the body politic.

On an initiative made by the Grand Imam of Al-Azhar, Professor Dr. Ahmad Al Tayyib, a group of Egyptian intellectuals gathered with several senior Al-Azhar scholars to assess vital concerns that confronted the Egyptian nation. Over the course of various meetings, intellectuals and scholars drawn from all walks of life, religious backgrounds and political views, discussed vital issues at this critical stage in Egyptian history, especially following the 25 January 2011 Revolution. They debated the future of Egypt, motivated by the quest to encourage prosperity and to guarantee their rights to freedom, dignity, equality and social justice.

Attendees agreed on the necessity to help pave a new way for the future of the country, according to comprehensive principles and rules discussed by different parties within Egyptian society, respecting laws that placed everyone on the right path.

Participants stressed the importance of Al-Azhar, whose unparalleled guidance of moderate Islamic teachings stood out, to play a critical role in determining the types of relations that ought to exist between the state and religious establishments. Moreover, discussants clarified the basics of appropriate legislative policies that needed to be voted in parliament, and applied by the executive branch.

The role played by Al-Azhar, based on its wide experience as well as its scientific and cultural legacies, may be summarized in the following:

1. Theological focus on reviving the science of religion according to the principles of the Sunnah [the verbally transmitted record of the teachings, deeds and sayings of the prophet], which integrate between those who refer to reason and those who refer to the Holy Qur'an and the traditions, and that reveal all required rules of interpreting religious texts.

2. Historical legacy to assist leading national movements toward freedom and independence.
3. Cultural heritage to restore various natural sciences, literature and artistic goals, including several subfields.
4. Learned perspectives to guide officials and the whole of Egyptian society.
5. Comprehensive abilities to champion scientific knowledge and culture throughout the Arab and Islamic worlds.

Participants were inspired in their discussions by the legacies of the great Shaykhs of Al-Azhar, including Shaykh Hassan Al Attar and his renowned student, Shaykh Rifa'at Al Tahtawih; the Imam Muhammad 'Abdu and his students, including [Mustafah] Al Maraghi, Muhammad 'Abdallah Daraz, Mustafah 'Abdul Razik, [Mahmud] Shaltut and others. Moreover, they were also inspired by senior Egyptian intellectuals, whose achievements and contributions to humanity and the development of knowledge was well established, and by philosophers, law-makers, literary figures, artists and others, all of whom helped participants underscore the importance of concentrating on common principles that shaped the country's intellectual contributions.

The Common principles that will determine relations between Islam and the State at this critical stage can thus be identified according to an agreeable strategy that will, in turn, shape the desired modern government and its ruling system. These should assist to achieve development, ensure democracy and social justice, provide prosperity and peace, and respect human and spiritual values while preserving Egypt's cultural heritage. They should also protect society from distortions or misinterpretations, and deny deviant parties the opportunities to use religion according to their needs and desires. Such violations of moderation and contempt of the Islamic principles of freedom and justice, which infringe on the rights of all heavenly religions, are intolerable and will not be allowed.

We therefore declare our agreement on the following conventions that rely on Islamic teachings, and which draw on sacrosanct and accurate religious texts.

First   Al-Azhar backs the creation of a constitutional democratic state, according to a universally accepted charter that unites Egyptians, who agree on the separation between state authorities and all governing legal institutions. Such a constitution should guarantee the rights and duties of all citizens on an equal basis, establish clear rules, and give the power of legislation to the people's representatives in accordance with true Islamic understandings. Muslim societies differed from others with respect to legislation. Yet, for cultural and historical reasons, especially when compared with Christian rulers [during the Middle Ages] that oppressed people, all of humanity suffered from excesses. The Muslim State nevertheless allowed individuals to manage their affairs and adopt the best mechanisms to promote and protect intrinsic interests. It also facilitated the application of Islamic jurisprudence as the main source of legislation, while it further guaranteed followers of other divine religions to rely on their religious institutions to settle personal matters.

Second Al-Azhar embraces democracy based on free and direct elections, which represent the modern formula to achieve the Islamic precept of "Shurah" (consultation), and that ensures pluralism and the rotation of power. Democracy permits the adoption of specialized institutions; allows citizens the right to monitor the performance of representatives; seeks to advance the public interest through legislation; safeguards the rule of law—and only the law—as the vehicle through which the state operates; tracks corruption; certifies accountability for all; and guarantees the right to access information.

Third Al-Azhar commits itself to freedom of thought and opinion, with full respect for human rights, as well as women's, and children's rights. It pledges to uphold multi-pluralism, the full respect of divine religions, and promises that citizenship will form the basis of responsibility within society.

Fourth Al-Azhar accepts full respect for opposing opinions and encourages open dialogue to avoid labeling people as believers or traitors. It discourages any means to exploit religion to disunite citizens, and to pit them against each other, and considers acts of religious discrimination, sectarianism and/or racism as crimes against the State. Al-Azhar supports dialogue and mutual respect between citizens based on equality of rights and duties.

Fifth Al-Azhar welcomes commitments to all international conventions, resolutions and achievements, which are consistent with the tolerant Arab and Islamic cultures. It builds on the experience of Egyptians throughout the ages, and the good examples that Egyptians set for peaceful co-existence, which promote the interests of all humanity.

Sixth Al-Azhar, which is dedicated to the protection of the dignity of Egyptians and to defending their national pride, pledges to guard and protect the places of worships of the followers of the three heavenly religions, as well as safeguard the free and unrestricted practices of all religious rites. Al-Azhar is also keen to uphold freedom of artistic and literary expression and creativity within the context of our universal cultural values.

Seventh   Al-Azhar considers education and scientific research as the principle means to advance culture in Egypt. Towards that end, it recognizes that there is a need to dedicate major efforts to compensate on the progress that society missed in these fields, apply significant investments to eliminate illiteracy, and harness human resources to achieve significant improvements in future endeavors.

Eighth   Al-Azhar recommends a focus on development and social justice projects, the necessity to fight oppression and corruption, the obligation to eliminate unemployment, along with the expansion of every sector ranging from the economy to socio-cultural accomplishments to media programs. It advocates the adoption of universal health care, a burden that ought to be assumed by the state towards all citizens, as a top priority.

Ninth   Al-Azhar hopes that Egypt will restore past ties with Arab, Muslim and African countries and with the rest of the world to protect its independence, and to support the rights of the Palestinian people. It expects Cairo to regain its leading historical role to accomplish mutually beneficial goals, and to maintain people's interests. Egypt should contribute to noble initiatives to strengthen and advance humanity, protect the environment, and achieve peace and justice among all nations.

Tenth   Al-Azhar backs the proposed independence of the institution from the executive branch, and the re-establishment of the Board of Senior 'Ulamah, which would thus be responsible for the nomination and election of the Grand Imam. Al- Azhar further supports renewing the syllabuses taught at Al-Azhar schools to regain its intellectual primacy and to rekindle its influence throughout the whole world.

Eleventh   Al-Azhar reflects the main authority on all Islamic affairs, ranging from scientific knowledge to heritage and thought without, however, depriving anyone from the right to express his opinion, as long as these are in conformity with the requirements of dialogue—to be conducted with respect and according to the norms of Muslim consensus as devised by the 'Ulamah of the nation.

Al-Azhar scholars and intellectuals who participated in drafting this "declaration" urge all parties and political organizations to apply themselves and improve political, economic and social conditions in Egypt, as discussed above.

May God bestow goodness to the nation.

Source: Adapted from the original. For an unedited English language version, see Republic of Egypt, State Information Service, *Al-Azhar Document*, 19 May 2016, at
http://www.sis.gov.eg/Story/56424?lang=en-us.

Appendix 3
The Al-Azhar Document on Basic Freedoms

8 January 2012

The Bayan al-Azhar 'an Manzumat al-Hurriyyah al-Asasiyyah *which follows was the third of a series of statements issued under the auspices of Grand Imam Shaykh Ahmad Al Tayyib, in the aftermath of the post-2010 Arab Uprisings that shook the entire Muslim World. Remarkably, this complex document was perceived as a Muslim "Magna Carta" or a "Bill of Rights," even if its call to "respect the believer but not necessarily the content of the belief" rattled some. Al-Azhar upheld Shari'ah Law, but sought "the correct, moderate understanding of religion," which highlighted dilemmas with which the venerable institution's scholars and Muslims in general struggled with. For example, the second section, under the heading "freedom of opinion and expression," commits the nation to respecting "the divine beliefs and rituals of the three Abrahamic faiths [precisely] to avoid threatening the national fabric and security." Still, and while it reaffirms that "No one has the right to raise sectarian or doctrinal strife in the name of freedom of expression," it nevertheless adds: "The right to present a scholarly opinion supported by relevant evidence, however, is far from incitement and shall be guaranteed, as outlined by the principle of freedom of scientific research."*

Notwithstanding such crucial quandaries, the mere fact that a Document on Basic Freedoms *was prepared and published by the premier Muslim religious institution in the Arab World, spoke volumes. It confirmed that Muslims addressed their own concerns to join, perhaps even lead, the nations of the world, assume the burdens associated with the search for knowledge, and otherwise aim to remain faithful, or become even better, believers. Equally important, it was revealed by the Grand Imam in the presence of the highest Christian authority in Egypt, the late Coptic Pope Shinuda [Shenouda] III, whose support was deemed critical by Al-Azhar.*

In the Name of God the Merciful
The Noble Azhar
Office of the Shaykh of Al-Azhar
Al-Azhar Statement on Basic Freedoms

In the wake of revolutions that fuel the spirit of freedom, Egyptians, along with all Arab and Muslim nations look to their scholars and intellectuals, to determine the relationship between the principles of Shari'ah Law and the set of basic liberties that are unanimously agreed upon by international conventions. These basic freedoms emerged from the cultural experiences of the Egyptian people, as they consolidate the nation's foundations, and reaffirm long-established principles. Scholars must therefore outline the foundations of these basic principles to determine the necessary conditions for development and to widen future prospects.

The freedoms referred to are those of belief, opinion, free speech, scientific research and literary as well as artistic creativity. All such freedoms must serve the overarching purpose of Shari'ah, as well as grasp the spirit of modern constitutional legislation along with requirements for the development of human knowledge. This relationship ought to channel the spiritual energies for the nation to fuel a renaissance and work as a catalyst for physical and moral progress. Towards that end, ongoing efforts ought to be harmoniously connected and remain consistent with both rational cultural discourses as well as enlightened religious dialogues. These two conversations must overlap and complement each other, in a pattern that is fruitful for the future, and which unites the goals and objectives agreed upon by everyone.

It is therefore important for Al-Azhar scholars and intellectuals—who drafted an Islamic Constitution and issued a statement in support of the Arab Uprisings—to examine the components involved in systems of human freedoms and rights, and to adopt a set of principles and rules that govern such freedoms. Aware of today's requirements and motivated by the needs to preserve the essence of compatibility in communities, these efforts consider the public interest through the democratization process, as the nation builds its constitutional institutions in peace and moderation with the blessings from God.

Such efforts can and must stop the spread of provocative summons and spread calls for prejudice, which tend to invoke the pretext of the call "to promote virtue and prevent vice," precisely to intervene in public and private freedoms. Indeed, this is incompatible with both the civilization and social development of modern Egypt, at a time when the country needs unity and the correct, moderate approach towards religion. This is the religious message of Al-Azhar and its responsibility to the community and the nation.

First   *Freedom of Belief*

Freedom of belief and the associated right to full citizenship for all based on full equality of rights and duties is considered a cornerstone of the modern social structure. It is guaranteed by authentic religious texts and explicit constitutional and legal principles.

In the words of God Almighty: "There shall be no compulsion in [acceptance of] the religion. The right course has become clear from the wrong" [2:256], adding "The truth is from your Lord, so whoever wills—let him believe; and whoever wills—let him disbelieve" [18:29]. These verses prohibit any appearance of coercion, persecution or discrimination in religion and legitimize their criminalization. Every individual in society can embrace ideas as he pleases without affecting the right of society to maintain monotheistic beliefs. In light of the sanctity accorded to all the three Abrahamic faiths, their followers should retain the freedom to observe rituals without facing aggression, directed either at their feelings or houses of worship, and without breaching public order.

As the Arab world has been the location of divine revelations that embrace heavenly religions, it is rigorously committed to the protection of their holiness, the respect of their rituals and the maintenance of the rights of their believers with freedom, dignity and brotherhood.

From freedom of belief follows recognition of the legitimacy of pluralism, the protection of the right to disagree, and the obligation of every citizen to respect the feelings of others that promote equality among citizens. This equality is based on a solid foundation of citizenship, partnership and equal opportunities in all rights and duties.

Furthermore, respecting freedom of belief entails rejecting exclusion and *takfir* [the declaration by a Muslim that another Muslim is a nonbeliever due to a certain creed, saying or action], and discarding trends that condemn the beliefs of others or attempt to inspect the consciences of the faithful. This is based on established constitutional systems and conclusive provisions decided upon by Shari'ah Law and expressed by many Muslim scholars inspired by the Prophet Muhammad who once responded to an faultfinder: "Have you opened his chest [and examined his heart]?" Similar sentiments were expressed by many Imams, including Imam Malik of Madinah who stated: "If a person says something that most probably denotes disbelief, yet still there is a remote possibility it does not, it should not be taken to denote disbelief." Notable Imams of jurisprudence and legislation in Islamic thought left us golden rules: "If the mind and the text are apparently in conflict, the mind should be given precedence and the text reinterpreted." This serves the objectives of Shari'ah while bearing in mind legal interests.

Second   *Freedom of Opinion and Expression*

Freedom of opinion, whether spoken, written, through art production or digital communication, is the foundation of all freedoms. It is the manifestation of social freedoms that goes beyond individuals to include among other things the formation of political parties and civil society institutions, the independence of the press and audio, visual, and digital media, as well as the free access to the information necessary to express an opinion. These liberties must be guaranteed explicitly by the constitution to transcend ordinary laws that are subject to change. As the Supreme Constitutional Court in Egypt broadened the concept of free speech to encompass constructive criticism, even if harshly worded, we must uphold what the court stipulated: that "it is not appropriate to restrict freedom of expression regarding public issues and that everyone must tolerate all opinions." Yet, we need to respect the divine beliefs and rituals of the three Abrahamic faiths, to avoid threatening the national fabric and security. No one has the right to raise sectarian or doctrinal strife in the name of freedom of expression. The right to present a scholarly opinion supported by relevant evidence, however, is far from incitement and shall be guaranteed, as outlined by the principle of freedom of scientific research.

We declare that freedom of opinion, and expression thereof, are the true manifestations of a real democracy. We call upon the nation to educate a new generation according to a culture of freedom and the right to disagree while respecting others. Furthermore, we urge those in the media who report on religious, cultural and political affairs to take this significant dimension into account, and exercise wisdom in the formation of public opinion, characterized by tolerance and broad-mindedness, which must emphasize dialogue and reject fanaticism. To achieve all of this, the cultural traditions of tolerant Islamic thought should be evoked. An example is a saying by one of the Imams: "I believe that my opinion is right, but may be wrong, and that the opinion of others is wrong, but may be right." The only way to fortify freedom of opinion is therefore by using sound arguments according to the ethics of dialogue and the cultural customs found in sophisticated societies.

Third *Freedom of Scientific Research*

Advanced scientific research in the humanities, sciences, sports and other fields is the engine of human progress and a means of discovering the ways and laws of the universe. Such knowledge must be harnessed for the good of humanity. However, this research cannot take place and pay off in a theoretical and practical sense without the nation devoting its energy and mobilizing all of its resources. Qur'anic scriptures urge analogical reasoning, review, deduction as well as measurement and meditation in cosmic and human phenomena to discover the laws of the universe. These criteria paved the way for the greatest scientific renaissance in the history of the East and recorded achievements for all of humanity. It is widely known that Muslim scholars carried the flames that lit the Western Renaissance. If thinking in general is an Islamic duty in all branches of knowledge and the arts, as held by the scholars of *ijtihad* [independent reasoning], theoretical and experimental scientific research is the instrument for the discharge of this obligation. The most important conditions are that research institutions and scientists enjoy full academic freedom to test their assumptions and probabilities and carry out experiments according to precise standards. It is also the right of such institutions to maintain creativity and harness the necessary experiences to ensure access to new results that add to human knowledge. Nothing can direct them to achieve this goal other than ethical standards and sound methods based on the constant principles of science.

Great Muslim scholars like Al-Razi, Ibn Al-Haytham, Ibn Al-Nafis, were leaders and pioneers of scientific knowledge in the East and the West for many centuries. The time has now come for Arab and Islamic nations to return to the race for power and to enter the era of knowledge. Science has become a source of military and economic power and a basis for progress, development and prosperity.

Furthermore, free scientific research has become the foundation of educational development. The supremacy of scientific thought and the prosperity of production centers, which shall be allocated large budgets, task forces and major project proposals, require securing the highest investments for research. Western powers retained all scientific progress in their hands, and would have monopolized this knowledge base were it not for the rise of Japan, China, India and Southeast Asia, which have provided illuminating models for the Middle East and the ability of the latter to break this monopoly and to embark on an age of science and knowledge too. The time has come for Egyptians, Arabs and Muslims to enter the competitive scientific and cultural arenas. They have what it takes in terms of spiritual, financial and human energy, as well as other conditions required for progress in a world that does not respect the weak and those falling behind.

Fourth   *Freedom of Literary and Artistic Creativity*

There are two types of creativity: scientific creativity related to scientific research as stated above and literary and artistic creativity found in the various genres of literature such as lyrical and dramatic poetry, fiction and nonfiction, theatre, biographical accounts, visual and fine arts, film, television, music and other innovative forms of art that have been newly introduced to these genres.

In general, literature and the arts seek to raise awareness of reality, stimulate the imagination, refine aesthetic feelings, educate human senses and expand their capacity, as well as deepen the human experience in life and society. Art and literature can also sometimes criticize society while exploring better and finer alternatives. All of these functions are significant and lead to the enrichment of language and culture, stimulation of the imagination and development of thought, while taking into account sublime religious values and moral virtues.

The Arabic language, which was characterized by its literary richness and remarkable eloquence, gained after the Holy Qur'an was revealed as the peak of eloquence, further increasing the beauty and genius of the language. The Qur'an nourished the art of poetry, prose and wisdom and launched the talents of poets and authors of all nationalities that embraced Islam and spoke Arabic. For years these individuals excelled in all the arts freely and without restrictions. Many Arab and Muslim scientists, including elders and Imams, were narrators of various types of poetry and stories. Nevertheless, the basic rules governing the limits of freedom of creativity must be the preparedness of society, on the one hand, and its ability to absorb the elements of heritage and renewal in literary and artistic creativity, on the other. Such rules should not touch upon religious feelings or established moral values. Literary and artistic creativity remain among the most important manifestations of a prosperous set of basic freedoms and the most effective at moving the community's awareness and to enrich its conscience. As this rational freedom becomes more entrenched, it becomes a symbol of modernization as literature and the arts are mirrors of a society's conscience and a sincere expression of its constants and its variables. They present a radiant image of society's aspirations for a better future, and may God bless that which is good and right.

Grand Shaykh of Al-Azhar Dr. Ahmad Al-Tayyib

8 January 2012

Source: Adapted from the original available at <u>http://freespeech</u> <u>debate.com/ar/discuss_ar/al-azhars-bill-of-rights/</u>. A different English version is available at the Dahrendorf Programme for the Study of Freedom at St Antony's College in the University of Oxford at, <u>http://freespeechdebate.com/en/discuss/al-azhars-bill-of-rights/</u>.

Appendix 4
Al-Azhar Backs Article 2 of Egyptian Constitution

11 July 2012

Shaykh Ahmad Al Tayyib, the Grand Imam of Al-Azhar, reiterated the institution's position regarding proposed changes or amendments to Article II of the Constitution of Egypt regarding the role of Shariʿah Law in crafting legislation. He stressed the need to preserve the current content of the article to preserve the nation's identity and rejected dropping the term "principles" of Shariʿah, which some wanted to drop. The distinction was important because some Salafi groups, including supporters of President Muhammad Mursi, opted for a more rigid version of the text. Al Tayyib asserted that he was against "any argument that drags down the nation," and reminded everyone that the ongoing controversy was a departure from what had been agreed upon in the Al-Azhar documents on the "Future of Egypt" and on "Basic Freedoms." He added: "In light of this controversy, which may confuse the nation and prevent it from achieving the desired level of stability, Al-Azhar—given its religious, national and historic standing—would like to reiterate its position, which calls for preserving the original content of Article II in the Egyptian Constitution: 'Islam is the official religion of the state, Arabic is its official language, and the principles of Shariʿah Law are the main source of legislation'."

A proposal by ultraconservative Salafis to give Egypt's main Islamic institution the final say on whether the law of the land adheres to Islamic laws threatens to bring the already painfully slow process of drafting the new constitution to a grinding halt.

The proposal would give the revered Al-Azhar power similar to a supreme court by making it the arbiter of whether a law conforms with the principles of Shariʿah, already cited in the constitution of ousted leader Husni Mubarak as Egypt's 'main source' of legislation.

Opponents say the move would only exacerbate Egypt's volatile politics and make it harder to heal social tensions in a country where one tenth of the population is Christian. The argument is also diverting energy away from other essential points of law—the balance of power between president and parliament, the influence of the army, defense of personal freedoms and an independent judiciary. "Lack of trust is so deep-seated now in Egypt," said Shadi Hamid, a political analyst at the Brookings Doha Center. "Anything in the constitution will be interpreted through this lens of mistrust." A constitutional assembly of 100 thinkers, scholars, professionals and political and religious leaders dominated by Islamists is drawing up the constitution, without which the country cannot hold elections to replace a parliament that a court declared void in June. Islamist President Muhammad Mursi holds lawmaking power for now, an awkward arrangement that erodes the credibility of his government, elected after Mubarak was overthrown last year. Some liberals committed to a more secular state have already boycotted the assembly and are challenging it in court, saying Islamists have too much control and want to turn Egypt into an Iran-style theocracy. "An assembly that doesn't reflect the intellectual diversity and a constitution in which core values aren't agreed on will lead to a deep social rift," Muhammad Al Baraday [El Baradei], former head of the U.N. nuclear watchdog, said on his Twitter account earlier this month. He has not responded to invitations to attend a hearing session at the assembly.

"BRING BACK SHARI'AH"

The assembly aims to complete a first draft of the constitution by late September, although a court has yet to rule on whether the assembly itself is legitimate. The assembly is working by breaking the document apart: four committees are handling one section each. After they agree the articles in their sections they send drafts to the phrasing committee, which is where the Al-Azhar proposal now sits for debate—now delayed—over the exact wording.

Articles will then be approved by general consensus, or if that fails by more than two-thirds vote, and if that fails, then after more discussion, with at least 57 votes. The draft constitution must finally be approved by public referendum. Analysts expect the new document to have a more Islamic flavor than its predecessor, including articles prohibiting criticism of God and establishing an institution to collect zakat, or charitable donations for the poor, while cancelling an article banning parties based on religion.

At the vanguard of this movement are the Salafis, who were kept out of politics under Mubarak but leaped onto the scene after his fall, taking second place in the country's first free and fair parliamentary vote in six decades. Their slogan was to "bring back Shari'ah"—laws derived from Islam's Holy Qur'an and the teachings of the Prophet Muhammad—in the belief it would solve Egypt's moral and social ills. They say that since Article 2 of the old constitution already says "the principles of Shari'ah" are the main foundation of legislation, they merely want to see this idea fully applied, if not by strengthening the role of Al-Azhar, then by changing the wording to make it just "Shari'ah" itself rather than its principles.

"Egypt is entering a new age that will witness a confirmation of the reference to Shari'ah Law in constitutions and a better application of it," said independent Salafi scholar Muhammad Yusry Ibrahim. Some liberals accept the idea of giving laws a religious seal of approval but say Al-Azhar's advice must not be binding. The head of Al-Azhar, founded over 1,000 years ago and widely respected among Sunni Muslims, is named by the president, but that arrangement is set to change. A new law will allow its leading Shaykh to be elected by a committee of 40 scholars proposed by the outgoing Shaykh and approved by the president, giving the prestigious institution more independence. Given the composition of the assembly, and the public's general support for a more Islamic political leadership, the Salafis proposal would have a good chance of passing if put to a vote. But it could also spark a wholesale boycott that would delay—and maybe even scupper—the entire process. "If there is no consensus, I think it will be difficult to have a draft constitution," said Wahid 'Abdul Majid, a liberal member of the assembly and its spokesman.

BACK TO FRONT

Egypt's military leadership threw out the legal rule book when they removed Mubarak from power in February 2011 to end mass street protests and embarked on 18 months of rule by decree. Mursi's election in June brought some clarity but the final extent of his powers still hangs on the deliberations of the constitutional assembly—an odd outcome caused by the back-to-front transition devised by the generals. Judges are wading through a flurry of court cases and appeals challenging decrees from Mursi, the legality of the Brotherhood's political party and the move to void parliament.

Mursi's Muslim Brotherhood allies, whose party was the largest in the dissolved legislature, have avoided weighing into the dispute over Article 2 in an attempt to forge a consensus. "We don't have a problem with it . . . because Egyptians are religious by nature," said Husayn Ibrahim, former head of the Brotherhood parliamentary bloc and a member of the assembly. Critics of the Salafis accuse them of trying to foist onto Al-Azhar a role that contradicts a tenet of Sunni Islam—that no one holds a monopoly in interpreting the word of God. Others say that making any Islamic body an arbiter of civil law ignores the rights of a Christian minority anxious at the growing assertiveness of Islamists in the nation of 83 million, the most populous in the Arab world. "When you take away the monitoring . . . from the constitutional court and give it to a religious entity, this is discrimination against Christians," said Hafiz Abu Sa'idah, head of the Egyptian Organization for Human Rights.

Salafis in the constitutional assembly say they have watered down their original demands, which included an article that would have stated that "sovereignty is with God." "We don't seek dramatic change," said Salafi ex-MP Yunis Makhyun. "We are a minority and nothing is passed except through consensus." But he added: "After the revolution, Egyptians chose Islamists. Egyptians want Islam and the application of Shari'ah. No one (opposes it) except TV personalities who have a loud voice and are trying to impose a different reality." If and when the Shari'ah debate is resolved, other vital details must be hammered out before the constitution can be put to a popular referendum, such as over-sight of the army's budget and the power of competing institutions. "How do you wield power? . . . To what extent does it guarantee freedom of expression? These are issues that will really have an effect on people's lives," said analyst Majid.

Source: Tamim Elyan, "Egypt Constitution Talks Stumble on Role of Islam," *Reuters*, 12 September, 2012, at http://www.reuters.com/article/us -egypt-constitution-idUSBRE88B0VB20120912.
Nabil Khalifé included a different report in his study, one that was repro-duced in the daily *Al Safir* on 11 July 2012, which highlighted some of the arguments advanced here. The translator opted for the more compre-hensive *Reuters* report to better acquaint the reader with the controversial positions adopted by Al-Azhar opponents.

Appendix 5
Al-Azhar Document Calls to Renounce Violence

31 January 2013

*Signed by twenty-eight leading religious and political figures repre-
senting major parties and institutions, the document that rejected
violence and encouraged dialogue stood as a powerful indictment of
revolutionary forces that rocked Egypt two years after the 25 January
2011 uprising that toppled President Husni Mubarak and his government and that shook that of his successor, President Muhammad Mursi.
Held under the auspices of, and presented by, the Grand Imam Ahmad
Al Tayyib, the manifesto aimed to tackle domestic conditions and the
means to achieve national consensus in Egypt. Shaykh Al Tayyib, who
emphasized that national dialogue was the only way to surmount political or partisan differences, insisted that Egyptians in particular, and
Arabs in general, must renounce violence and sabotage to accomplish
political objectives. He repeatedly urged all youths engaged in revolutionary activities to discard all forms of violence and called on
authorities to punish criminals who violated the law. In a significant
departure from similar pledges made by Egyptian elites, the meetings
that produced this document were attended by, and included representatives from, the National Salvation Front (NSF), an anti-Muhammad
Mursi coalition that involved 35 secular groups, President Muhammad
Mursi's Freedom and Justice Party (FJP), the Islamist Development and
Building Party (DBP), as well as the equally ultra-conservative (and
Islamist) Al-Nur Party. Bringing all of these groups together and
securing pledges to renounce violence was a unique achievement and a
singular victory for Al-Azhar and Grand Imam Ahmad Al Tayyib.*

Egyptian youths engaged in the revolution gathered at the revered Al-
Azhar mosque and university under the auspices of the venerable
Al-Azhar National Science Foundation, and in the presence of senior

scholars and representatives of Egyptian churches, committed to the national patriotic principles and higher values of the 25 January 2011 Revolution. Intellectual figures, the heads of political parties and coalitions, as well as religious and political authorities, are all determined to protect the spirit of the revolution. Towards that end, we the undersigned pledge to the following:

1. The right to life is one of the most fundamental rights guaranteed by all religions and laws. There is nothing good in any nation or society that fails to recognize the sanctity of life and dignity. Reckoning for misdeeds must, by definition, be done according to the law.

2. A full recognition of the sanctity of human life must be upheld, along with the essential distinction between political action and criminal acts of violence and sabotage, as well as the preservation of public and private property.

3. The State, along with all of its security institutions, is duty bound to protect every citizen. It must uphold constitutional rights and freedoms and protect public and private property without breaching the laws of the land or the human rights of its inhabitants.

4. We unequivocally and explicitly denounce and condemn violence in all its forms and manifestations, call for the criminal prosecution according to the law, and invite national and religious leaders to deny such individuals heavenly protection.

5. We condemn any incitement, justification, promotion, defense or exploitation of violence.

6. We denounce the incitement of, and calls to, violence, slander and defamation, along with the spreading of rumors and all forms of moral assassination of public figures and entities. All parties must acknowledge what these actions are ethical crimes and renounce them unequivocally.

7. We commit ourselves to nonviolent means in our political activities and to instill a culture of peaceful discourse among the nation's youth.

8. We pledge to hold serious dialogue among all parties and political groups, especially in times of crisis and conflict, to establish a culture of respect for diversity and pluralism precisely to achieve consensus for the sake of the homeland. Nations rise with tolerance and fall with intolerance and division.

9. We promise to protect the nation from sectarian strife, whether real or contrived, from calls to racism and discrimination, from unlawful militant groups, and from illegal foreign intervention, as well as from all that may threaten the safety and security of the nation, the solidarity of its sons and daughters, and the unity of its territory.

10. The protection of the Egyptian State is the responsibility of all parties—government, people, opposition forces, youth, the elderly, political parties, groups, movements and institutions. Everyone will be implicated if political discord leads to the dismantling or weakening of state institutions.

As we declare our faith in these principles, and uphold the culture of democracy, national unity and revolutionary experience that they reflect, we call on all politicians, leaders and activists to abide by the same. We must cleanse our political life of all risks and forms of violence, whatever the justifications or slogans.

We call all citizens, rulers and ruled alike, in the farthest corners of upper Egypt and its oases, in the depths of Egypt's Delta and its deserts, and in the Suez Canal region and in the Sinai, to reconciliation, denouncing violence, and activating dialogue. For serious dialogue is the only way out of all matters of dispute. We must let justice prevail, respect the will of the people, and uphold the rule of law, in order to complete every objective of the 25 January Revolution.

LIST OF SIGNATORIES:
1. Abul 'Ila [Ela] Madi, Wasat Party.
2. Dr. Ahmad Sa'id, Free Egyptians Party.
3. Ahmad Mahir, Initiative Youth.
4. Islam Lutfi, Initiative Youth.
5. Reverend Munir Hanna, Bishop of the Episcopal Church in Egypt.
6. Bishop John Kolta, Deputy Patriarch of Catholic Copts in Egypt.
7. Dr. Ayman Nur [Nour], Ghad Al-Thawrah Party.
8. Pope Tawadros II, Pope of the Coptic Orthodox Church.
9. Hamdin Sabbahi, former presidential candidate.
10. Dr. Sayyid Badawi, Wafd Party.
11. Dr. Safwat Bayadi, President of the Anglican Church.
12. Mr. Safwat 'Abdul Ghani, Jama'ah Islamiyyah.
13. 'Abdul Rahman Yusif, Initiative Youth.
14. Dr. 'Abdul Munim Abul-Futuh, Strong Egypt Party.
15. Dr. 'Amr Hamzawy, Egypt Freedom Party.
16. 'Amr Musa [Moussa], former presidential candidate.
17. Dr. Muhammad Al Baraday [El-Baradai], Constitution Party.
18. Muhammad Al-Qassas, Initiative youth.
19. Muhammad Anwar Sadat, Reform and Development Party.
20. Shaykh Muhammad Hassan, Muslim Preacher.
21. Muhammad Sami, Karama Party.

22. Dr. Muhammad Sa'ad Katatni, Freedom and Justice Party.
23. Dr. Mahmud 'Izzat, Muslim Brotherhood Vice-Chairman.
24. Mustafah Al-Najjar, Initiative youth.
25. Nasr 'Abdul Salam, Building and Development Party.
26. Wa'il [Wael] Ghunaym [Ghoneim], Initiative youth.
27. Walid 'Abdul Munim, Misr Party.
28. Yunis Makhiyun, Nur (Light) Party.

Source: Adapted from the original available on SkyNews (Arabic) at http://www.skynewsarabia.com/web/article/72647/. A different English version is available at the Muslim Brotherhood (Cairo, Egypt) web-page at http://www.ikhwanweb.com/article.php?id=30619.

Appendix 6
The Al-Azhar Document on Women's Rights

26 February 2012

During a 2012 meeting with the head of the Egyptian National Council of Children and Motherhood (NCCM)—who was accompanied by several other members of the Council—Grand Shaykh Ahmad Al Tayyib stressed to Dr. Mirvat Al Ta'lawi that Islam granted women many rights that were not explicitly identified in other religions, and that Al-Azhar intended to prepare a new document to safeguard women's rights as enshrined in Shari'ah Law.

Al Tayyib called for the formation of a new committee to include Al-Azhar scientists, education experts, media officers and seasoned social workers, to draft a blueprint for Egyptian women and to promote their rights to education, work, and other privileges as well as duties. Dr. Al Ta'lawi agreed and backed an Al-Azhar role in updating the prevalent social culture that preserved a Muslim woman's identity.

When the document appeared, many were pleased to read how a Muslim woman's legal right to divorce was restored, including specific references that allowed her to receive all of her financial rights from her divorcing husband. In addition, the document called for the protection of women from harassment in the workplace and on public transportation. Above all else, it stressed that there were and are no differences between males and females, and that both genders enjoyed equal rights, duties and job opportunities. In was worth noting that Al-Azhar Shaykhs argued in the 1950s and 1960s that a woman's instincts and emotions always dominated over her reason and wisdom. Consequently, it was important to note that this new statement was revolutionary, and to conclude that if men were considered to be superior to women and that they alone had the right to divorce or that women were not allowed to travel without a male guardian (mahram) in the past, that Al-Azhar was on the vanguard of the many changes coming to Egyptian society in particular, and Muslim counterparts in general.

On a request from senior Al-Azhar scholars and Egyptian intellectuals to issue a definitive declaration on women that affirmed full equality between genders, Shaykh Ahmad Al Tayyib met with leading women personalities to formally present the "Al-Azhar Declaration on Women's Rights." This initiative complemented two earlier documents that clarified the identity of the nation and the promotion of liberties at the height of the 25 January 2011 Revolution. Al-Azhar thus guided Egyptian society—and the Arab world in general—to rationalize ongoing debates on the nature of the State and the Arab quest for freedom and democracy. Towards that end, and building on earlier declarations that spoke of basic freedoms, it provided the following guidance regarding women in contemporary society, their active roles in public life, and the need to develop a comprehensive framework for their rights on the basis of the Shari'ah principles of tolerance and in conformity with international conventions.

Accordingly, participants agree to the following:

First *Human and Social Value*

The status of women in Islam is based on full equality with men, both in terms of her humanity and in terms of her membership in the nation, which is based on a principle revealed by the Almighty Creator in the verse: "And their Lord responded to them, 'Never will I allow to be lost the work of [any] worker among you, whether male or female; you are of one another' [3:195]."

Just as the principles of equality and shared responsibilities are clearly enunciated in the Holy Scriptures, so this is the basis for understanding all relationships between genders.

Women's political and economic rights are thus equal to those of men as far as the development of the areas, functions and systems of political and economic roles in contemporary societies are concerned, all to serve the interests the nation, according to Shari'ah. What may vary requires due diligence from the nation's scholars to interpret and explain, which is an ongoing historical and cultural process in which women have the right to participate.

Second *Women's Legal Identity*

Women enjoy intrinsic abilities and assume financial independence as well as the right to fully dispose of their properties, as enunciated by the Prophet (peace be upon him), who declared: "Muslims are equal in respect of blood. The lowest of them is entitled to give protection on behalf of them, and the one residing far away may give protection on behalf of them" (Sunan Abu Dawud—Book of Jihad, 2751). And as the Lord said: "The believing men and believing women are allies of one another. They enjoin what is right and forbid what is wrong and establish prayer and give zakah [alms] and obey God and His Messenger. Those—God will have mercy upon them. Indeed, God is Exalted in Might and Wise" [9:71)].

Furthermore, women have legitimate rights to inheritance, which the State must guarantee, and that scholars, the sages of the nation, as well as the leaders of public opinion must defend. Every effort must be made to end unjust customs and traditions that disrupt the application of religious texts, which protect women's inheritance, and that God described as the "imposed inheritance," and for which HE developed legal guarantees.

Third   *Women and the Family*

The family is the foundation of society. Its unity is a physical as well as a moral imperative, which requires that every measure be taken to support and safeguard this entity. The family is thus a contractual entity that is created voluntarily and within an agreed upon relationship, which can end either in agreement or through a judgment that may or may not include compensations. A man and a woman who enter into such a contractual relationship engage on an equal basis in the establishment of the family and are therefore equally responsible to empower it or dissolve it, which must occur according to the Shari'ah, as outlined in several verses and as required by the terms of their marriage contract. Such engagements must be entered into on the basis of compromise and mutual acceptance, and of available documents, to protect both parties but especially the rights of women.

The Family is based on participation, consultation, justice, love and compassion. God dictated man to assume the burdens associated with the welfare of the family and granted women the natural privilege of procreation and the rearing of children. Therefore, looking after women and children is a duty that God assigned men, which does not mean that women loose their identities, but that both men and women have different and multiple roles within the family.

Fourth   *Women and Education*

One of women's fundamental rights is education. Both the State and all of society must provide for, and support access to, women's education without discrimination. This right must also apply to the family, where no discernments are allowed between boys and girls, so that all may receive the education needed to ensure financial and moral success.

Fifth   *Women and Labor*

Contemporary economic obligations, or advanced educational requirements, can impose on women a duty to work alongside men. All assume the burdens of human necessities, as work is a noble objective that allows one to earn a living, and which is not rejected by religion if the circumstances of the couple and their children require it as long as it is accompanied by the preservation of Muslim morals. Moreover, the duty of the State towards women and children, as it is for men when confronted by unemployment or the inability to provide, is to ensure a decent standard of living and housing. Every effort must be made to provide remedial education to allow for a return to the labor field.

Sixth   *Women and Personal Safety*

Islam adopts an integrated vision for the human body, "and its various faculties," as a responsibility before God Almighty who said: "And do not pursue that of which you have no knowledge. Indeed, the hearing, the sight and the heart—about all those [one] will be questioned" [17:36] that, unfortunately, is used for aggression in all its forms. Therefore, harassment and other forms of sexual assault—especially against women—is one of major human tragedies throughout history. If every individual is responsible for keeping the human body safe from immorality, it is also the responsibility of the community as a whole, especially in extenuating circumstances, to protect women. Consequently, it is a legitimate necessity to uphold moral principles at the psychological and religious levels.

Seventh   Women and Public Service

Women have the right to assume public service positions whenever they acquire the qualifications required for specific professions. The State must provide equal opportunities to men and women. It is well known that qualified women served in Muslim societies and assumed major public posts in the fields of education, commerce, and health.

Women have also the right to volunteer and serve whatever their potential, talents or personal motivations compel them to. Volunteerism and public service are rights as well as duties for all human beings, men or women, whose wealth, knowledge and efforts can assist society as a whole.

Finally, women have inherent rights within society and the privileged—as well as the duty—to give advice, consult, and to participate in just causes. Such developments burden those entrusted with public service, whether as voters or elected officials, to deliver justice and protect the rights and interests of the public. They also impose upon all those in charge of decision-making in the national community to seek consensus.

Source: Adapted from the original available at the *Al-Bawaba* web-page at http://www.albawabhnews.com/18603. A different Arabic version is available at the Oasis web-page at http://www.oasiscenter.eu/ar/
"Oasis: Christians and Muslims in a Global World," was founded in 2004 in Venice, out of an intuition sponsored by Cardinal Angelo Scola, whose aim is to encourage mutual understanding and opportunities for dialogue between Western and Muslim societies. Nabil Khalifé did not include this document in his study but reproduced a newspaper essay dealing with a discussion of the document published in *Al-Sharq Al-Awsat* on 19 June 2012.

Appendix 7
The Shi'ah Alliance

The photo-montage distributed on Arab social media outlets shows manipulation. This young man poses behind a rally, presumably held somewhere in the United States, where what appears to be Iraqi and American flags are on display. The young man is then shown in front of the Qa'abah [Kaabah] in Makkah, Sa'udi Arabia, and even inside the Holy Mosque, displaying the same flag whose logo reads "The Shi'ah Alliance."

٥٣٪   ٢:٣٤ م   STC

التغريدة

ردًا على جمال خاشقجي

ALIABDULLAH
@ali_g5559

@JKhashoggi @Almatrafi استاذ جمال هم
لايستطيعون فعل هذا في الحرم والصورة فوتوشوب
ومزورة حفظ الله حجاج بيت الله

٢:١٣ ،٢٠١٦/٩/٩ م

الرد على ALIABDULLAH، جمال خاشقجي، خالد الم..

 الرئيسية   التنبيهات   الرسائل   أنا

Appendix 8
Perceptions of the War for Iraq

This photo-montage, which circulated on social media outlets throughout the Arab World, presumed to illustrate the consequences of the 2003 War for Iraq. The Arabic text reads: "These two individuals [President George W. Bush and Prime Minister Tony Blair] destroyed two countries . . . killed 5 million human beings and displaced another 12 million . . . all without anyone labeling them terrorists . . . it is a world without a conscience."

هذان الشخصان دمرا بلدين ... قتلا خمسة ملايين انسان
وشردا 12 مليون اخرين ... كل هذا ولم يطلق احد عليهما
تسمية ارهابي .... انه عالم بلا ضمير

This is what
democracy looks like
when we bring it

2 countries destroyed, 5 million people
killed 12 million displaced and no
one calls them terrorists???

Appendix 9
Russia and the War for Syria

This photo-montage, which circulated on social media outlets throughout the Arab World, was meant to show how Washington and Moscow were aligned, and presumably wished to perpetuate the conflict.

Appendix 10
British Support to Iranians

Kuwaiti newspaper *Akhbar al-Kuwayt* dated 29 March 1964 with the headline: "Britain Arms Iranians" with the subtitles asserting that British aircraft are bombing targets in Yemen, that British forces in the Arabian Gulf are using Iranian ships to distribute weapons to Iranians, and even arming Persians living in Dubai.

Appendix 11
Benjamin Netanyahu at the United Nations

Israeli Prime Minister Benjamin Netanyahu at the United Nations General Assembly in September 2012. The clip-art drawing that shows the official drawing lines over a bomb led many cartoonists to add their own take to it and was published on *Al-Arabiya News*, and subsequently circulated widely on all social media networks. See "'Bibi and the bomb': How Netanyahu's U.N. sketch exploded online," *Al-Arabiya*, 29 September 2012, at https://english.alarabiya.net/articles/2012/09/29/ 240814.html

Appendix 12
Ayatollah Ruhallah Khumayni

Although the Iranian revolutionary leader gained notoriety in the after-math of the 1979 crisis that saw U.S. diplomats taken hostage for 444 days, Iran grew in importance at the height of the war with Iraq (1980–1988). The cleric graced the cover of several magazines in memorable portraits that pitted his country against the world, though rumors circulated regarding the Ayatollah's background.

See "Khomeini—An Agent of the UK and US Governments," *hormozgan 96*, 5 November 2012, at https://hormozgan96.word press.com/2012/11/05/british-ruholla-khomeini/.

Ruhollah Khomeini – Made in Britain

1979 in Tehran, while watching Iranian students executions

Picture, taken 1972 while living in London with shaved beard

Appendix 13
Ibrahim al-Baghdadi:
The Great Departed

Beirut cabaret performance by the band *al-Rahil al-Kabir* [The Great Departed] on Abu Bakr al-Baghdadi. The complete four-minute-long song with English subtitles is available on YouTube, at https://www.youtube.com/watch?v=UjaSGXmUjWI&index=3&list =RDD-4Am98nSyA.
Photograph courtesy of *NOW Lebanon*.

Appendix 14
Daliah al-'Aqidi

Iraqi news anchorwoman Daliah al-'Aqidi, a Sunni Muslim, wearing a cross in support of Assyrians/Christians in Mosul, Iraq. Courtesy of the Assyrian International News Agency, see "Muslim Iraqi News Anchorwoman Wears Cross in Support of Christians," 29 July 2014 at http://www.aina.org/news/20140729162850.htm.

Appendix 15
Khumayni Commandment for War

In 1983, Ayatollah Ruhallah Khumayni granted an interview to, and graced the cover of, an independent Arabic language weekly magazine, *Al Dustur*, published in London, which quoted him saying: "This is my commandment: When the war with Iraq ends, we need to start another one; I dream that our flag will flutter over 'Amman, Riyadh, Damascus, Cairo and Kuwait." *Al Dustur* [Ad-Dastour], Number 297, 1 August 1983.

Index